FEMINISM AND SOCIAL CHANGE

Feminism and Social Change

Bridging Theory and Practice

EDITED BY HEIDI GOTTFRIED

UNIVERSITY OF ILLINOIS PRESS
Urbana and Chicago

Manufactured in the United States of America

1 2 3 4 5 C P 5 4 3 2 1

This book is printed on acid-free paper.

Library of Congress Cataloging-in-Publication Data

Feminism and social change : bridging theory and practice / edited by Heidi Gottfried.

p. cm.

Includes bibliographical references and index.

ISBN 0-252-02198-3 (alk. paper). — ISBN 0-252-06495-X (pbk. : alk. paper)

1. Feminism—Research—United States. 2. Feminist theory—United States. 3. Social change—United States. I. Gottfried, Heidi, 1955– .

HQ1181.U5F43 1996

305.42'01—dc20 95-5922

CIP

Contents

PART 3: PARTICIPATORY AND LIBERATORY ADVOCACY

Preface

Feminism and Social Change represents a collective endeavor whose original purpose began as a series of papers presented at the Society for the Study of Social Problems in 1991. The session evoked a revival more than a professional meeting; one person after another chronicled the ambivalence and rewards of doing feminist research over the past two decades. Twelve years of Reaganomics had created a hostile climate for and backlash against feminist scholarship, culminating in the debate over political correctness. Women's studies programs came under siege from a New Right bent on polishing what they saw as the tarnished image of the ivory tower. In the name of saving the canon, these troubleshooters took aim at interdisciplinary programs. By bringing together sociologists from North America, the session served as a much needed antidote to a decade of antipathy and neglect.

A positive impulse within feminism also inspired the development of this collection. Many who gave testimonials spoke passionately about their work as the accomplishments of several generations of activist feminist research. Participants who crowded in the hotel ballroom recalled projects ranging from participatory research with women in battered women's shelters to cultural exchange with Hmong women in California. Another influence came from Black, Latina, Asian, and lesbian feminists who challenged white feminists in the academy to develop a more inclusive feminism and to rethink feminist theories and methodologies. *Feminism and Social Change* becomes part of this self-reflexive effort to engage women's communities toward the goal of social change.

No project reaches fruition without the encouragement and aid of many friends and colleagues. My collaborator, Patty Sotirin, deserves special mention for her storehouse of ideas that launched the initial project. In her subsidized graduate student house without air conditioning on sweltering days in the summer of 1990, we sat together at her computer terminal composing "Research for Women: Notes toward the Development of a Liberatory Research Project," which served as the impetus to organize the conference session. Patty continues to influence and shape my thinking on feminism and methodology.

The women's studies program at Purdue came to my rescue at early stages of the book's development. Lyn Kathlene and Elizabeth Grauerholz provided insightful comments on the prospectus draft. Berenice Carroll, director of women's studies, offered her usual good advice throughout the process.

The manuscript would still be a rough, hard copy if Barbara Puetz and Janet Neel had not typed several of the chapters. Their professional input kept the book on track. Chrystal Struben came on board as an independent study student and later as an assistant. Her careful attention to detail allowed me to focus on other tasks. From the beginning, Carole Appel, senior editor, and her assistant, Cat Warren, have guided me through the editorial maze. Karen Hewitt, senior editor, took over this task. The periodic postcards kept me informed. Becky Standard copyedited the book, Stacey Copenhaver prepared the index and handled the proofreading, and Matt Bahr tracked down missing reference material while I was on sabbatical in Hamburg, Germany. Thanks are due also to Mary Margaret Fonow, whose two extensive reviews offered instructive advice.

Several other friends lent their support during the development of this project: Penny Weiss, Jane Hassinger, Cynthia Stohl, and Dena Targ spent hours discussing various aspects of feminism and methodology with me.

I reserve for final mention my partner of thirteen years, David Fasenfest, who stood by me even when the specter of frustrations threatened to terminate the project. His patience, love, and encouragement enabled me to keep on keeping on. The last few months of manuscript preparation were enlivened by Bernhard Gottfried Fasenfest, the newest addition to our household. May he learn about feminism from this and other books.

FEMINISM AND SOCIAL CHANGE

Introduction

HEIDI GOTTFRIED

Engaging Women's Communities: Dilemmas and Contradictions in Feminist Research

This volume explores the problems, dilemmas, contradictions, and prospects for doing feminist research, not only *on* women or even *for* women, but also *with* women. In feminist research gender operates as a "basic organizing principle which profoundly shapes/mediates the concrete conditions of our lives. . . . Through the questions that feminism poses and the absences it locates, feminism argues the centrality of gender in shaping our consciousness, skills, and institutions as well as in the distribution of power and privilege" (Lather 1988:571). These essays form a collection of original research on the topic, in some cases presenting revised or revisited arguments made in previously published work.

Each chapter discusses principles of feminist inquiry, contains illustrative examples from each author's own research, and evaluates research practices for their potential to promote social change. Detailed case studies follow the actual research process, starting with the selection of questions for investigation, through the establishment of relationships with a community, to conducting research and dissemination of the research findings. By building a bridge between theory and practice, these chapters highlight the dilemmas and the possibilities for social change posed by different feminist research methodologies. The book serves as a practical guide to making connections with different women's communities, to representing different feminist (women's) voices, and to discussing possibilities and problems for the production of knowledge inherent in different research methods and theoretical strategies.

In contrast to other collections, this volume includes a broader range of social science methods, new contexts, and a selection of essays written about North American cases. While most texts focus on a single method, *Feminism and Social Change* covers a diversity of methodologies, including interpretive research strategies and techniques such as ethnographic study, in-depth interviewing, naming, and going public; consultative relationships between academic researchers and activist organizations; participatory and advocacy research processes; and coalition building. Contributors address a range of questions:

1. Who will have ultimate control over the results?
2. Should the results promote a specific set of policies or programs?
3. How best can an academic researcher represent women's voices in the results of research?
4. What methods best engage women in the process and products of research?
5. Is there a privileged standpoint from which to discover the real relations among human beings?
6. What is the relationship between standpoint and experience (theory and practice)?
7. Must we forsake scientific standards to conduct feminist research?
8. If science is always partial, situated, and a cultural product, then what standards (if any) could be applied?

To demonstrate how this volume adds to feminist research, I will review recent literature on the topic. The review of research on feminist methodology highlights the gaps and issues that are grist for continuing debate.

RESEARCH ON FEMINIST METHODOLOGY

The explosion of feminist research has produced several excellent anthologies on feminist methodology.[1] *Feminism and Methodology,* edited by Sandra Harding (1987), compiles an interdisciplinary selection of chapters addressing the unique feminist contributions to several disciplines. This collection directs attention to and makes theoretical claims about the existence of an uniquely feminist epistemology[2] and methodology. The interdisciplinary essays in Harding's book add a strong voice to a larger chorus of feminist challenges to the traditional canon. Unfortunately, research issues are posed at a very high level of abstraction. All too often, the authors resort to rarefied philosophical language to make their cases. In so doing, the book is most useful for constructing reasonable arguments in favor of conducting feminist scholarship. The authors, however, tend to remain silent on research methods and rarely come down to the concrete level to discuss their own methods or the research methods implied by their arguments (as acknowledged by Harding in her introduction). As a consequence, one is left without practical knowledge about how to conduct research in accordance with the various theoretical positions.

At the other end of the spectrum stand *Doing Feminist Research,* edited by Helen Roberts (1981), and *Theories of Women's Studies,* edited by Gloria Bowles and Renate Duelli Klein (1983), much earlier endeavors to assert feminism as a method of conducting research. In contrast to *Feminism and Methodology,* these texts primarily rely on experiential-based research practices. The contributors celebrate a woman's experience or voice that can be apprehended by and informs the necessity for feminist research methods. They insist that gender is integral to research practices and grant priority to experience as the primary source of knowledge. Yet basing research claims on the authority of experience can be limiting and exclusionary. Since the publication of these books, feminists have turned away from a search for either a single feminist theory, methodology, or authentic woman's voice. As a consequence, research practices premised on experience represent only one out of many choices for doing feminist research.

Assembling a group of interdisciplinary scholars from diverse racial, national, and ethnic backgrounds, two recent collections, *Women's Words,* edited by Sherna Berger Gluck and Daphne Patai (1991), and *Feminist Praxis,* edited by Liz Stanley (1990), offer a much needed corrective to these earlier volumes. Although *Women's Words* purports to focus exclusively on the feminist practice of oral history, as evidenced in the subtitle *The Feminist Practice of Oral History,* the volume includes informative discussions about other interpretive methods, such as ethnography, life history, testimonials, and interviewing. The authors of the chapters attempt to problematize as well as identify the conditions of possibility for the production of cultural representation. Such a pursuit, while tightly focused, should not be mistakenly interpreted as a narrow one because it spans multiple disciplines and methodologies.

Feminist Praxis begins with excellent theoretical chapters on the production of knowledge within a specific academic mode of production and on method, methodology, and epistemology in feminist research, followed by several chapters of substantive feminist research processes. This exemplary text contains substantive essays about British cases. However, the case material is less readily accessible to a U.S. audience. Both volumes weave together theoretical insights with illustrative examples from feminist research practices.

Two other books warrant mention: *Beyond Methodology,* edited by Mary Margaret Fonow and Judith A. Cook (1991), and *(En)gendering Knowledge,* edited by Joan Hartman and Ellen Messer-Davidow (1991). Fonow and Cook bring together noted feminist scholars, primarily from sociology, who examine feminist epistemology and methodology through a sociology of knowledge perspective. The chapters reprise four major themes extant in feminist scholarship: reflexivity, action-orientation, attention to the affective components of research, and the use of the situation at hand.

One of the most interdisciplinary collections is the recently published *(En)gendering Knowledge.* Whereas social sciences or the philosophy of science dominate most other texts on feminist methodology, Hartman and Davidow add to these the classics, biology, physical sciences, literature, and art history.

The above-mentioned volumes remain limited in their representation of research strategies and of women's diverse communities. Much of this writing on feminist methodology remains highly abstract, and the applied/practical/political side still requires closer attention, both by way of more abstract reflection and especially in the context of specific research projects in varied settings. *Feminism and Social Change* incorporates these criticisms, builds on previous insights, and tries to fill in some of the gaps.

ENGAGING WOMEN'S COMMUNITIES

This book begins with a discussion of broad epistemological and methodological concerns and then moves to the nitty-gritty of actual research projects, proceeding in three parts: part 1 explores dilemmas and contradictions in feminist research; part 2 presents case studies of research practices developed while engaging different women's communities; and part 3 considers various strategies of activist research, including participatory research, advocacy research, and coalition building.

As Harding (1987) notes, debates about feminism often conflate method, epistemology, and methodology. Some argue that feminism is a mode of doing research (Stanley and Wise 1983); others that it offers a theory of research practice (McRobbie 1982); still others that it constitutes a frame through which inquiries about the world can be made (Hartsock 1987a).

Those who argue for feminism as method distinguish between feminist methods and those same methods practiced in accordance with alternative theories. For example, ethnography and interviewing have been viewed as giving expression to women's experiences. As Judith Stacey notes in her essay in this volume, "In ethnography, the researcher is the primary medium, draws on those resources of empathy, connection and concern that many feminists consider to be a woman's special strength." Joan Acker, Kate Barry, and Joke Esseveld, along with Judith Stacey, caution that empathy is not always possible, nor is it a defining quality of feminist research. Feminist researchers may work on topics that require interviews with women and men who have more power or different political aims than the researcher (see, for example, Kaufman 1991). Feminism as method sees the representation of women's experience as the beginning and often the end of the production of knowledge claims. Sophie Laws (1986 as cited in Kelly 1988) argues that sociological literature on feminist research has favored women interviewing women as a research strategy because of its parallel to consciousness-raising. Consciousness-raising as feminist method privileges experiential knowledge.

Granting priority to experience as the primary source of knowledge can lead to a "politics of identity." A politics of identity bases research claims on the authority of experience. In so doing, a politics of identity can be both limiting and exclusionary, since no personal experience is inclusive enough to encompass all human experience. Further, premising insights into oppression on the verities of personal experience can be atomistic and relativistic.[3] "Naming" one's own experience is only the first step toward collective self-liberation (Combahee River Collective 1984; hooks 1984).[4]

Yet, insight into and appropriation of experience is critical to feminist projects of social transformation. It is theory that facilitates the mutual understandings among diverse experiences upon which collective action can be taken. Theory makes understanding another's point of view possible (Kelly 1988), but theory is not a substitute for political action. Alison Jaggar observes that "theory alone will not liberate women. But women's liberation seems equally unlikely to result from simple activism, not grounded in systematic understanding of women's situation" (1983:289).

The recognition of a bond between theory, research, and experience denies the conventional social science attitudes of disinterest and disembodiment. For example, the researcher attempts to narrow the distance between herself and other subjects and engages with them—a process Helen Roberts (1981) calls "reflexivity." Angela McRobbie (1982) situates the feminist researcher both personally and politically; she contends that feminism forces the researcher to locate her own autobiography and experience inside the questions asked. Similarly,

Sandra Harding (1987) and Dorothy Smith (1987b) claim that in the best feminist research, the inquirer places herself on the same critical plane as the other subjects. "Thus the researcher appears to us not as an invisible, anonymous voice of authority, but as a real, historical individual with concrete, specific desires and interests" (Harding 1987:9). Feminism can situate the researcher within the problematics from which inquiry begins. The intimate connection between theory, research, and experience is realized in a mutual engagement among concrete, historical individuals.

The first section in this volume discusses these feminist debates over the relationship between theory, research, and experience. Dissatisfied with the equation of feminism and method, Sherry Gorelick reviews both feminist critiques of dominant methodological paradigms (especially positivism) and early feminist methodological claims. Feminist scholars have an important role to play beyond giving voice to our silent sisters. Simply letting women speak for themselves will neither address internalized oppression nor allow the subjects of research to uncover the hidden bases of gender, class, and race oppressions. Gorelick suggests that voice(s) offer the researcher raw materials, but that theory provides the interpretive frame to make visible the daily and concrete social relations through which men and women create their worlds. An emancipatory social science, then, should provide women with understandings of how their everyday worlds, their trials and troubles, were and are generated by the larger social structure (see also Acker, Barry, and Esseveld in this volume).

Still, voice remains a valuable concept in feminist research. Since the publication of Carol Gilligan's (1982) influential book *In a Different Voice,* the concept of voice has become ubiquitous in feminists' writings. Feminists have used "voice" to convey agency on the part of women speakers. However, the application of the concept has not always been consistent, shifting from literal to metaphoric meanings—sometimes in the same work. In its literal sense, voice purports to simply represent women in their own words, that is, to let women speak for themselves, a method particularly prevalent among feminist symbolic interactionists. The metaphoric meaning refers to the logic of the speech act. To say that women speak in a "different voice" is to suggest that frames of reference differ, as in Gilligan's example of women adopting a needs (caring) and men a rights (justice) discourse to ground moral claims. To escape both the empiricism implied by symbolic interactionists and the essentialism implied by Gilligan's formulation, Gorelick and Acker, Barry, and Esseveld advocate problematizing representation of women's voices and examining the connections between women's everyday experience and the relations that underlie them.

The remaining chapters in part 1 continue the focus on the politics of doing feminist research. As the contributors turn their gaze back to assess feminism's second wave, optimism gives way to ambivalence about the political possibilities for feminist scholarship to help transform the oppressive conditions affecting women's lives. Some attribute partial blame to the retreat of feminism into the academy, arguing that academic feminism may be the victim of its own past successes. Dorothy E. Smith offers a trenchant critique of sociology as a disciplining discourse. She uncovers the hidden political ground of the academy that deprives feminist social scientists of perspectives other than those that sediment in our disciplines. As an alternative mode of inquiry, Smith proposes an engaged sociology constructed from standpoints of women both inside and outside of the academy. Joan Acker, Kate Barry, and Joke Esseveld agree that once the production of knowledge for women became fully embedded in the academy, the ties linking it to the concerns of women outside became attenuated.

Qualitative research methods are discussed in the final chapter of part 1. Judith Stacey extends the discussion by formulating a question, "Can There Be a Feminist Ethnography?" In conducting fieldwork on family and gender relationships in California's Silicon Valley, she found herself wondering whether the appearance of greater respect for and equality with research subjects in the ethnographic approach masked a deeper, more dangerous form of exploitation. There are no easy answers to the question she poses. Through a feminist dialogue with the "new," "postmodern," or "reflexive" ethnography,[5] she puts to rest any quest for an unproblematic feminist methodology. She concludes: "A fruitful dialogue between feminism and critical ethnography would continue to address their complementary sensitivities and naivetés about the inherent inequalities and the possibilities for relationships in the definition, study, and representation of the Other."

The volume as a whole moves beyond the old log jam of qualitative (supposedly more feminist) versus quantitative methods, what Geoff Skoll (1993) calls a false divide. Roberta Spalter-Roth and Heidi Hartmann and Ronnie J. Steinberg show that quantitative techniques can serve social change purposes and that such techniques can be innovatively fashioned to produce outcomes favorable to women. For example, to make quantitative data more accessible to a lay audience, Spalter-Roth and Hartmann have fashioned new techniques such as "reconstituted diaries." Yet going beyond this false divide is only the first step. We face other complex issues of how to choose the most appropriate method(s) for what we are studying, how to be more reflective and innovative in handling the drawbacks of each method, and how to be more creative in reshaping methods to more fully account for women's varied lives and experiences.

ENGAGING WOMEN: VARIED SETTINGS AND DIFFERENT COMMUNITIES

Chapters in part 2 detail the actual process of doing feminist research. As several of the essays illustrate, feminist scholars seek to transgress the boundaries of insider/outsider, observed/observer, and subject/object. Personal narratives chronicle the authors' attempts at negotiating these relationships.

Pierrette Hondagneu-Sotelo addresses the melding of research and activism in a project called "Immigrant Women and Paid Domestic Work," based on eighteen months of participant observation and in-depth interviews. In spite of many handicaps (legal, class, race, and gender), the research reveals that undocumented immigrant women workers construct and utilize informal social networks to stabilize their employment and to enhance their working conditions and pay. One of the more innovative aspects of the project involves its intimate connection to an ongoing advocacy project, the Coalition for Humane Immigrant Rights in Los Angeles. The coalition utilized Hondagneu-Sotelo's findings to construct *novelas*, didactic informational handouts using caricature scenarios and text. These handouts are now being distributed to domestic workers who ride Los Angeles public buses and to Latina nannies who congregate with their young charges in public parks.

Linda Carty discusses feminist research projects involving Caribbean women who were either current or former domestic workers and documented or undocumented immigrants. Being from the Caribbean and understanding the culture and some Creole dialects afforded her the privilege of initially approaching these women, but this insider status did not allow her total acceptance. The women's suspicion was predicated on Carty's positional difference as an academic and her political self-identification as a feminist. The research revealed the contested and politically charged nature of feminism and the implications of using the concept when trying to solidify participatory relationships and to achieve feminist and antiracist goals.

Further pursuing the theme of insider/outsider, Verta Taylor and Leila J. Rupp reflect on and present richly descriptive case material to illustrate the problems and advantages involved in the process of making lesbian existence central to their research. In assessing their research on the women's movement, they discovered that many of the women lived together in marriagelike relationships and formed communities with similar couples. This led them to question how to discuss lesbianism in cases where the subjects themselves did not self-identify as lesbians. Taylor and Rupp "believe that it is important to pay attention to women's relationships, to describe carefully and sensitively what we do know about them, keeping in mind both the historical development of a lesbian identity and the individual process that we now identify as 'coming out.'" Their next project focused on women's cultures produced in lesbian communities. As insiders they gained access unavailable to outsiders: "It is not that insider status gave us a privileged vantage point on some 'true' story of the community, but rather that we had knowledge of ephemeral developments that might not appear in any written sources or oral histories and were able to interview women who were willing to speak with us because they knew that we were lesbians and trusted that we would generate our analysis from a lesbian feminist standpoint."

Nancy A. Naples and Emily Clark add a new voice to the literature on participatory research, mixing personal narrative and theoretical explication. Their narrative emerges out of the reflexive bond between theory, research, and practical action as they "go public" with their experiences of child sexual abuse. Naples explores the role feminism plays as an alternative discourse in shaping the storytelling process and as implicated in the articulation of survivors' discourses. The unfolding research process comes to life in the dialogue between Nancy and Emily, who bring different, albeit overlapping, interests (e.g., healing, consciousness-raising, career building) to the project.

FEMINIST ACTIVIST RESEARCH: MULTIPLE STRATEGIES

The chapters in part 3, taken together, provide entre into feminist activist research, including participatory, advocacy, and coalition-building types. Many styles of activist research have existed both within and outside of the academy as alternatives to conventional social science methods. Activist researchers share in common a commitment to social change and to empowerment of the subjects of research but use different methods to realize these goals.

The starting point of participatory research is the "problem-posing" educational program popularized by Paulo Freire (1972) and extended to feminism most notably by Patricia Maguire (1987) and most recently by Francesca M. Cancian (in this volume). Participatory research exemplifies one of the most radical and activist elements of feminist methodology by enlisting a community's participation and collaboration in social change projects. Participation and collaboration are more than terminological hallmarks of participatory research: they specify the practices, subjects, and possibilities for such research projects (Hall 1981; Brown 1985; Brown and Tandon 1983). Cancian describes the components and process of conducting participatory research and analyses and identifies the strengths and weaknesses of several feminist and nonfeminist participatory research projects based on interviews with activist researchers. Various forces within and outside the university (e.g., careerism and the academic power structure) conspire to suppress participatory research methods.

In contrast to participatory research with its emphasis on grass-roots participation and collaboration, advocacy researchers operate in a policy context, often use available data sets, and stress the use of numbers as an important code in policy debates, that is, "counting is as important as naming." Unlike participatory researchers who engage directly with a community, those who work with advocacy organizations implicitly assume a division of labor between research organizations (who do the research) and national advocacy groups (who do the advocacy). According to Roberta Spalter-Roth and Heidi Hartmann, the advocacy researcher relies on others to tell us "what is important to women, what needs to be researched, and how that research will be used" rather than working directly with constituencies of women and learning about their needs directly through our own experience. Thus the connection between theory (research) and practice (the grass roots) is attenuated at best.

Spalter-Roth and Hartmann frame these issues by situating the debate within the historical context of two generations of feminist advocacy research. The first group of women received training as social scientists in the new research universities of the late nineteenth-century United States, which were centered around the University of Chicago and Hull-House. This important but lost history provides a unique vantage point to compare the second generation that includes the Institute for Women's Policy Research. They contrast today's division of labor model with the "Hull-House model" of feminist policy research, a model in which data collection, research, and analysis; policy change and advocacy; service and education to the community; and politics were all done simultaneously by Hull-House members. Proposing "the dual vision of feminist policy research," Spalter-Roth and Hartmann attempt to synthesize the views of the two generations—to create research that meets both the standards of positivist social science and the feminist goals of doing research *for* rather than *on* women.

Reflecting on fifteen years as an advocacy researcher, Ronnie J. Steinberg assesses problems that have plagued policy-based researchers. Throughout her work on comparable worth and pay equity, she and others have utilized scientific credentials and social science methodologies as a "power resource" to further policy goals. Feminist advocacy research encompasses a variety of activities that bring scholarship to bear on social issues explicitly for the purpose of achieving change in power relations and in structural arrangements—in this case, on behalf of women. According to Steinberg, "for research to serve as a power resource, it is necessary that it be impeccably designed and carried out, given the ease with which any scientific study can be pulled apart by those of other ideological persuasions." The need for legitimacy in the face of hostile adversaries adds pressure on advocacy researchers to adopt methodological tools common in conventional social science. "While feminist advocacy researchers are critical of science and feel all too strongly the limitations of its claims to objectivity and universal truth at a practical level, we use [conventional] methods because they legitimate our expertise and because they legitimate the findings we introduce into the policy arena."

Steinberg and Spalter-Roth and Hartmann acknowledge that advocacy researchers purposively adopt conventional social science methodologies characteristic of academic research, but distinguish between conventional and advocacy research methods. Advocacy research differs in several aspects, as enumerated by Steinberg: in the context in which the research is conducted; in the need for the researcher to establish scientific credibility, in that, as an advocate, she is not assumed to be an objective scientist seeking one uncontested truth; and in the amount of control that the researcher can exercise in the design of the research and in the selection of the indicators. Steinberg concludes that the unique and combined characteristics of advocacy research make it more difficult to do effectively than conventional social science research.

Shifting the focus to the theoretical bases of coalition building, Nancy C. M. Hartsock discusses the challenge of postmodernism to feminism. In a political excavation of postmodernist thought (particularly of Richard Rorty and Michel Foucault), Hartsock reads postmodernism as the "destabilized voice of the powerful being forced to come to terms with the voice of the disenfranchised." In her chapter she argues for the utility, validity, and even necessity of political theory in developing feminist liberatory politics. It would be folly to follow post-structuralist's injunction for the abandonment of theory or the death of the subject. Those on the margins need to understand the world systematically in order to change it (Hartsock 1989:7). Feminist politics today should involve building new coalitions and strategic alliances; and in any effort at coalition building or alliance formation, close attention must be given to the specific situations (identities) of each group as defined by axes of gender, race, class, and sexuality. As Hartsock summarizes in this volume: "Recognizing our experiences in the lives of others can strengthen our resolve to do the difficult political work of coalition building."

Activist researchers appear to be more self-conscious about the impact that the choice of methods have on their intended audiences and try to address different, and sometimes conflicting, audiences, such as academics, policy-makers, and grass-roots groups. Cancian, Smith, and Acker, Barry, and Esseveld discuss how academic audiences and academic structures, including career building in academic women's studies, affect our work, sometimes in cooptive and depoliticizing ways. Spalter-Roth and Hartmann and Steinberg argue for the legitimacy of numbers and scientific rhetoric and the dilemmas this poses for altering research to speak to the experiences of the less powerful and to appeal to and serve other, also politically important audiences instead of just policy-makers. Grass-roots activists are emphasized by Cancian, Taylor and Rupp, Hondagneu-Sotelo, and Naples and Clark, while Hartsock uses a more direct political-organizing and theoretical focus.

FROM SINGULARITY TO PLURALITY

A summary of feminist theories and methods suggests that the terrain has moved from singularity to plurality.[6] Feminists no longer argue for a single procedure that produces one true story. Similarly, the privileging of experience has given way to accounts premised on different feminisms and on differences between women.[7] This current plurality of feminisms was most notably "motivated by the enormous and continuing political impact of black women's critique of the racist and ethnocentric assumptions of white feminists" (Barrett and Phillips 1992:4; see also Collins 1990). Invoking the abstraction "woman" tended to privilege gender over other oppressions and failed to represent adequately the diversity of women's lived experiences, legacies, and possibilities (Spelman 1988). Most feminists now acknowledge the importance of difference(s); at stake is whether or not some differences matter more than others (di Stefano 1990; Bordo 1990, 1992; Hartsock, this volume) and how various axes of difference relate to each other (Fraser and Nicholson 1990).

This focus on diversity and difference has led many (Harding 1989; Collins 1990; as well as many in this volume) to question whether a feminist standpoint or even a hierarchy of standpoints can adequately capture multiply configured positions and identities of women. For example, Acker, Barry, and Esseveld are "critical of theory developed from a universalistic male perspective, [and they would] counterpose to this a women's perspective that also is universal." In their afterword, they point out that their earlier formulation assumed a universal, mostly heterosexual, woman's standpoint. Any new research would recognize the diversity of women's experiences.

Feminists have proposed more contingent and less deterministic theories and concepts to ground a critique of phallocratic, racist, homophobic, and capitalist institutions. The concept of "situated knowledges," developed by Donna Haraway (1988) and used by both Hartsock and Cancian, offers a way to incorporate diversity of women's lived experiences. Situated knowledges imply qualities of multiplicity, are locatable in time and space and particular cultures, are embodied in specific ways, and operate as social and collective points of view. As an aspect of being situated, these knowledges represent a response to and an expression of a specific embodiment.

By extension Cancian draws the conclusion that a partial and situated science implies limits to the achievement of science. Despite these limits, she argues that feminist researchers can build minimal standards of science. This would include a commitment to good evidence and a consideration of alternatives—i.e., the openness to debate, allowing for the play of competing explanations. She suggests feminist standards of evidence, starting with what's useful in positivism, while recognizing that positivism favors the dominant.

Gorelick's notion of a "complex of many determinations" opposes either "academic feminist pluralism" or a fragmentary science and a simple hierarchy of standpoints: "A methodology based on a 'complex of many determinations' implies a cumulative social science that is not merely additive. The visions of each subgroup of women must refocus or revision the knowledge of all."

Harding (1989:22) advocates a "perverse" research stance that constantly seeks to reveal and examine the privileged identities and the unequal power relations that facilitate the collusion of research in the perpetuation of conditions of domination, oppression, and privilege and corrode the interpersonal dynamics of research relationships. Feminist researchers who seek relations of mutuality must continually invent "monstrous" identities out of step with the conventions and comforts of acceptable selves; it is a painful process that involves an ongoing struggle against social and psychic complacency and comfort (Harding 1989:27). Research should not just reproduce experience but should develop procedures that allow for the production of contrary readings, which can play an active role in social debate.

Feminists' contingent (partial) view of science emphasizes multiplicity and diversity and criticizes deterministic accounts as well as accounts premised on indeterminacy. Concepts such as situated knowledges oppose, on the one hand, modernists' uncritical faith in reason and rationality and, on the other hand, postmodernists' rejection of the possibility of knowledge. It is neither a call for the abandonment of theory nor for a ceding of the possibility of knowing the Other.[8] To reject a universalizing and totalizing voice, that of the transcendental scientist, does not necessitate a displacement or negation of theory. By using concepts like situated knowledges, we can begin to counter essentialism inherent to standpoint theories, to recognize that the knowledge we claim is conditioned by the locations we occupy (Hartsock 1987a:32), to take as reference points positions other than white, industrialized world, and heterosexuality, and to allow for multiple and shifting perspectives that enable us to learn about ourselves from the experiences and knowledges of others (Martin and Mohanty 1986).

RESEARCH AS POLITICAL PRACTICE: PROBLEMS AND FUTURE POSSIBILITIES

> How we can use our educational apparatuses and institutions to make social change—how we can reinvigorate "our capacity as agents to act as well as to know otherwise, to intervene in the world as well as the academy, to have an effect."
>
> —Gayle Greene

This book highlights research as political practice, examining both the possibilities and contradictions posed by feminist research at the conjuncture of a third wave of feminism. Research is inherently political, structured in hierarchies of power among researchers, between sponsors of research and researchers, and between researchers and the subjects of their research (Bell and Roberts 1984). These political relations present feminist researchers with an array of counterforces to the development of liberatory research practices, including the insinuation of relations of control and dependency, the material privileges of researchers, and the influence of institutional interests on research conduct.

First, the reinscription of the researcher into a position of power and privilege opens possibilities for exploitation that subvert empowerment and mutuality. While there may be an effort toward the collaborative, reciprocal quest for knowledge, Stacey cautions that the research project ultimately is that of the researcher—it is the researcher who narrates and "authors" the final text.

Second, writing is always an act of translation rather than simply a transcription of women's words. It is neither desirable nor possible to simply represent the "voices" of women. Women's voices are always mediated through the filter of the researcher and conventions of language. Ultimately the researcher must objectify the experience of the researched and must translate that experience into more abstract and general terms if an analysis that links the individual to processes outside her immediate social world is to be achieved.

Third, the researcher intervenes into a system of power relations that she is free to leave upon completion of a research project. By disengaging, the researcher leaves the subjects on their own to negotiate the power dynamics they mutually have uncovered and often abdicates responsibility for the political implications of the research results.

Fourth, the interests of the academic researcher may conflict with those of the community. In the process of doing research, a researcher may come to learn what Steinberg has called "guilty knowledge," any information that potentially compromises an individual's or a group's interest. Stacey faced the decision of whether or not to reveal the sexual orientation of one of her respondents. To "out" a "closeted" lesbian would have had political repercussions for the woman, yet to suppress the knowledge about sexual orientation would distort Stacey's research. Do we have an obligation to disclose information uncovered during the process of research even if it could damage community efforts toward social change? Does failure to report guilty knowledge violate tenets of good research practice? The authors offer different strategies for dealing with these dilemmas and contradictions.

Research involves power relations and the conduct of research is embedded in the hierarchies and constraints of academic life. Doing research in academic institutions raises difficult questions: How can the material privileges rooted in academic positions be used in the service of oppressed women rather than in the interests that such privileged academic positions represent, i.e., those of the academy and the powerful groups in society that support it? How can disciplinary protocol and the conventional standards of social science research be confronted in ways that assert rather than accede the legitimacy of liberatory research practices? How can universities be sites of struggles while serving as sites for the reproduction of power and privilege (Bannerji et al. 1991:5)?

These constraints cannot be overcome by simply altering the methodology or applying a particular theory. Methodological change ultimately depends on changing the structure of the university. "The task of dismantling the master's house with the master's tools, always problematic, has become more vexed the more institutionalized we've become; our dilemma is now, . . . how to dismantle the masters' houses while we are trying to get computers for their offices we have set up inside them" (Bammer 1991 as quoted in Greene 1992:25). Possibilities do exist for reforming parts of the university by taking advantage of feminist spaces such as feminist journals or women's studies programs. These programs create spaces in which debates over power and the production of knowledge can take place (Lather 1988:569). If, as Kelly (1988) suggests, one of the basic principles of feminist practice is to challenge social relations based on power, then feminist research must critically confront the power dynamics of academic expectations, conventions, and traditions in order to establish an alternative practice. Research itself can be a vehicle for consciousness-raising.

However, to remain cloistered behind the walls of the university, safely entrenched in the day-to-day battles that preoccupy us, will serve to attenuate feminism's base in broader communities of women and to sever feminism's connection to wider women's movements. Acker, Barry, and Esseveld sound a cautionary note in their observation that "as feminist scholarship feminism has become institutionalized within the academy, increasingly abstract theoretical concerns seem to have less and less to do with practical problems of women's everyday lives." Feminist researchers thus must renew and maintain links with various communities of women in order to ground their research in women's everyday lives.

None of the problems discussed in this book come with easy answers. The authors have raised questions and have provided answers to a wide range of vexing research problems. Hopefully, readers will come away with a renewed spirit to carry on feminist research both inside and outside of the university. Future generations of feminist researchers can reflect on our triumphs and defeats in order to fashion new feminist practices aimed at promoting social change.

NOTES

Many of the ideas for this chapter were developed in "Research for Women: Notes toward the Development of a Liberatory Research Project," coauthored with Patty Sotirin, and expanded upon in "Notes towards the Development of a Liberatory Research Project," in *Trade Unions and Social Research,* edited by Keith Forrester and Colin Thorne (Aldershot, England: Avebury, 1993).

1. Methodology is the study of actual techniques and practices used in the research process.

2. Harding states that "an epistemology is a theory of knowledge, it answers questions about who can be a 'knower' (can women?); what tests beliefs must pass in order to be legitimated as knowledge (only tests against men's experiences and observations?); what kinds of things can be known (can 'subjective truths' count as knowledge?), and so forth. . . . Feminists have argued that traditional epistemologies, whether intentionally or unintentionally, systematically exclude the possibility that women could be 'knowers' or agents of knowledge; they claim that the voice of science is a masculine one; that history is written from only the point of view of men (of the dominant class and race); that the subject of a traditional sociological sentence is always assumed to be a man" (1987:3).

3. Relativism assumes that all explanations are subjectively grounded and therefore have equal weight. When all accounts are equally valid, the search for "how it actually works" becomes meaningless (see Acker, Barry, and Esseveld in this volume).

4. Spender advocates naming as "the means whereby we attempt to order and structure the chaos and flux of existence which would otherwise be an undifferentiated mass. By assigning names, we impose a pattern of meaning which allows us to manipulate the world" (1987:163).

5. "The favored postmodern solution to the reflexive anthropological predicament has been to fully acknowledge the dialogic and discursive character of the ethnographic process and product and to deconstruct their own claims to ethnographic authority" (Stacey, this volume).

6. Barrett and Phillips (1992:4) find that early formulations in feminist theory instantiated a "modernist" impulse whose starting point assumed that one could specify a cause of women's oppression; feminists differed on what this cause might be, alternatively stressing either male control of women's fertility, a patriarchal system of inheritance, or capitalists' need for a docile labor force.

7. Multiplicity and diversity of approaches resist simple dichotomies such as emancipatory versus subordinative research. The idolization of experience as the beginning and end of research is seen as a romantic fallacy that denies the specificity of social and scientific practices. These ideas benefited from the comments by Erik Kats and Folks Galstra in personal correspondence.

8. Symbolic interactionists and postmodernists converge in their arguments when they contend that we can never truly know the Other and refuse to speak for or about the Other.

REFERENCES

Bammer, Angelika. 1991. "Mastery." In *(En)gendering Knowledge: Feminists in Academe,* ed. Joan Hartmann and Ellen Messer-Davidow. Knoxville: University of Tennesse Press. 237-58. Quoted in Gayle Greene, "Putting Principle into Practice," *Women's Review of Books* 10, no. 1 (1992): 25.

Bannerji, Himani, Linda Carty, Kari Dehli, Susan Heald, and Kate McKenna, eds. 1991. *Unsettling Relations: The University as a Site of Feminist Struggles.* Boston: South End Press.

Barrett, Michelle, and Anne Phillips, eds. 1992. *Destablizing Theory: Contemporary Feminist Debates.* Stanford: Stanford University Press.

Bell, Colin, and Helen Roberts, eds. 1984. *Social Researching: Politics, Problems, and Practice.* London: Routledge and Kegan Paul.

Bordo, Susan. 1992. "Postmodern Subjects, Postmodern Bodies." *Feminist Studies* 18 (1): 159–75.

———. 1990. "Feminism, Postmodernism, and Gender Skepticism." In *Feminism/Postmodernism,* ed. Linda J. Nicholson. New York: Routledge. 133–56.

Bowles, Gloria, and Renate Duelli Klein, eds. 1983. *Theories of Women's Studies.* London: Routledge and Kegan Paul.

Brown, David. 1985. "People-Centered Development and Participatory Research." *Harvard Educational Review* 55 (1): 69–75.

Brown, David, and Rajesh Tandon. 1983. "Ideology and Political Economy in Inquiry: Action Research and Participatory Research." *Journal of Applied Behavioral Science* 19 (3): 277–94.

Collins, Patricia Hill. 1990. *Black Feminist Thought: Knowledge, Consciousness, and the Politics of Empowerment.* Boston: Unwin Hyman. Reprint. New York: Routledge, 1991.

Combahee River Collective. 1984. "A Black Feminist Statement." In *Feminist Frameworks,* ed. Alison Jaggar and Paula Rothenberg. 2d ed. New York: McGraw Hill. 202–9.

di Stefano, Christine. 1990. "Dilemmas of Difference: Feminism, Modernity, and Postmodernism." In *Feminism/Postmodernism,* ed. Linda Nicholson. New York: Routledge. 63–82.

Fonow, Mary Margaret, and Judith A. Cook, eds. 1991. *Beyond Methodology: Feminist Scholarship as Lived Research.* Bloomington: Indiana University Press.

Fraser, Nancy, and Linda Nicholson. 1990. "Social Criticism without Philosophy: An Encounter between Feminism and Postmodernism." In *Feminism/Postmodernism,* ed. Linda Nicholson. New York: Routledge. 19–38.

Freire, Paolo. 1972. *Pedagogy of the Oppressed.* Trans. Myra Bergman Ramos. New York: Herder and Herder.

Gilligan, Carol. 1982. *In a Different Voice.* Cambridge: Harvard University Press.

Gluck, Sherna Berger, and Daphne Patai. 1991. *Women's Words: The Feminist Practice of Oral History.* New York: Routledge.

Gottfried, Heidi. 1993. "Notes towards the Development of a Liberatory Research Project." In *Trade Unions and Social Research,* ed. Keith Forrester and Colin Thorne. Aldershot, England: Avebury. 45–60.

Gottfried, Heidi, and Patricia Sotirin. 1991. "Notes toward the Development of a Liberatory Research Project." Ms.

Greene, Gayle. 1992. "Putting Principle into Practice." *Women's Review of Books* 10 (1): 25.

Hall, Bud. 1981. "Participatory Research, Popular Knowledge, and Power: A Personal Reflection." *Convergence* 14 (3): 6–19.

Haraway, Donna. 1988. "Situated Knowledges: The Science Question in Feminism and the Privilege of Partial Perspective." *Feminist Studies* 14 (3): 575–99.

Harding, Sandra. 1989. "After the End of 'Philosophy.'" Ms.

———, ed. 1987. *Feminism and Methodology: Social Science Issues.* Bloomington: Indiana University Press.

Hartman, Joan, and Ellen Messer-Davidow. 1991. *(En)gendering Knowledge: Feminists in Academe.* Knoxville: University of Tennessee Press.

Hartsock, Nancy C. M. 1989. "Epistemology and Politics: Developing Alternatives to Western Political Thought." Ms.

———. 1987a. "The Feminist Standpoint: Developing the Ground for a Specifically Feminist Historical Materialism." In *Feminism and Methodology: Social Science Issues,* ed. Sandra Harding. Bloomington: University of Indiana Press. 157–80.

———. 1987b. "Rethinking Modernism: Minority vs. Majority Theories." *Cultural Critique* 7 (Fall): 187–206.

hooks, bell. 1984. *Feminist Theory: From Margin to Center.* Boston: South End Press.

Jaggar, Alison. 1983. *Feminist Politics and Human Nature.* Totowa, N.J.: Rowman and Allanheld.

Kaufman, Debra. 1991. *Rachel's Daughters.* New Brunswick, N.J.: Rutgers University Press.

Kelly, Liz. 1990. *Feminist Practice.* London: Routledge, Chapman, and Hall.

———. 1988. *Surviving Sexual Violence.* Minneapolis: University of Minnesota Press.

Klein, Renate Duelli. 1983. "How to Do What We Want to Do: Thoughts about Feminist Methodology." In *Theories of Women's Studies,* ed. Gloria Bowles and Renate Duelli Klein. London: Routledge and Kegan Paul. 88–104.

Lather, Patti. 1988. "Feminist Perspectives on Empowering Research Methodologies." *Women's Studies International Forum* 11 (6): 569–81.

Laws, Sophie. 1986. "The Social Meaning of Menstruation: A Feminist Investigation." Ph.D. diss., Warwick University. Cited in Liz Kelly, *Surviving Sexual Violence* (Minneapolis: University of Minnesota Press, 1988).

McCarl-Nielsen, Joyce. 1990. *Feminist Research Methods: Exemplary Readings in the Social Sciences.* Boulder, Co.: Westview Press.

McRobbie, Angela. 1982. "The Politics of Feminist Research: Between Talk and Action." *Feminist Review* 12:46–58.

Maguire, Patricia. 1987. *Doing Participatory Research: A Feminist Approach.* Amherst: Center for International Education, School of Education, University of Massachusetts.

Martin, Biddy, and Chandra Mohanty. 1986. "Feminist Politics: What's Home Got to Do with It?" In *Feminist Studies/Critical Studies,* ed. Teresa de Lauretis. Bloomington: Indiana University Press. 191–212.

Maynard, Mary. 1990. "The Re-shaping of Sociology?: Trends in the Study of Gender." *Sociology* 24 (2): 269–90.

Oakley, Ann. 1989. "Women's Studies in British Sociology: To End at Our Beginning?" *British Journal of Sociology* 40 (3): 442–70.

———. 1981. "Interviewing Women: A Contradiction in Terms." In *Doing Feminist Research,* ed. Helen Roberts. London: Routledge and Kegan Paul. 30–61.

Reinharz, Shulamit. 1992. *Feminist Methods in Social Research.* New York: Oxford University Press.

Roberts, Helen, ed. 1981. *Doing Feminist Research.* London: Routledge and Kegan Paul.

Skoll, Geoff. 1993. "On the Natural Superiority of Women in the Human Sciences." Ms.

Smith, Dorothy. 1987a. *The Everyday World as Problematic: A Feminist Sociology.* Boston: Northeastern University Press.

———. 1987b. "Women's Perspective as a Radical Critique of Sociology." In *Feminism and Methodology: Social Science Issues,* ed. Sandra Harding. Bloomington: University of Indiana Press. 84–96.

———. 1979. "A Sociology for Women." In *The Prism of Sex: Essays in the Sociology of Knowledge,* ed. Julia A. Sherman and Evelyn Torton Beck. Madison: University of Wisconsin Press. 135–87.

Spelman, Elizabeth V. 1988. *Inessential Woman: Problems of Exclusion in Feminist Thought.* Boston: Beacon Press.

Spender, Dale. 1987. *Man Made Language.* 2d ed. London: Routledge and Kegan Paul.

Stanley, Liz, ed. 1990. *Feminist Praxis: Research, Theory, and Epistemology in Feminist Sociology.* London: Routledge and Kegan Paul.

Stanley, Liz, and Sue Wise. 1983. *Breaking Out: Feminist Consciousness and Feminist Research.* London: Routledge and Kegan Paul.

Treichler, Paula A., Cheris Kramarae, and Beth Stafford, eds. 1985. *For Alma Mater: Theory and Practice in Feminist Scholarship.* Urbana: University of Illinois Press.

PART I

Doing Feminist Research: Dilemmas and Contradictions

CHAPTER 1

SHERRY GORELICK

Contradictions of Feminist Methodology

Feminist methodology grows out of an important qualitative leap in the feminist critique of the social sciences: the leap from a critique of the invisibility of women, both as objects of study and as social scientists, to the critique of the method and purpose of social science itself. This is the leap from a sociology *about* women to a sociology *for* women, as Dorothy Smith (1974) put it. Smith argued that male-dominated science objectifies, but something very fundamental happens when both the knower and the known are women. When the pronoun applied to the knower is *she,* rather than the *seemingly* impersonal *he,* the knower is changed immediately from The Scientist to a person with a gender. And when this scientist with a female personal pronoun studies women, she is apt to feel a different relationship with her subjects, because she is subject to finding herself mirrored in them, a fact with revolutionary implications for the relationships among observer and observed, theory and experience, science, politics, race, and class. In the past two decades, however, we have learned that this mirroring process has its own limits, reflecting divisions based on race, class, and other forms of oppression and requiring that we push the methodological revolution even further.

FEMINIST CRITIQUES OF THE DOMINANT METHODOLOGICAL PARADIGMS

Feminist methodological critiques have been made on several interrelated levels: philosophical, moral, and practical. The *philosophical* level has involved a critique of positivism: the pretense of value-free science and the presumption of objectivity conceived of as a set of procedures or an achievement, rather than a process (Gorelick 1989; Keller 1980).

On a *moral* level, feminists have criticized the objectification of subjects and their exploitation by researchers using the dominant methods.[1] Objectification rests on positing a radical difference between the roles of scientist and subject in which, in the most extreme positivist approaches, studying human beings is, in principle, no different from studying things. George Lundberg wrote that there is, for the social scientist, no difference between a paper flying before the wind and a man flying before an angry crowd (1963:45–46).

In contrast to this reduction of human beings to social facts, feminism, building on the interpretative approach in sociology, emphasizes the human agency and subjectivity of the people studied. The production of science is not an operation (or indeed an autopsy); it is a relationship. That relationship is exploitative when a researcher studies people for the benefit of the researcher's career or of the sponsors of the research without regard for any positive or negative effect on the people being studied. Feminists have also criticized the entire structure of inequality in the conduct of research, especially the hierarchical structure of large-scale research projects.

This moral critique of research hierarchy is directly related to feminists' *practical* critique of the dominant methodologies. The opposed interests of researcher and researched in the dominant, hierarchical methodological approaches lead to distortions, lying, even farcical results (Gorz 1972; Klein 1983:91). A subject population does not tell the truth to those in power. Not only that, large-scale research projects generate *two* subject populations: the people being studied and the people doing the routine labor involved in studying them. In "hired hand research" (Roth 1966; Reinharz 1983:171), low-level research staff may find myriad ways of cutting short their work, constituting a "labor problem" in the truth factory. Between the creative dissimulation of the objectified research subjects and the subversive creativity of the research workers, each responding to their different modes of exploitation, the results are often not science, but science fiction.

Two feminist methodological alternatives emerged: the Marxist-feminist and the experiential-inductionist, often affiliated with ethnomethodological and interactionist scholarly traditions and with the new social history emphasizing "the view from the bottom." Some feminists have attempted to integrate these two approaches (e.g., Acker, Barry, and Esseveld 1983; Smith 1987). After reviewing this literature, I propose to explore some contradictions involved in the development of a Marxist-feminist-interactionist methodology. These contradictions concern the role of theory and "false consciousness" in the relationship between researcher and participant; the implications of race, class, and other inequalities for feminist research; and the implications of the social biography of the researcher for the development of a liberatory feminist standpoint. I argue that the feminist inductionists fail to take account of the hidden structure of oppression (the research participant is not omniscient) and the hidden relations of oppression (the participant may be ignorant of her relative privilege over and difference from other women). Women's oppression is a complex of many contradictions and requires a new standpoint-based methodology created by researchers and participants of diverse race, class, and other oppressed groups, refocusing and revisioning knowledge based on theory, action, and experience.

EARLY FEMINIST METHODOLOGICAL MANIFESTOS

In 1978 Maria Mies set forth methodological guidelines for feminist research that proposed that the hypocritical "postulate of *value-free research,* of neutrality and indifference toward the research objects, has to be replaced by *conscious partiality"* toward the oppressed, engagement in their struggles for change, and the creation of a form of research that fosters *conscientization* of both the researcher and the researched (1983:122–26). The guidelines set the dominant formula for research practice on its head. The dogmas of positivism—its hands-off approach, its clinical fastidiousness about mutual contamination, its insistence that research must precede change, that indeed change is the business of politicians and not scientists—were overturned. For feminist methodologists, as for the Marxist and interpretive sociologists on whose work they built, social science is much more profound than the mere collection of "facts." Said Mies: "Most empirical research on women has concentrated so far on the study of superficial or surface phenomena such as women's attitudes toward housework, career, . . . etc. Such attitude or opinion surveys give very little information about women's true consciousness. Only when there is a rupture in the 'normal' life of a woman, i.e. a crisis such as divorce, end of a relationship etc., is there a chance for her to become conscious of her true conditions" (1983:125). As Judith A. Cook and Mary Margaret Fonow put it much later: "Feminism is a vision of freedom as future intention and this vision must indicate which facts from the present are necessary knowledge for liberation. Description without an eye for transformation is inherently conservative and portrays the subject as acted-upon rather than as an actor or potential actor" (1986:12). The implication is quite clear: Merely collecting descriptive statistics or experiential data about women does not constitute feminist research. Feminist research must be part of a process by which women's oppression is not only described, but challenged. Similarly, beginning in 1974, Dorothy Smith argued that sociology as currently practiced expressed unreflectively the distortions of a male, ruling-class standpoint. She urged that instead research must be done "from the standpoint of women," taking "the everyday world as problematic" and beginning from women's ordinary, everyday experience (1974, 1979). Smith specifically cautioned against *confining* the inquiry to the world of experience (1974:12, 1979:174). Some later feminist methodologists, however, have argued for a social science that is "inductive rather than deductive," that "focuses on processes rather than structures," and that is "interested in generating concepts *in vivo*, in the field itself" rather than using "predefined concepts" (Reinharz 1983:172, 168). According to Shulamit Reinharz, whereas the validity criteria of "conventional or patriarchal" science are "proof, evidence, statistical significance [and] replicability," the validity criteria of feminist science are "completeness, plausibility, . . . understanding, [and] responsiveness to readers' or subjects' experience; [the] study cannot, however, be replicated" (1983:171). The role of the researcher is to "give voice" to hitherto silenced groups and facilitate their own discoveries (Kasper 1986).

GIVING VOICE IS NOT ENOUGH: THE LIMITS OF FEMINIST EMPIRICISM

"Giving voice" was a progressive development in the history of feminist theory. It went beyond criticism of the use of "mainstream" social science as a tool of oppression and began the quest for a liberatory social science. But the more radically empiricist forms of the feminist critique have their own limitations that threaten to encapsulate feminist social science within each specific milieu being studied and even preclude understanding the very milieu being examined. For example, use of such techniques as interviews, participant observation, and oral history helps to describe the world as perceived by the persons studied, but it may remain confined within their perceptions and thus not be able to provide them with much that they do not already know.

The agonizing and cumulative process of feminist discovery over the years has revealed how much of sexism is deeply internalized and therefore buried beneath the conscious level (MacKinnon 1987). Consciousness-raising as a technique of research and political action may enable women to "give voice" to knowledge that they did not know they had. But this knowledge, too, is limited to what each group of women is able to discover anew. Maria Mies's emphasis on the importance of crises or ruptures in the pattern of normality, so that the pathology of the normal may be perceived, is of crucial importance. Even so, giving voice is not enough. Women know much and may learn more about their own pain, but some of the underlying causes of that pain may be very well hidden from them (cf. Maguire 1987:37).

THE HIDDEN DETERMINANTS OF OPPRESSION

In *Capital,* Marx showed that the most fundamental social relations occur "behind the backs" of the actors. That is, much of the underlying structure of oppression is hidden, not only by means of ideology, but also by means of a contradictory daily life. Appearance contradicts reality: Workers feel dependent on capitalists for employment and wages, yet in reality they produce daily, in surplus value, the wages with which they are paid and the wealth that permits their continued subjugation. The "developing" world appears dependent on the "industrializing" world for technology and investment, yet in reality the imperial world is dependent on the colonized world for raw materials, markets, and cheap labor. Wives appear to be dependent on husbands for support and protection, yet in reality it is husbands that are dependent on wives for their unpaid labor, emotion management, and much else. Suniti Namjoshi's amusing but chilling fable "The Monkey and the Crocodiles" (1981:26) shows women's need for male physical protection to be little more than a protection racket. In reality each of these dependencies is substantially reversed, yet none of these realities is immediately apparent to those most oppressed by them.

In "Women's Perspective as a Radical Critique of Sociology," Dorothy Smith described the dependence of professional and managerial men practicing "the abstracted conceptual mode of ruling" on the concrete invisible labor of women as computer specialists, secretaries, administrative assistants, wives, and so on. Their own social determinants are invisible to the men (1974:10), yet the importance of their own role may be invisible to the women themselves, for two reasons. First, the dominant ideology obscures their role: "ideas and social forms of consciousness may originate outside experience, coming from an external source and becoming a forced set of categories into which we must stuff the awkward and resistant actualities of our worlds" (1987:55). Second, women's vision of their own oppression is masked by the development of corporate capitalism, in which local events are determined by social forces far from the site (1979:161). In short, although oppression can *only* be understood from the standpoint and experience of the oppressed, the very organization of the everyday world of oppression in modern capitalism obscures the structure of oppression: "The everyday world is not fully understandable within its own scope. It is organized by social relations not fully apparent in it nor contained in it" (1979:176; 1987:92).

In contrast to the reified conceptualizations of social structure produced by functionalist (and radical functionalist) social scientists (Gorelick 1977), the feminist concept of social relations does not connote a rigid and reified social structure impervious to human action. Rather, social relations are relatively enduring relationships among people, relationships that embody contradiction and change (Acker, Barry, and Esseveld 1983:425). Some of the methodological implications of the structure of social relations were developed in Nancy Hartsock's pivotal "The Feminist Standpoint: Developing the Ground for a Specifically Feminist Historical Materialism" (1984). According to Hartsock, "if material life is structured in fundamentally opposing ways for two different groups, . . . the vision of each will represent an inversion of the other, and in systems of domination the vision available to the rulers will be both partial and perverse" (232). It is perverse because it enforces and justifies oppression, even including murder. Both the partiality and perversity of this view undermine the claims of objectivity made by those who practice establishment science. Yet although the standpoint of the ruling group is perverse and self-serving, it cannot be dismissed as simply false, because "the vision of the ruling class (or gender) structures the material relations in which all parties are forced to participate" (232). If the ruling class and gender have the power to structure ideology, reality, and perception, then everyday material reality will obscure the causes of oppression. "In consequence, the vision available to the oppressed group must be struggled for and represents an achievement which requires both science to see beneath the surface of the social relations in which all are forced to participate, and the education which can only grow from struggle to change those relations" (232).

To some extent these hidden relationships can be discovered (and are discovered) by the oppressed themselves as they begin to interact, collectivize their experience (for example, through consciousness-raising), and start to change their situation. For the very act of trying to change the structure tends to bring the nature of the system of oppression into bolder relief (Mies 1983). To some extent, the hidden structure of oppression must be discovered anew by each group of women because of the great educative power of direct experience and because each concrete situation of oppression has its own historical specificity, its own specific lessons.

Direct experience has its limitations, however. Besides the lack of cumulative knowledge, there are some hidden aspects of oppression that no amount of direct struggle will reveal. In view of these limitations, the researcher may play a role that is quite different from that of the participants. For example, in their study of industrial homework in Mexico City, Lourdes Benería and Martha Roldán (1987) not only interviewed homeworkers but they also traced the subcontracting links from those homeworkers on up through major corporations. Decisions of managers to employ women rather than men, and to employ them directly in factories or to subcontract out the work, had a major impact on the lives of the women who were assembling parts, polishing plastics, sorting pieces, and finishing textiles in their homes. Yet the women themselves would never have been privy to these decisions if Benería and Roldán had not had the institutional resources giving them access to these managers and the theory leading them to seek that access. Because the structure of oppression is often hidden, a feminist standpoint "is achieved rather than obvious, a mediated rather than immediate understanding" (Hartsock 1984:234).

Hartsock was not proposing an abstract, ivory-tower science; she did insist, however, on the necessity of scientific analysis. It would be extremely difficult, if not impossible, to derive that analysis purely inductively. In her study of lacemakers in India, Mies (1982:2–3) criticized the androcentric conceptualizations of Marxism: "Labor," "productive labor," and other concepts have been defined with inappropriate biologistic assumptions. She forcefully rejected abandoning those concepts altogether, however. It would be foolish, she said, not to reclaim, reform, and use them. The concepts—which are, after all, the essential links between theory and method—must be redefined "from below." The social scientist can, in collaboration with research participants, provide, question, and test theoretical understandings that reveal the hidden underlying structure of oppression.

FALSE CONSCIOUSNESS AND THE SOCIAL RELATIONS OF RESEARCH

The notion of hidden determinants—the determination of women's oppression by factors beyond their immediate experience—raises the issue of false consciousness, an idea that exposes some of the contradictions in Marxism. If social relations occur "behind the backs of the actors," how can the researcher know them, unless she claims a source of knowledge or understanding beyond that of her respondents? If she makes that claim, doesn't she run the risk of elitism? But if she does *not* attempt to uncover social relations and structures of oppression that may be hidden from her respondents' view, is she not limiting her contribution to them and to feminist science and political practice? If we reject the solipsism of feminist empiricism, from what standpoint does the scientist know the "reality" masked by appearances? If structural conflict produces opposing worldviews, then the social biography of Marxist theorists becomes problematic. In conceptualizing the false consciousness of a group, its imperfect comprehension of its own interests, what is the theorist's relation to the multifaceted structures of oppression?

In her excellent study *Life and Health in Three Palestinian Villages,* Rita Giacaman describes how her team of health scientists discovered their own class and urban bias and the limitations of their attempt to apply an unalloyed Marxist-feminist analysis:

> The women interviewed had their own agendas, and we were incessantly grilled with such questions as "How many children do you have?" "Why aren't you married?" "Where are your parents?" As we were being interviewed we would try to slip in a question or two in the midst of the confusion. The experience slowly led us away from the stereotyped images we had of "poor, weak and obedient" peasant women. . . . We had begun by looking at the women condescendingly: We were there to help them, to "raise their consciousness." But these women did not necessarily need their consciousness raised. They knew what was going on and . . . how to solve their problems. What they needed was the power and authority to change their lives. (1988:37)

The concept of false consciousness has been passionately criticized by many feminists, most notably Liz Stanley and Sue Wise:

> We reject the idea that scientists, or feminists, can become experts in other people's lives. . . . Feminism's present renaissance has come about precisely because many women have rejected other people's (men's) interpretations of our lives. Feminism insists that women should define and interpret our own experiences. . . . Feminists must attempt to reject the scientist/person dichotomy and, in doing so, must endeavor to dismantle the power relationship which exists between researcher and researched. (1983a:194–95)

Stanley and Wise took pains to state that they were "in no way opposed to theorizing as such": Instead they espoused symbolic interactionism because it "adopts a non-deterministic attitude towards social life and interaction, . . . [and] insists that structures are to be found *within* [the] processes [of interaction] (1983a:201–2). They also embraced ethnomethodology because it "accords well with the egalitarian ethos of feminism" (204).

The Struggle for Egalitarian Feminist Methodologies

If it is true that women's oppression is created entirely within the process of social interaction, then women can come to understand their oppression themselves, through ethnomethodological and symbolic interactionist techniques. The researcher's role would be limited to facilitating that process of discovery "from the ground up." In *Street Corner Society,* one of the original, paradigm-founding exemplars of symbolic interactionism, William Foote Whyte (1943) showed that the "corner boys" in a Boston slum created, through their patterns of interaction, the social and symbolic hierarchies in their gangs, their religion, and their politics. The structure he analyzed could have been made visible by the "members," since to a great extent, it was already known by them. But why were thirty-year-old men hanging out like "boys" on street corners? Because it was the Great Depression and they were unemployed. The depression was certainly not a result of their patterns of interaction. Looking at their own patterns of interaction, they would only have been able to blame themselves, each other, and the people they knew.

If women make their own history, they can uncover the roots of their oppression in the patterns of their own making. But if women "make their own history, but not under conditions of their own choosing" (Marx 1963;[2] Personal Narratives Group 1989:13), then women must be able to examine those conditions as well as their own patterns of interaction and understanding. While it may be more egalitarian to reject the notion of outside determination, that does not stop the president of Ingersoll Rand from making decisions in his New Jersey office that affect the work lives, choices, and susceptibility to cancer of women in Singapore (Fuentes and Ehrenreich 1984). Nor does it prevent those decisions from being influenced by the investment climate in Brazil. Understanding the implications for Singapore women of those international investment patterns and capital flows, understanding the location of Mexican homeworkers in the labor process requires theories that generalize from realities outside of the immediate experiential frame of the Singapore and Mexican women, theories more derived from Marxist-feminism than ethnomethodology (Benería and Roldán 1987).

The difficulty with the concept of false consciousness is not, in my view, that it asserts that people may have an imperfect understanding of their own conditions. Nor does the solution lie in asserting that their understanding is perfectly valid, as if the nature of the world were merely a matter of opinion (cf. Acker, Barry, and Esseveld 1983; Fisher 1984, on relativism). The difficulty with the concept of false consciousness lies in the implications that there is a true consciousness that is known and complete and that the researcher/activist knows it and the participant does not.

Joan Acker, Kate Barry, and Joke Esseveld began their research on women going out to work at midlife with a commitment to egalitarian relations; they discovered that the women demanded a more complex understanding of their respective roles:

> What they wanted, they said, was more of our own sociological analysis. They wanted us, the researchers, to interpret their experience to them. . . . If we were to fulfill the emancipatory aim for the people we were studying, we had to go beyond the faithful representation of their experience, beyond "letting them talk for themselves" and put those experiences into the theoretical framework with which we started the study, a framework that links women's oppression to the structure of Western capitalist society. (1983:429–30)

Exploring the "incompatibilities between various components of our feminist approach to social research," they conclude with a commitment to "reconstructing women's experience in a way that accounts for both their and our explanations of that experience and the relation between the two" (430). This reconstruction must include both the active voice of the subject and the researchers' own dialectical analysis (431). Similarly, the Personal Narratives Group concluded that the social context of the women they studied "had to be considered from the standpoint of the subject of the personal narrative, as well as from the standpoint of the interpreter's analysis of a particular cultural and social system" (1989:12).

Paradoxically, the ideology of complete equality between researcher and researched reintroduced the notion of value-free science in a new guise because it obscured the differences of their roles and the power complexities of their relationship (Stacey 1988; Personal Narratives Group 1989:13). The researcher is not a mere vessel of consciousness-raising or social action any more than a psychotherapist is merely a neutral facilitator of personal growth. The newer notion of research as a sort of dialogue or contrapuntal duet, while recognizing that the viewpoints of researcher and participants are not necessarily compatible (Personal Narratives Group 1989:264), remains somewhat problematic, however, as long as the vast majority of researchers (or "interpreters") remain predominantly white and privileged (Riessman 1987).

To her interaction with the participants, the researcher brings her social location, culture, motivations, limitations, ignorances, skills, education, resources, familiarity with theory and methodology, trained incapacities of socialization in dominant institutions, and an outside perspective that may be useful as well as troublesome (Acker, Barry, and Esseveld 1983; Riessman 1987; Gorelick 1989; Stanley and Wise 1983b). The researcher is transformed in the process of research—influenced and taught by her respondent-participants as she influences them. Theory and practice emerge from their interaction. The researcher is ultimately responsible for the final version, however. She cannot avoid this responsibility (Acker, Barry, and Esseveld 1983:428–29; Benería and Roldán 1987:27–28; Gorelick 1989:352; Mbilinyi 1989: 224–25; Sacks 1989; Stacey 1988).

Stanley and Wise's critique of the researcher-respondent relationship was similar to the critiques many of us made, during the 1960s and 1970s, of the elitism involved in teacher-student, psychologist-patient relationships. In no way do I wish to associate myself with the reactionary arrogance, the suffocating smugness, with which social pundits of the eighties look back (and down) on the radical and creative spirit of the sixties and seventies. We have learned from our experience of living and struggling in a backlash era, however, that these relationships are a set of contradictory interactions, and our successes and limitations in resolving them are historically determined. Teachers cannot *alone* undermine their own oppressive power over students, nor can researchers in relation to respondents. Even the possibility of their working together to overcome these oppressive relations is shaped by outside forces (Sacks 1989).

Even in the worst of times, however, we must not simply succumb to the institutional forces recreating hierarchy. We must always push at the margins, push at the limits, push at ourselves. In the worst of times, we must be most on guard against the hierarch within ourselves. But we must, collectively, try to understand the times and how they frame our possibilities of transcendence.

THE HIDDEN RELATIONS OF OPPRESSION

A purely inductive research project such as that advocated by the feminist empiricists can generate only those progressive understandings available to the women studied. If the participants are white, heterosexual, middle class, or North American, they are likely to generate a standpoint that is on the wrong side of racial, sexual, class, and imperial oppression. If they are Christian, they may not be able to find within their milieu the basis for understanding their own anti-Semitism. Hartsock's observation regarding the ruling class and gender applies here: "There are some perspectives on society from which, however well-intentioned one may be, the real relations of humans with each other and with the natural world are not visible" (1984:232). If generalizations are not to be made from one field situation to another, none of these groups of women can learn from each other and all must remain mired in the ignorance of their various privileges.

Combining interviews, participant observation, and an extensive historical analysis of domestic work, Judith Rollins found that maids and their employers had very different views of themselves, each other, domestic work, wages, and their relationship:

> Domestics were able to describe in precise detail the personalities, habits, moods, and tastes of the women they had worked for. (The descriptions employers gave were, by comparison, less complex and insightful—not, it seemed to me, because employers were any less capable of analyzing personalities but rather because they had less need to study the nuances of their domestics.) . . . The domestics I interviewed knew the importance of knowledge of the powerful to those without power. (1985:213–16)

Rollins, a Black sociologist doing participant observation as a domestic, was able to reveal contradictions her white respondents could not see: "The middle-class women I interviewed were not demanding that their husbands play a greater role in housekeeping; they accepted the fact that responsibility for domestic maintenance was theirs, and they solved the problem of their dual responsibilities by hiring other women to assist" (104). Her work reveals the white employer as caught in a contradictory location: oppressed as a woman, oppressing another woman as her employee, under the particular conditions of race, gender, and political economy in the late twentieth century (cf. Fisher 1988:223–24). It is for this reason that a methodology based purely on induction, and on the conclusions that the participants are able to generate for themselves, cannot even help them to understand their own milieu completely. As Stanley and Wise put it, discussing Frye (1983), "maleness, heterosexuality and whiteness all 'work' . . . by being states of *unawareness* in which the key privilege of the privileged group is not to notice that they are such" (1990:33). "Feelings are useless with-out facts," said Adrienne Rich, and "all privilege is ignorant at the core" (1986:226).

To understand both the domestics and their employers, therefore, and for them to understand themselves, Rollins needed both perspectives, but they were not equal. The maids' perspective had primacy. Consistent with the insights of all of the feminist methodologists, *theirs* is the "view from below." This idea goes beyond "different perspectives" and "difference" to the nature of oppression as a multifaceted structure of unequal social relations.

In this sense, *Interpreting Women's Lives* (Personal Narratives Group 1989) is a way station along the road "from feminist empiricism to feminist standpoint epistemologies" (Harding 1986:136). Its authors recognize the necessity and inevitability of interpretation and theory and the likelihood that the perspectives and motivations of "narrator" and "interpreter" may differ (4–6). Yet the Personal Narratives Group does not adequately analyze the consequences of the interpreter's social biography (her race, class, nationality, sexuality) for her interpretation. Although the authors are excruciatingly, fascinatingly honest about their difficulties, ideological commitments, errors, and contradictions, they generally do not mention their own social characteristics, even when exploring race and class differences among their narrators. As Acker, Barry, and Esseveld pointed out in 1983, "the interpretation must locate the researcher in the social structure and also provide a reconstruction of the social relations that produce the research itself" (431; see also Riessman 1987).

The Personal Narrative Group's solution to the problem of different perspectives (between narrator and interpreter and among women of different race, class, and nationality) is limited to invoking the necessity of substituting "truths" for "Truth," and urging "a reconstruction of knowledge that admits the fact and value of difference into its definition" (1989:263). Understanding the necessity and problematics of interpretation, they have moved from "giving voice" to hearing voices. That is, they dissolve the structure of inequality into a cognitive pluralism supplanting standpoint (cf. Stanley 1987). To solve the problem of different conditions of oppression by focusing on different "truths," however, is to equalize what is not equal, to spread a patina of equivalence over brutal realities and their inverse insights.

STANDPOINT AND MOVEMENT: A COMPLEX OF MANY DETERMINATIONS

In *Feminism and Methodology,* Sandra Harding considers whether the critiques of science by both the "postmodernists" and by women of color mean that no unitary science is possible:

> For instance, Bell Hooks insists that what makes feminism possible is not that women share certain kinds of experiences, for women's experiences of patriarchal oppression differ by race, class, and culture. Instead, feminism names the fact that women can federate around their common resistance to all the different forms of male domination. Thus there could not be "a" feminist standpoint as the generator of true stories about social life. There could, presumably, only be feminist oppositions, and criticisms of false stories. (1987:188; she is referring to hooks 1984)

I believe that this is a misreading of hooks and of the implications of the works by women of color for the creation of a feminist standpoint (in contrast see Fisher 1989; Hartsock 1987; Smith 1987:121–22, 134). Hooks did not call her book "Another Country" or "A Different Voice." She called it *Feminist Theory: From Margin to Center.* She argued that as a result of the dominance of feminism by relatively privileged women, "feminist theory lacks wholeness, lacks the broad analysis that could encompass a wide variety of human experiences" (1983:x). To create such an analysis, the perspectives of women of color must move to the center of feminist theory and the feminist movement. White feminists' definitions of feminism must be overturned by the view from below or from "the margin."

The notion that there must be "many stories," that is, a fragmentary science, is similar to men's assumptions that the study of gender is only about women's worlds. On the contrary, difference of condition does not mean absence of relationship. Black women's experiences are relevant not only to other Black women but also to understanding the situation of white women, and indeed of Black and white *men.* It is only because Black women empty bedpans that white men can run hospitals. It is only because Native American women are poor that ruling-class men and women are rich. It is only because Guatemalan peasant women are oppressed that North American businessmen have power. And it is not only lesbians but all women who are oppressed by the compulsory heterosexuality that lies at the heart of sexism (Rich 1986).

Theory making, therefore, cannot be ghettoized because reality does not come in separate boxes. We must uncover not only the different experiences of diverse groups of women but also the processes creating these differences. We must trace how these processes of oppression—racist, imperialist, class, national, religious, and sexual—are connected to each other and determine, in very different patterns, the lives of all and each of us.

Within a feminist approach, we need an analysis of racism from the standpoint of women of color, national oppression from the standpoint of oppressed minorities, Christian chauvinism from the standpoint of Jews and other ethnoreligious minorities, class from the standpoint of working-class women, and heterosexism from the standpoint of lesbians. All of these systems (or axes) of oppression intersect and implicate virtually everyone (at least in U.S. society), since everyone stands on one or the other side of these axes of oppression and privilege. Therefore, every piece of research must include an analysis of the specific social location of the women involved in the study with respect to these various systems of oppression.

Such an analysis requires that someone be able to step back and do that analysis, or facilitate its emergence among the participants, raising again the questions of the segregation of milieux, the social biography of researchers, the researcher-participant relationship, and so on. Ultimately, what we can build toward is an understanding of the "complex of many determinations" as a set of dynamic interrelations (Marx 1970:206).

The notion of a "complex of many determinations" goes beyond "academic feminist pluralism" (Stanley and Wise 1990:47), beyond the notion of a fragmentary science, and beyond a simple hierarchy of standpoints (Stanley and Wise 1990:28; Harding 1986). Rather, a methodology based on a "complex of many determinations" implies a cumulative social science that is not merely additive. The visions of each subgroup of women must refocus or revision the knowledge of all. The field is continually decomposed and reconceptualized at deeper and more complex levels of understanding (Smith 1987:215–16, 222–23), always giving primacy to the vision of the oppressed.

Such a science may imply an amazing goodwill transcending opposing interests, for example, between white employers and "their" maids. That is, the idea of such a cumulative social science may seem to ignore conflict. The conflicts are real, however. The problem of creating a women's social science encompassing the diverse consciousness and conditions of different women is similar to and related to the problem of creating a nonoppressive women's movement. Are there any material supports for unity? Are there at least creative contradictions to counter the differences in material interests? Can we begin to analyze our present situation as a "complex of many contradictions?" And will "we" all want to do so?

We have learned this much: The old top-down methods of politics and science will no longer do. To end the oppression of women we need a political movement and a social science that "gives voice" to women. But because of the multifaceted structure of oppression, giving voice is not enough. To understand the different milieux in which women experience their oppression and to trace their connections with each other, we need a social science produced by women of various social conditions (race, class, sexual preference, nationality, ethnicity), a social science that reveals the commonalities and structured conflicts of the hidden structures of oppression, both as they are felt and as they are obscured. The quest for such a science confronts and comprises a dynamic tension among the researcher and the researched, struggle and science, action, experience, method, and theory.

CONTRADICTIONS OF FEMINIST METHODOLOGY: A POSTSCRIPT

Unlike my earlier article "The Changer and the Changed: Methodological Reflections on Studying Jewish Feminists" (1989), this essay did not grow out of my own research. Rather, it was born of my strong reaction to reading what I call the "feminist empiricists." I originally called this essay "Giving Voice Is Not Enough." "Giving voice" is not enough because of the hidden determinants of oppression (the respondent may be unable to know the structure of her own situation) and the hidden relations of oppression (she may not be aware of her own implication in the oppression of others).

My current research focuses on Jewish feminists' responses to the Israeli-Palestinian conflict. In working with the transcripts of my interviews, I do not merely "give voice" to the views of my respondents. Dealing with as controversial an issue as the Israeli-Palestinian conflict and questions of Jewish identity, I realize that I cannot simply "give voice" to their views even if that were all that I wanted to do. After all, it is I who asked the questions, I who read the transcript, I who selected the materials to be placed in the text. It is when I am trying to be most faithful to their meaning, and particularly when I am trying to portray the political consciousness of women with whose politics I may disagree, that I am most painfully aware that simply "giving voice" is not so simple after all. It is fraught with interpretation.

Even if I simply published the transcripts verbatim, without editing, I would only be giving voice to those thoughts that the women were willing or able to express on the day of the interview. They might express themselves quite differently by the time their words are solidified into print.

But I do not simply reprint unedited transcripts. Their words, thoughts, and feelings are filtered through the selections that I, with my own political views, my own (changing) convictions and contradictions, make. Nor do I think that simply giving my respondents voice would be enough of a contribution. I am attempting to analyze the way that Jewish feminists deal with being in a contradictory social location: the contradiction of being oppressed as women and as Jews (vis-à-vis anti-Semitism) while being in a structurally privileged position, at least by implication, with respect to the Palestinian question (and, of course, for most—but not all—North American Jews, with respect to race, although I am not studying this aspect currently). I am trying to analyze the interviews I held with them in historical perspective, in light of the historical events that have influenced their (and our) lives. In that sense too, I have the chutzpah to think that I may have something to say that is relevant and that comes from outside the immediate frame of the interview.

Yet although in my essay in this book I argue that the researcher *may* discover determinants of which the respondent is unaware, she may not always do so. In my current research, as I have read and reread my respondents' testimonies, over the years of this study, I have continued to see those testimonies differently, as I myself change, partly under their influence and partly under the influence of other events and forces in my own life, including historical events and outside circumstances. I am impressed more by what I learned from my respondents—not only about their own consciousness but about anti-Semitism and the Israeli-Palestinian conflict—than by what I have to offer them in insights and "hidden determinants."

That might be because I am myself very much like them and subject to some of the same social forces, some of the same distortions and limitations. There are hidden determinants in my life also, and I am both the worst and the best person to uncover them. Worst, because structural barriers mislead me too (in the way that Hartsock describes); best because only I am in my skin. I am closest to my own experience.

In that sense, being in the same "critical plane" as my respondents has both advantages and disadvantages. I may be better placed than another student to achieve an empathic understanding (*Verstehen*) of their situation and their contradictions; I may be less able to perceive our common "hidden determinants" and "hidden relations" of oppression, our common contradictions.

When Smith's feminist sociologist found herself mirrored in her respondents, social science took a great leap forward. She moved social science from a false universalism to a discovery of the particular characteristics and limitations of white, male scholars. Then, prodded by women of color, lesbians, and others,[3] feminist scholars discovered the solipsism of the mirror. White, "middle-class" feminist scholars had mirrored *themselves* only *too* well—and yet still with a distorted lens.

Does the standpoint-based critique of feminist scholarship mean, therefore, that only Black lesbians can study Black lesbians, that only working class Jews can study working class Jews?

Yes and no.

I have argued that the structure of oppression hampers those who are in the dominant position, so that we are severely impaired in our ability to perceive the oppression in which we are implicated; privilege limits even our ability to understand our *own* circumstances, let alone exercise *Verstehen* toward the oppressed. Our privileges in the structure of oppression leave us severely hampered, but depending on the circumstances, not fully disqualified from collaboratively engaging in the work.

Furthermore, the implication of my critique of *both* feminist empiricism and standpoint theory is that although oppression gives the oppressed a vantage point, a standpoint, by which Black lesbians and working-class Jews have the potential to better understand our own conditions, the structure of oppression, and the complexities of multiple oppression, hamper our own search for clarity. Thus our relationship to oppression, as either privileged or oppressed, has implications for the quality of our research, but our relationship to it is contradictory, complex, and, to some degree, up to us. That is, in part, why I called this essay "*Contradictions* of Feminist Methodology."

Dialogue—multilogue—the noise of debate are absolutely essential correctives to the contradictory limitations of privilege and oppression. We will not be able to perceive our diverse, interlocking, structurally induced errors unless we can point them out to each other and learn from each other's work across the boundaries of race, class, and other conditions of oppression.

Nor are purely academic "discourses" sufficient. If we truly learn from Cook and Fonow (and from Marx before them) that the point is not merely to describe the world but also to change it, then it is in the crucible of activism, of coalition work to produce feminist change simultaneously confronting racism, heterosexism, and the other forms of oppression, that greater clarity may be forged. And it is in this sense that the separation over the past two decades of academic feminism from the active feminist movement has seriously handicapped both theory and practice.

Beyond a critique of feminist empiricism, the unique contribution of this chapter is, I believe, my suggestion that "ultimately . . . we can build toward . . . an understanding of the 'complex of many determinations' as a set of dynamic interrelations." I introduced this model as a possible way of dealing with the problem created by the multiplicity of "standpoints" within multiple systems of oppression.

But what does the phrase "complex of many determinations" mean? What does it imply? It means that things are not unicausal or unidirectional, that each element of the complex (e.g., the subject being studied or an instance of oppression or society considered as a whole) affects and is affected by all of the other elements in multiple (specifiable) ways. It means that cause and effect are not a unilinear chain; rather, cause and effect are dialectically interrelated. It is our job to systematically trace these interrelationships.

The notion of creating (or analyzing) the "complex of many determinations" moves beyond the fragmentary "postmodern" description of "difference" in two ways. It is not *fragmentary*—rather, it conceptualizes difference as an expression of a relationship, not merely a separation. It moves beyond *description* to analysis of the forces producing those differences and relationships and the (dynamic) structure of which they are a (changing) part. When Adrienne Rich moved beyond complaining about the exclusion of lesbians from feminist writing to analyzing "compulsory heterosexuality," lesbians—and indeed feminism itself—moved beyond discussing "difference" to analyzing the determinants of lesbian existence. More than that: The concept of compulsory heterosexuality determines not only lesbianism but also heterosexuality as a set of institutions and ideological practices; compulsory heterosexuality shapes sexuality, economics, and gender inequality.

The task now is to find the comparable underlying elements with regard to race, nationality, and—more germane to my own work—anti-Semitism and Jewish existence. We can readily find in the works of people of color this comparable analysis at the core of racism and nationalism/nationality, for example.[4] Now we must further explicate the interrelations (in as painstaking and exhaustive a way as Marx did with Production-Distribution-Exchange-Consumption) between racism and compulsory heterosexuality and between each of these and social class. I have not even begun to make this type of analysis with respect to anti-Semitism and Jewish existence. I still consider the "complex of many determinations" to be a model for analyzing the (changing) system of interlocked and crosscutting oppressions in patriarchal, capitalist society. It is a model yet to be achieved, a methodological aspiration, a path, a promise, a task for our collective work.

NOTES

This is an updated version of an essay published as "Contradictions of Feminist Methodology" in *Gender and Society* 5, no. 4 (Dec. 1991): 459–77.

1. I use the term *dominant* methodology, rather than *traditional* or *mainstream,* because *traditional* connotes a benign antiquity that modern-day social science does not have, and because *mainstream,* a rather bucolic metaphor, seems to imply that alternative methodologies are mere tributaries, rivulets of the mainstream, rather than real alternatives with opposing assumptions and consequences. The term *mainstream* also washes over the power structure that maintains the dominant methodologies in place and relegates alternative methodologies to the periphery.

2. Of course, Marx said, "*Men* make their own history, but . . . they do not make it under circumstances chosen by themselves" (1963:15).

3. See, for example, Collins (1990) and hooks (1984) among many, many others.

4. McCluskey (1994).

REFERENCES

Acker, Joan, Kate Barry, and Joke Esseveld. 1983. "Objectivity and Truth: Problems in Doing Feminist Research." *Women's Studies International Forum* 6 (4): 423–35.

Benería, Lourdes, and Martha Roldán. 1987. *The Crossroads of Class and Gender.* Chicago: University of Chicago Press.

Bowles, Gloria, and Renate Duelli Klein, eds. 1983. *Theories of Women's Studies.* London: Routledge and Kegan Paul.

Collins, Patricia Hill. 1990. *Black Feminist Thought: Knowledge, Consciousness, and the Politics of Empowerment.* Boston: Unwin Hyman. Reprint. New York: Routledge, 1991.

Cook, Judith A., and Mary Margaret Fonow. 1986. "Knowledge and Women's Interests: Issues of Epistemology and Methodology in Feminist Sociological Research." *Sociological Inquiry* 56 (Winter): 2–29.

Fisher, Berenice. 1989. "Feminist Academics at Mid-life Crisis." Ms.

———. 1988. "Wandering in the Wilderness: The Search for Women Role Models." *Signs* 13 (Winter): 211–33.

———. 1984. "What Is Feminist Method?" *New Women's Times Feminist Review* 33 (May/June): 10, 11, 14.

Frye, Marilyn. 1983. *The Politics of Reality: Essays in Feminist Theory.* New York: Crossing Press.

Fuentes, Annette, and Barbara Ehrenreich. 1984. *Women in the Global Factory.* Boston: South End Press.

Giacaman, Rita. 1988. *Life and Health in Three Palestinian Villages.* London: Ithaca Press.

Gorelick, Sherry. 1989. "The Changer and the Changed: Methodological Reflections on Studying Jewish Feminists." In *Gender/Body/Knowledge: Feminist Reconstructions of Being and Knowing*, ed. Alison M. Jaggar and Susan R. Bordo. New Brunswick, N.J.: Rutgers University Press. 336–58.

———. 1977. "Undermining Hierarchy: Problems of Schooling in Capitalist America." *Monthly Review* 29 (5): 20–36.

Gorz, Andre. 1972. "Workers' Control: Some European Experiences." *Upstart* 1 (Jan. 1971); reprinted in *The Capitalist System*, ed. Richard C. Edwards, Michael Reich, and Thomas E. Weisskopf. Englewood Cliffs, N.J.: Prentice Hall. 479–91.

Harding, Sandra, ed. 1987. *Feminism and Methodology: Social Science Issues*. Bloomington: Indiana University Press.

———. 1986. *The Science Question in Feminism*. Ithaca: Cornell University Press.

Hartsock, Nancy C. M. 1987. "Rethinking Modernism: Minority vs. Majority Theories." *Cultural Critique* 7 (Fall): 187–206.

———. 1984. "The Feminist Standpoint: Developing the Ground for a Specifically Feminist Historical Materialism." In *Money, Sex, and Power: Toward a Feminist Historical Materialism*. Boston: Northeastern University Press. 231–51.

hooks, bell. 1984. *Feminist Theory: From Margin to Center*. Boston: South End Press.

Jaggar, Alison M. 1989. "Love and Knowledge: Emotion in Feminist Epistemology." In *Gender/Body/Knowledge: Feminist Reconstructions of Being and Knowing*, ed. Alison M. Jaggar and Susan R. Bordo. New Brunswick, N.J.: Rutgers University Press. 145–71.

Kasper, Anne. 1986. "Consciousness Reevaluated: Interpretive Theory and Feminist Scholarship." *Sociological Inquiry* 56 (Winter): 30–49.

Keller, Evelyn Fox. 1980. "Feminist Critique of Science: A Forward or Backward Move?" *Fundamental Scientiae* 1:341–49.

Klein, Renate Duelli. 1983. "How to Do What We Want to Do: Thoughts about Feminist Methodology." In *Theories of Women's Studies*, ed. Gloria Bowles and Renate Duelli Klein. London: Routledge and Kegan Paul. 88–104.

Lundberg, George. 1963. "The Postulates of Science and Their Implications for Sociology." In *Philosophy of the Social Sciences*, ed. Maurice Natanson. New York: Random House. 33–72.

MacKinnon, Catherine. 1987. "Feminism, Marxism, Method, and the State: Toward Feminist Jurisprudence." In *Feminism and Methodology: Social Science Issues*, ed. Sandra Harding. Bloomington: Indiana University Press. 135–56.

McCluskey, Audrey Thomas. 1994. "Multiple Consciousness in the Leadership of Mary McLoed Bethune." *NWSA Journal* 6 (1): 69–81.

Maguire, Patricia. 1987. "Doing Participatory Research: A Feminist Approach." *National Women's Studies Association Perspectives* 5 (3): 35–37.

Marks, Shula. 1989. "The Context of Personal Narrative: Reflections on Not Either an Experimental Doll—The Separate Worlds of Three South African Women." In *Interpreting Women's Lives: Feminist Theory and Personal Narratives*, ed. Personal Narratives Group. Bloomington: Indiana University Press. 39–58.

Marx, Karl. [1859] 1970. *A Contribution to the Critique of Political Economy.* Moscow: Progress Publishers.

———. [1867] 1967. *Capital.* Vol. 1. New York: International.

———. [1851] 1963. *The Eighteenth Brumaire of Louis Bonaparte.* New York: International.

Mbilinyi, Marjorie. 1989. "'I'd Have Been a Man': Politics and the Labor Process in Producing Personal Narratives." In *Interpreting Women's Lives: Feminist Theory and Personal Narratives,* ed. Personal Narratives Group. Bloomington: Indiana University Press. 204–27.

Mies, Maria. 1983. "Towards a Methodology for Feminist Research." In *Theories of Women's Studies,* ed. Gloria Bowles and Renate Duelli Klein. London: Routledge and Kegan Paul. 117–39.

———. 1982. "The Dynamics of the Sexual Division of Labor and Integration of Rural Women into the World Market." In *Women and Development,* ed. Lourdes Benería. New York: Praeger. 1–28.

Namjoshi, Suniti. 1981. *Feminist Fables.* London: Sheba Feminist Publishers.

Oakley, Ann. 1981. "Interviewing Women: A Contradiction in Terms." In *Doing Feminist Research,* ed. Helen Roberts. London: Routledge and Kegan Paul. 30–61.

Personal Narratives Group, ed. 1989. *Interpreting Women's Lives: Feminist Theory and Personal Narratives.* Bloomington: Indiana University Press.

Reinharz, Shulamit. 1983. "Experiential Analysis: A Contribution to Feminist Research." In *Theories of Women's Studies,* ed. Gloria Bowles and Renate Duelli Klein. London: Routledge and Kegan Paul. 162–91.

———. 1979. *On Becoming a Social Scientist: From Survey Research and Participant Observation to Experiential Analysis.* San Francisco: Jossey-Bass.

Rich, Adrienne. 1986. *Blood, Bread, and Poetry: Selected Prose, 1979–1985.* New York: W. W. Norton.

Riessman, Catherine Kohler. 1987. "When Gender Is Not Enough: Women Interviewing Women." *Gender and Society* 1 (2): 172–207.

Rollins, Judith. 1985. *Between Women: Domestics and Their Employers.* Philadelphia: Temple University Press.

———. 1984. "Employing a Domestic: A Case of Female Parasitism." Paper presented at the annual meeting of the American Sociological Association. San Antonio, Tex.

Roth, Julius. 1966. "Hired Hand Research." *American Sociologist* 1 (4): 190–96.

Sacks, Karen Brodkin. 1989. "What's a Life Story Got to Do with It?" In *Interpreting Women's Lives: Feminist Theory and Personal Narratives,* ed. Personal Narratives Group. Bloomington: Indiana University Press. 85–95.

Smith, Dorothy E. 1987. *The Everyday World as Problematic: A Feminist Sociology.* Boston: Northeastern University Press.

———. 1979. "A Sociology for Women." In *The Prism of Sex: Essays in the Sociology of Knowledge,* ed. Julia A. Sherman and Evelyn Torton Beck. Madison: University of Wisconsin Press. 135–87.

———. 1974. "Women's Perspective as a Radical Critique of Sociology." *Sociological Inquiry* 44 (1): 7–13.

Stacey, Judith. 1988. "Can There Be a Feminist Ethnography?" *Women's Studies International Forum* 11 (1): 21–27.

Stanley, Liz. 1987. "Biography as Microscope or Kaleidoscope?" *Women's Studies International Forum* 10 (1): 19–31.

Stanley, Liz, and Sue Wise. 1990. "Method, Methodology, and Epistemology in Feminist Research Processes." In *Feminist Praxis: Research, Theory, and Epistemology in Feminist Sociology,* ed. Liz Stanley. London: Routledge and Kegan Paul. 20–60.

———. 1983a. "'Back into the Personal'; or, Our Attempt to Construct 'Feminist Research.'" In *Theories of Women's Studies,* ed. Gloria Bowles and Renate Duelli Klein. London: Routledge and Kegan Paul. 192–209.

———. 1983b. *Breaking Out: Feminist Consciousness and Feminist Research.* London: Routledge and Kegan Paul.

Whyte, William Foote. 1943. *Street Corner Society.* Chicago: University of Chicago Press.

CHAPTER 2

DOROTHY E. SMITH

Contradictions for Feminist Social Scientists

I am unreservedly committed to securing for women the resources institutionalized in the academy that create knowledge, build and transmit intellectual tradition, house and foster debate, and sustain continuities across generations. While we have lacked these, in the past twenty years or so we have begun to secure them but at a cost. Twentieth-century North American universities have never been directly subjected to state control. But buried historically in their foundations is a powerful class politics. It is a politics that, at crucial periods during the thirties, fifties, and again in the nineties, has sought to isolate the university bases of the intelligentsia from local and regional connections, from linkages with the working class and the activism of the trade union movement, and from organizations identified with oppressed and marginalized groups. This politics is institutionalized in the university system. Most of the time it is taken for granted. It only comes into view when it has to be enforced. Freedom of thought, speech, and the pursuit of knowledge, however imperfectly realized in the university system, create an endemic pressure threatening to authority. When it breaks out of bounds, as it did during the early fifties, the sixties, and the seventies, it is actively repressed. Discourse, the across-time-and-space conversation of the intelligentsia, builds in the boundaries of the institutional order, adopting its standpoint and incorporating its relevances and interests. So long as it observes the class boundaries imposed by that order and does not serve the need to know of people subordinated to it, discourse is not exposed to repressive political pressure.

By relations of ruling I mean that complex of extra locally organized relations that are specialized *as* forms of organizing, regulating, communicating, and so forth. They are text-based and entirely reliant on technologies of the text, including, of course, computers. We know them variously as text-mediated discourse, professional organization, formal organization, management, administration, bureaucracy, the state, at all levels, and so forth. The categories naming them overlap because they have been evoked by the theories, issues, and topics of different disciplines, but they identify a variety of institutional forms that act in and regulate the local actualities of people's lives. The relations of ruling rely on and generate specialized systems of concepts, theories, categories, technical languages, and so forth that define their objects and situations as actionable on their terms. These specialized language systems generalize the distinctive organizational competence of each institutional form across the many and various sites of people's actual living.

The work of the social sciences sediments the logic of these controls. The sociology we have adopts the boundaries of its terrain; it is hooked up dialogically to its relations at multiple points, often incorporating their categories directly and always preserving their standpoint of ruling in its conceptual and theoretical order; it knows how to harvest information, data, and knowledge from people and to bring it home to the text-based discourses that have universities as their local bases. Social scientific knowledge represents the world from a standpoint in the relations of ruling, not from the standpoint of those who are ruled.

The relations of ruling are far from monolithic. Multiple and diverse interests and voices operate within it. Nonetheless, generally its terrain is never conceded to or opened up to use and influence by people who are exploited, marginalized, or subordinated by the relations of contemporary capitalism. As a system of control it has been particularly effective in ensuring that the knowledge produced is not oriented toward the needs and interests of the mass of people, but to the needs and interests of ruling. When loopholes are found and leakages occur, they are stopped; when those privileged with access desert and go over to the other side, their access is cut off. Breached during the sixties, this system of control has been reformed and tightened.

The women's movement has its distinctive history and its distinctive struggle against and within the relations of ruling because these relations encysted the gender hierarchy we call "patriarchy." Its critique of patriarchy has often been also a critique of the relations of ruling, proposing radically alternative forms of organizing the social relations of knowledge and communication. It revealed, for many women, the taken-for-granted class, gender, and racial subtexts of academic institutions—the hidden boundaries, exclusions, and positionings on which the texts and practices of ruling rely.

The women's movement has struggled to make women's voices heard in universities and colleges and within academic disciplines. Those of us who were active in universities and colleges were, in the early stages of this struggle, activists in the women's movement outside as well; what we worked for in the academy was inseparable from what we were working for outside it. We wanted the immense resources vested in the university and college systems to sustain the development of thought, knowledge, and culture by women and for women. We had discovered, were and are discovering an intellectual and political world to which women were marginal if present at all. The intellectual, cultural, and political achievements of our foremothers had been for their own time only—if at all. The academy has never vested its resources in preserving and advancing their thought and work. If there was no ongoing intellectual tradition among women, no conversation extending from the past into the present, it was in part because the resources of the academy were never dedicated to this project.

• • •

To remind us that the women's movement didn't begin with us, we have called this a new phase or wave of the North American and European women's movement. But this phase has been and is distinctive in making us conscious of the complex of power relations we have named "patriarchy" and in the development of organization aimed at transforming it. Whatever that term might mean when subjected to refined definition, it showed us the institutionalized barriers and exclusions that we had for so many hundreds of years taken for granted. And though women are everywhere in the society, established channels of communication—academic discourses and universities, book publishing, the mass media of television, newspapers, even women's magazines—were not for us, as women, to use in organizing among women, speaking and writing as women for women, developing issues, innovating expression, and remaking academic and professional discourses from women's standpoint.

A radical critique speaking from the experience of women has been integral to the politics of the women's movement. Recognizing women's right to speak from the actualities of our experience is always potentially disruptive; there is always something new to be heard; there is always rethinking to be done. The "we" of the women's movement has been open; hence settled positions in it are always subject to challenge. The perspectives and relevances of white, heterosexual, middle-class women built into the definition of women's issues have been disrupted by working-class, lesbian, and nonwhite women opposing that hegemony. Elsewhere women of "developing" countries were and are evolving a women's movement or women's movements independent of and in many respects more radical than those of North America and Europe.

New bases of organization have been emerging constantly; rifts and rows resulted in new activism, realigning and expanding the women's movement's system of communication. We published newspapers and newsletters, created new publishing houses, established bookstores. And of course we also tried to convert the established structures for women, most often by creating within them a shell, such as a women's caucus or committee, or in universities and colleges, a women's studies course, even a program. We took seriously in practice and in theory the universality lent our project by the category "women." Though established exclusions and barriers of race, class, politics, and imperialism were implicit in women's movement practice, they were, and are, always subject to confrontation and disruption. The very claim to speak *as women* and *for women* as the speaker creates its own instability as the speaker is found not to be speaking for me, for you, for her, for us.

Today women like myself working in the academy most often learn of other women's experiences in the disembodiments of the text wherein they appear only as "voices." But in the early days of the women's movement, we were also connected in multiple ways through organization and activism. Of course these may have been the peculiarities of my own experience growing up as a feminist in the women's movement in Vancouver, Canada, a city then of some one and a half million. The women's movement of those times was a many-headed organization, a hydra of contending groups. Yet despite contention, or perhaps because of it, there was an interlacing of multiple relationships crosscutting factional differences.

Our challenges to the ruling relations weren't only voices, they were challenges created by activism and experience acquired in activism; issues of gender, sexuality, and class were raised not as a matter of theory but as a matter of political practice (much more rarely at that time they were challenges raising issues of race). The activism and debates of the women's movement were embedded in and responsive to other forms of activism and organization of the time—the openings created by the movements of the sixties, the idealization of the Chinese revolution, the renewal of Marxism-Leninism. The dogmatisms and sectarian forms of organization were hooked in to a footloose women's movement whose participants moved in and out of organizations, quarreled, made friends and enemies, debated positions, and created new organization out of dissatisfaction with what was already in existence or recognizing newly a gap where action was called for.

The splitting, trashing, passionate quarrels, debates out of which opposing sides came, resolving never to speak again to former friends and allies, were the dynamic of a movement that was grounded in multiple ways in the society. What had seemed at first a simplicity of our sisterhood, what we confronted as patriarchy, what we found as the bases of our oppression in the control of our bodies, for example, turned out to be magnificent but untenable simplifications. Because women were everywhere in the society and because the forms of what we named patriarchy turned out to be multiple and various, the women's movement came to take up issues not as a generality crosscutting such divisions but as based in particularities of experiences in paid employment, in the home, in the community, in relation to children, in political organization, in sexual relationships, of racism—wherever our daily/nightly lives located us.

Differentiation did not mean separation. Arguments and debates were intense and passionate; they engaged others in opposition as well as in agreement. In them, positions became defined, were given theoretical formulation, were dissolved, and were reformed. The debates, alignments, conflicts, shared experiences, and issues linked women across institutional barriers. The connections were *active,* partly in and through the media of the women's movement, partly in organization around issues of shared concern, and partly just in informal support and discussion.

Women taking up the women's movement in the academy were part of this connectedness. We participated with women outside the university attempting to create linkages that broke with its traditional isolation and its traditional claims to authority. Certainly this was my experience. And I found that the institutional barriers that detach the university from the local community had two sides: on the one hand, there was nothing in the university that supported making connections outside. If anything it made difficulties; and, on the other, as we became active in off-campus organizations, we found that the women we worked with were antagonistic to the implied superiority of knowledge derived from the institutional dominance of the academy. We were under constant critical pressure in this encounter, constantly challenged by thinking and theories originating outside academic discourse, and by being confronted with bases of knowing grounded in experiences other and beyond our own.[1]

In universities and colleges, we sought alternatives to institutional connections and to use the skills and resources the academy commands *for* women. The women's studies courses that we established also relied on experience and understandings grounded outside the academy. Since there was little or nothing in the way of books or articles that we could teach from in more orthodox styles, we didn't speak in our classes from an established discourse that we were trying to pass on to our students. Rather, we encouraged and evoked their and our speaking from our experience as women, beyond the comprehension of the academic discourses as they were then.

• • •

In the years since that time, we have achieved extraordinary things in the academy. Of course, we do well to take nothing for granted, but women's studies are now part of the normal course of business in many if not most universities and colleges of English-speaking North America. We now enjoy resources that we did not have before. We made rich and brilliant achievements. The contrast between the early days of teaching women's studies and today is very marked. Then we had extraordinarily little material to learn and teach from. Now the wealth of women's scholarly, cultural, and political writing is vast. It is powerfully enriched by the progressive displacement of white women from the center and the advent of the authoritative presences of Latina, Black, Asian, and native women. Whereas once each individual could think she could know it all—read a little later at night, get up a little earlier in the morning—we now know that is impossible. And for better or for worse, we now have specializations, subdisciplines, schools, academic factions, hierarchies.

We have, I do believe, been successful in vesting at least some of the institutional resources of the academy in preserving, transmitting, and advancing knowledge of and for women. We have also been somewhat successful in breaking down the radical one-sidedness of the male-dominated discourses of the disciplines and sciences, particularly in the humanities and social sciences. If we have not succeeded altogether in overturning the claims to generality based on gender partiality, we have at least succeeded in creating a richness of critique and alternatives that is astonishing given the relatively brief period of our "renaissance."

But there is a cost. There are powers operating at a less-visible level in the university that pull our feminist work in unseen ways. In establishing ourselves in the academy, in making a place for women and women's experience in social science and the humanities, to a modest degree in law and the life sciences, and at least marginally in medicine, we have also become increasingly detached from our former linkages with activism and organization outside the academy. This is partly due, no doubt, to the changing organization of the women's movement itself, to growth and advances that have meant more specialization and less place for the multiconnected activism of the earlier movement. In the academy, it has meant a progressive conforming of the discourses of women's studies and feminist theorizing to the institutional boundaries of the university. Once the production of knowledge for women became fully embedded in the academy, the ties that hooked its characteristic forms and directions of development with the concerns of women outside the academy became increasingly attenuated. Not that such knowledge production has not continued; this is particularly true for Black and Latina women with ongoing activist ties outside the academy. European-American women have also continued to do work that serves women, but the pull these earlier forms of activism and organization exercised over our minds, imaginations, energies, and loyalties has been attenuated. Increasingly feminists working in the academy with ties to activism beyond it are hooked into the relations of ruling—professions, public service, political life, scholarly careers, and so on. As our own thinking becomes more articulated to disciplines sedimenting the hidden political ground of the academy, we become increasingly detached from independent sources of resistance and from the profoundly different take on the world they represent. Our feminism becomes professionalized.

And there *is* a hidden political ground. It has a history that is part of the developing organization of class in North America. The recurrent politicization of university campuses stimulating alternative approaches to teaching and research have encountered, sooner or later, repressive political responses. The pressure may come via boards of governors representing very directly the interests of a regional ruling class or from university administrators and organizations of administrators or from within the academic community itself or from external and indirect pressures from the media or politicians. Clyde Barrow's study of the "reconstruction" of U.S. higher education during the early years of the twentieth century describes a major political shift from faculty to administrative and board of governors control of universities. He details the specific practices, now institutionalized in universities, by which that control was secured, in particular over the freedom of faculty to develop knowledge independent of the interests of business (Barrow 1990:250–59). Capacities established then have come into play during the recurrent waves of campus political activism since that time.

The public target of McCarthyism was the Communist party, but its effective, perhaps intended, aim was the broader-based political activism of students and faculty after World War II (Schrecker 1986:84–85). Student organizations created linkages with labor, took up civil rights issues, proposed foreign relations radically opposed to "cold war" thinking, and were involved with left-wing presidential politics. Earlier campus radicalism in the forties had been repressed. The attack on radicalism in the fifties, now identified with McCarthyism, confronted and repressed a new and more general political activism on campus. The attack on communism has been called a witch-hunt because merely to come under suspicion was to be damned. Faculty members were frightened, particularly liberal faculty. They might not have changed their views, but they were afraid to act on them.[2] In some instances, political activism on campus was prohibited altogether—the issue that eventually, in the sixties, sparked the free speech movement on the Berkeley campus of the University of California.

Emphasis on the ideological dimensions of campus radicalism tends to obscure the extent to which it breached a class-enclosure institutionalized as the effect of various repressive moves. I've sometimes thought that faculty members could be as radical as they wished in their writing and in the classroom so long as radicalism did not lead to an activism that built relationships between a university intelligentsia and a society's marginalized and exploited people. Writing of the early decades of this century, Barrow describes repression directed against individual faculty members who undertook research in the interests of local communities and against those of "big business." An agricultural chemist, for example, was penalized for bringing evidence to a state legislature about the damage done to local crops by copper smelting (1990:241). The notion of the scholarly and academic as detached from concerns and interests external to discourse itself is constructed and reconstructed recurrently in the context of an endemic campus activism. Writing of the period following the seventies, Paul Diesing describes how administrative and budgetary powers of university administrations and boards were used to tame radical faculty: "We found faculty resolutions ignored by the university administration and tenure recommendations overruled; library budgets cut and class sizes increased; tenured professors fired with three months' notice or less; educational policy and resources shifted without consulting us. . . . Our illusions crumbled; we began soberly to face our real conditions of life" (1982:262).

Political repression had its effects in social scientific thinking. The McCarthy period of sharp divorce between intellectual activity and what it might imply in terms of the society at large can be traced in sociology's shifts from the influences of Marxism or native North American traditions of radicalism, such as those embodied in C. Wright Mills's work. The "systems" thinking of Talcott Parsons, in which issues of class and racial oppression disappear, assumed a dominant role (Diesing 1982). "Mass society" theory was briefly popular, perhaps because it offered a striking redefinition of the intelligentsia's relationship to the masses, proposing that an elite's ability to sustain democratic values could only be effective if it preserved its detachment from the people. Marxist conceptions of class and class struggle were displaced by and sublated in the new politically purified notion of "social stratification." Durkheim's devices for converting the world of actual people into a subjectless phenomenal universe became standard practice (Smith 1989). The popular methodological artifice of the Archimedian point constituted a discursive space for sociology outside class relations; race was an object but lacked subjects; and gender was not yet even a whisper. The artifices of objectified discourse concealed the real subtexts of race, class, and gender oppressions. In the contemporary context, postmodernism has written the constitution that eliminates from the phenomenal domain of social and cultural thinking the bases of oppression that Marxism had brought into view, replacing it with a self-reflexive critique of discourse within discourse.

Feminist postmodernism is feminism's own variant of the post-McCarthy redesigning of sociological discourse that stripped social science of its relation to political activism beyond the academy. It insists on the subject as existing only in discourse, creating a discursive seclusion that restricts speakers and speech, writers and writing, to discourse's objects and conventions (Butler and Scott 1992; Smith 1993). It repudiates the speaking from experience that was so powerful in the beginnings of this phase of our women's movement and that has been so powerful in the disruptions and displacements of white, middle-class, heterosexual hegemony in feminism. At an earlier period, women would speak up from and for the margins that had been created by the focus of a conference or meeting. They could speak from their own realities and that had its own authority; others might not agree or believe, but had to attend to what was said and take it seriously. But the conventions of postmodernist feminism, for all its denial of the unitary subject of modernism, set up barriers to such speech. Take this striking tale by Susannah Radstone of her experience at a conference held at Glasgow University in Scotland in 1991. She is describing her uneasiness with the kinds of exclusion that the theoretical commitments of the conference set up.

> My first, and perhaps keenest intimation of unease came . . . when . . . Glasgow's Lord Provost—a woman—delivered a heart-rending speech of welcome. She felt, she told us all, an abiding sense of gratitude for and commitment to the struggles which had enshrined women's—and especially working-class women's—right to education, since, as a child of the Glasgow tenements, it was via education that she had accomplished her undoubtedly tough journey from the Gorbals to the civic hall. This was a story that moved me, a story told bravely, and a story told from the heart—a story, though, which appeared destined to fall into the void. For, unlike at Ruskin [a women's movement conference twenty-one years before], at Glasgow there remained no place, apparently, for the questions implicitly raised by the Lord Provost's welcoming address—questions about women and class, women and education, and women and the welfare state, to name but a few. (Radstone 1992:87)

The effect of "there remaining no place" points to how feminist theory organized the discursive enclave on that occasion, what could be said and what could be admitted to the talk of women there. The ongoing discussions were impenetrable to speech that would address what might be actually going on in the lives of women in Glasgow or the lives of women anywhere.

I emphasize that this isn't a matter of individual responsibility or guilt. It is a matter of the social relations in which our work comes to be embedded, who its readers are, how it is funded (and let's not pretend that we can go on forever doing work on shoestrings and night oil), and how it is recognized for purposes of publication and hence serves not only our survival in the academy (and I don't trivialize the issue of survival) but also our means of reaching others through our work. The political ordering of the academy is less significant in our choice of subject matter than it is in ensuring that we write from a standpoint that fits our work within the dialogic parameters of the relations of ruling.

• • •

Here is our difficulty, our problem, and our problematic. On one side, there's the problem of how to write a sociology that speaks in and of the world as it is in women's, in people's, actual experience. If we are to be writing a sociology that serves people, we have to create knowledge from their standpoint that provides maps or diagrams of the dynamic of macrosocial powers and processes that shapes their/our lives.

We want to create a systematically extended consciousness of society from women's standpoint and therefore we want more than short-run applications of our sociological skills. We also need to advance the technicalities of such a knowledge so that our research can be responsible in terms of "truth," accuracy, and relevance. And we have to contend with the jungle created by the in-text organization of sociology's object world, so that we can put in place a sociology or sociologies oriented to exploring the extended social relations of people's lives. Such a sociology or sociologies would recognize that, as Marx saw, the social comes into being only as the doings of actual people under definite material conditions and that we enter into social relations that our own activities bring into being but we do not control them. Thus our own powers contribute to powers that stand over against us and "overpower our lives" (Marx and Engels 1973:90).

On the other side is the problem of connecting such a sociology to those for whom it might be useful and who might use it. There must be real and equal interchange. Solving this problem is essential to how such a knowledge can be developed; knowledge is not abstract but is embedded in a discourse or discourses. How could a knowledge of the kind sketched in the previous paragraph develop if it were embedded in discourses wholly within the academic circuits of sociological and feminist theory? My own experience has been telling in this respect. For I started work on a sociology for women in the very practical contexts of a women's research center that was oriented, outside the university context, to working *for* women in the community and my thinking was pulled by the exigencies of doing this kind of research properly and finding that the sociology I knew would not do. But as my thinking on a sociology for women became known in academic contexts, I was invited to speak in (usually U.S.) universities to audiences of women scholars who were interested in issues of theory and epistemology and I became a participant in discourses of quite a different order. These were discourses that were framed within the academy and were "determined" largely by a feminist dialogue with established disciplines rather than with activists. My thinking began to orient toward these debates, and in consequence, more than functionally toward the theoretical and epistemological frames of academic discourses. My work was certainly strengthened in this process, but if the other term of the relationship had continued to be as strongly present as it was when I started on this line of inquiry, my work could only have benefited from being pulled more immediately and vitally into relevance to women outside the academy. In its absence, the effect was to redirect my energies and thinking—and time—toward a theoretical discourse that it had not intended originally. I could feel how my focus began to shift, a process that was progressive as the great political impetus of the sixties faltered and was repressed.

Any work and its development becomes what it is and will do in discursive settings. Discursive settings that are insulated from activism produce research and theorizing that is oriented elsewhere than activism. The theory may still be "radical" but nonetheless it is withdrawn from its anchorage with the actualities of people's lives, as we see with contemporary Marxist theorizing.

There are no easy solutions here. Since it's not a matter of an individual's intentions, or individual guilt, it is also not something that can be changed simply by an act of will. The implicit political organization of the ivory-tower university is still effective. It is not easy to go against it, though we can sometimes get things done within its scope. Indeed the recent attack on what is described by its opponents as the "political correctness" movement on North American campuses suggests that we have been more successful than perhaps we'd realized.

But this isn't the only isolation. The disciplinary norms to which we are subject sediment the politics of the ivory tower. They were put into place during the fifties and sixties in the process of moving sociology away from its earlier dubious connections with class struggle and the suspect ties of the North American intelligentsia of the forties and fifties to the working class. The academy creeps up on us. How do we get to keep our jobs? By writing papers that will be published in academic journals. To get our papers published we have to conform to procedural and methodological canons that have no relationship to what might be conceived of as the canons of relevance of women activists. Of course we have made and preserve our openings into the relationships in which so much of what we have done as feminists originate; we are ingenious. But it becomes increasingly difficult, and increasingly difficult as new feminist theories are established, even popularized, that conform to the class contours of the academy, the more so now that universities themselves are being increasingly pulled into direct subservience to the requirements of a global capitalism.

The academy is not seamless. I've shown earlier how repressions have followed on initiatives among students and faculty opposing injustices, oppressions, suffering in the society. Universities bear, I believe, the hidden radicalism of the Enlightenment and in teaching, in talk, and in the access to stored knowledges become, every now and again, reconnected to this long historical project. Here, for feminism, is our distinctive project in the academy. It is one in which, in fact, many of us are involved. I propose that we become more conscious of it and of each other.

The idea of developing a social science *for* women, which has been my own project, is not, of course, exclusively mine. There are women in the academy all over North America who in different ways are also engaged. We can change the way sociology knows the world because it is still a site of debate; because the academy is changing; because we know that there's desperation in society and our social sciences don't know how to know this new and frightening world; and because we know as women that we have the power and capacity to change and to create a social science that serves people rather than servicing their ruling. But the problem of how to create and preserve linkages with women working in sites outside the academy remains and hence the problem of how to create intersections between the in- and extra-academy discourses of feminism remains as well.

No intellectual enterprise can subsist in a social vacuum. Every such enterprise participates in something we could call a community. Because we are working with texts, reading and writing texts, the existence and significance of that community is often invisible to us. Yet it is always implicit in what we write. How then are we to defend and intensify connections beyond the academy against the multiple ways it inhibits them? In the session at the annual meetings of the Society for the Study of Social Problems at which the ideas of this essay were originally presented, a woman activist spoke of her dismay in finding how distant the sociology she had been hearing at the meetings was from the concerns and interests of activists and the women they represented. We had no answer then. This essay has no answer. But it has a diagnosis. It does not locate the issue in the individual intentions of women sociologists or in "careerism." The issue is not a matter of individual guilt. Rather it is to be located in the social relations embedding a politics at a level of the organization of the academy where it is not visible as such. Making it visible is a first step in addressing how we can overcome, bypass, and, as a minimum, avoid consciously replicating and reaffirming a politics that is neither for women nor for people in general.

NOTES

1. Of course, women are not the only group that has developed these relations. Here is a more current instance of exactly the kinds of relationships that the regulators of the academy fear: "Throughout this protracted struggle [for a Chicana/o Studies Department], a student-community alliance matured and campus mobilizations at UCLA began to take the shape of a crucial community struggle. Equally important, as the movement gained concessions from a resistant administration, Chicana/o student-faculty relations were strength-

ened by the presence of seasoned community organizers who mediated disputes and challenged all parties to keep the goal of the department at the heart of each action. This resulted in several key philosophical victories. Chief among these was a faculty pledge to include students and community people in the governance of Chicana/o Studies. Faculty were also pushed to develop curriculum focusing on current problems of the Latina/o community. Finally, faculty members were challenged to reaffirm through concrete action the basic aims of Chicana/o Studies—the development of an informed and community-minded leadership among our college youth" (Lizardo 1993:13).

Though unusually well-organized, struggles of this kind aimed at connecting the intellectual resources of the university with the needs of people in a local community are an endemic feature of campus activism and I suspect that it is this kind of activism that is most likely to invite repressive moves. An activism dedicated to causes elsewhere in the world is much less threatening. The latter does not jeopardize the monopoly control of intellectual resources and "production" by the class or classes that dominate in contemporary capitalism. Hence the carefully crafted controls that have been built into the academy and the discourses it sustains and the progressive shift of intellectual resources into organizations such as "think tanks" that can be more directly and consistently regulated.

2. Reported in Lazarsfeld (1958) according to Schrecker (1986:309).

REFERENCES

Barrow, Clyde W. 1990. *Universities and the Capitalist State: Corporate Liberalism and the Reconstruction of American Higher Education, 1894–1928.* Madison: University of Wisconsin Press.

Butler, Judith, and Joan W. Scott. 1992. Introduction to *Feminists Theorize the Political,* ed. Judith Butler and Joan W. Scott. New York: Routledge. xiii–xvii.

Diesing, Paul. 1982. *Science and Ideology in the Policy Sciences.* New York: Aldine.

Lazarsfeld, Paul, and Wagner Thielens, Jr. 1958. *The Academic Mind.* Glencoe, Ill.: Free Press.

Lizardo, Rubén. 1993. "Building Bridges, Demolishing Divisions." *Crossroads,* no. 34 (Sept.): 11–14.

Marx, Karl, and Frederick Engels. 1973. *Feuerbach: Opposition of the Materialist and Idealist Outlooks.* London: Lawrence and Wishart.

Radstone, Susannah. 1992. "Postcard from the Edge: Thoughts on the 'Feminist Theory: An International Debate' Conference Held at Glasgow University, Scotland, 12–15 July 1991." *Feminist Review* 40 (Spring): 85–93.

Schrecker, Ellen W. 1986. *No Ivory Tower: McCarthyism and the Universities:* New York: Oxford University Press.

Smith, Dorothy E. 1993. "High Noon in Textland: A Critique of Clough." *Sociological Quarterly* 34 (1): 183–92.

———. 1989. "Sociological Theory: Methods of Writing Patriarchy." In *Feminism and Sociological Theory,* ed. Ruth Wallace. Newbury Park, Calif.: Sage. 34–64.

CHAPTER 3

JOAN ACKER, KATE BARRY,
AND JOKE ESSEVELD

Objectivity and Truth: Problems in Doing Feminist Research

What methods should be used in a feminist[1] analysis of society? Are there modes of thinking, data collection, and analysis that are more appropriate than others for studying the situation of women from a feminist perspective? These questions were raised early in the contemporary feminist critique of the social sciences (Bart 1971; Bernard 1973; McCormack 1975; Smith 1974) and are still being explored and developed. Feminist scholars have analyzed the male bias in the social sciences (see, e.g., Sherman and Beck 1979) and are beginning to make a distinctive contribution to long-standing debates about theory and method (Smith 1977, 1979, 1980; Westkott 1979), sharing the concern of others with basic and enduring controversies such as the nature of science, its epistemological foundation, the possibility of a science of society, and the role of science in maintaining or undermining systems of power (see, e.g., Blumer 1969; Berstein 1978; Hughes 1980). In addition, we are beginning to consider how these debates become translated into problematic methodological issues for those doing empirical studies within a feminist perspective (e.g., Roberts 1981).

The goals of feminist social science have developed in the context of the criticism of the established natural science model of sociology and related disciplines (Bernard 1973). Extending that critique, some feminist perspectives share the critical view of the Marxist and interpretative traditions within the social sciences, while adding their own emphasis and content (Smith 1974, 1977). These feminists have argued that the traditional approach to social science is compatible with the aims of those in particular locations or positions of management and control in society (Smith 1977) whose goals include such things as managing workers more effectively, dealing with civil disorder, and encouraging women to enter or leave the work force in accord with changing economic conditions; thus, what is taken as problematic in much of social science has also been what is problematic for those who control and manage the society. Moreover, in addition to problem definition, the concepts, frames of reference, and perspectives that define traditional sociology express the interests of and arise out of particular social institutions in which the governing and organizing of society takes place (Smith 1979). Almost all those who rule and manage are male; interesting and important phenomena are identified from a male perspective as well as from the perspective of those who manage and control. Women are largely absent from this world; the female domain of production and reproduction that provides the necessary infrastructure for the male world is, despite its importance, invisible, uninteresting to many social scientists, and largely unconceptualized. Thus, in the history of sociology, the development of an approach to knowledge with the goal of control has contributed to the failure to study the situation of women, as well as to a conceptualization of women that is consistent with continuing male dominance (Acker 1973). Beginning around 1970, attempts to deal with the exclusion, distortion, and neglect of women have produced many useful theoretical and empirical studies. One significant result of this research has been the identification of many regularities and correlations that describe women's situation. However, this has limitations for building a tradition of research for women because it leaves largely unexamined the social processes lying behind the correlations. Understanding the processes that result in inequalities is a necessary step toward changing women's position. For us this understanding comes from a theoretical perspective that has its roots in feminism, Marxism, and critical theory. This means a commitment to a social science that can help change the world as well as describe it. "Women's devaluation—and the consequences of this devaluation are reinforced by a social science which records these conditions while systematically ignoring alternative possibilities" (Westkott 1979:428).

The goals of a sociology for women, one that is in the interests of women rather than only about women, must be emancipatory (Esseveld 1980; Hartsock 1979; Westkott 1979). *Emancipation*, as we use the term, means the eventual end of social and economic conditions that oppress women and the achievement of a free society. The ideal is that women should be self-emancipating and our conviction is that social scientists can contribute to this process (Karabel 1976) by analyzing how the personal is political and by pushing that analysis beyond individual experience to comprehension of "its determination in the larger socio-economic structure" (Smith 1977:22). An emancipatory social science would provide women with understandings of how their everyday worlds, their trials and troubles, were and are generated by the larger social structure. The emancipatory aim of a women's sociology derives from its close connections with the contemporary women's movement as well as from our particular position as women researchers. Women's research is intimately connected with the political aims of the women's movement in a number of ways. The movement provided the necessary social basis for legitimation and political support that allowed women researchers to start publicly asking some of the questions they had long been asking privately. Moreover, the women's movement outside of academia posed new questions and new formulations of women's situation that then could be taken up in the academic setting. Women researchers, in addition, were usually members of the women's movement and had, and still have, a political commitment to ending women's oppression. This commitment supplied a general standard against which to assess the kinds of questions and problems that should be dealt with. At the same time women researchers were developing analyses of their own locations in the larger socioeconomic structure, for in some fundamental ways their positions were and are similar to those of their subjects. As women they too may have husbands and children, they too keep house as well as work, they too have to cope with sexism in their daily lives. Thus, a sociology for women has emancipatory possibilities for the researchers as well as the researched, for as women researchers we also have been absent and unheard within the male sociological traditions.

Having accepted the above critique of traditional social science and recognizing that in all social science women have been peripheral and their lives misrepresented, it is clear that a radical rebeginning is needed in feminist research.

For us, a radical rebeginning has meant understanding gender as central in constructing all social relations and taking individual women's lives as a problematic (Hartsock 1979; Smith 1980). What is to be explained is what actually happens in women's everyday world and how these events are experienced. We begin, then, with the ordinary life of women but neither stop there nor move into a search for individual psychological sources of feelings, actions, and events. Although we view people as active agents in their own lives and as such constructors of their social worlds, we do not see that activity as isolated and subjective. Rather, we locate individual experience in society and history, embedded within a set of social relations[2] that produce both the possibilities and limitations of that experience. What is at issue is not just everyday experience but the relations that underlie it and the connections between the two. In this analysis, we use a dialectical method in order to arrive "at adequate description and analysis of how it actually works. Our methods cannot rest in procedures for deciding among different formalized 'opinions' about the world" (Smith 1977:26). Rather, this is a method of exploration and discovery, a way to begin to search for understandings that may contribute to the goals of liberation. Exploration, in our usage, means an open and critical process in which all the intellectual tools we have inherited from a male-dominated intellectual tradition are brought into question, including ideas about the basic nature of human beings, the nature of social life, the taken-for-granted worldview of traditional science, what concepts and questions might help to illuminate our shared condition, and how we should go about developing such knowledge.

In developing this knowledge we also try to maintain a critical perspective toward some of the assumptions made within the social sciences. For example, the assumption that the researcher must and can strive to be a neutral observer standing outside the social realities being studied is made by many who use quantitative and qualitative methods in a natural science model. This assumption is challenged by the feminist critique of social science that documents the male bias of theory and research that has previously been taken as a neutral account of human society. A feminist methodology must, therefore, deal with the issues of objectivity in social science and, in the process, deal also with the issue of the relationship between the researcher and the researched. As researchers, we must not impose definitions of reality on those researched, for to do so would undermine our intention to work toward a sociology for women. Our intention is to minimize the tendency in all research to transform those researched into objects of scrutiny and manipulation. In an ideal case, we would create conditions in which the object of research enters into the process as an active subject.

Recognizing the objects of the research as subjects in their own right suggests that researchers must take care not to make the research relationship an exploitative one. This has been a concern at least since the 1960s, when New Left criticism of the subtle and obvious repressions of bureaucratic society included an evaluation of the research process as oppressive. It becomes a critical issue for feminist researchers who themselves might be cast in the role of the research object and who, as women, have experienced the objectification of women in society. Perhaps more important, research that aims to be liberating should not in the process become only another mode of oppression. But, this aim poses an ongoing contradiction; ultimately the researcher must objectify the experience of the researched, must translate that experience into more abstract and general terms if an analysis that links the individual to processes outside her immediate social world is to be achieved. Objectification would be minimized and the emancipatory goal furthered if both researcher and researched could participate in the process of analysis. But this is not always possible because the preconditions of such participation, some similarity of interest, ideology, and language between researcher and researched, are sometimes absent. Even with a similarity of interest, there are still problems of a practical nature. The impossibility of eliminating all objectification exists in all social research, and the problem cannot be solved by creating the illusion that no relationship exists between the researcher and the research object.

In summary, the following are some of the principles of feminist research with which we began this project:

1. Our goal was to contribute to women's liberation through producing knowledge that can be used by women themselves.
2. The methods of gaining this knowledge should not be oppressive.
3. We should continually develop the feminist critical perspective that questions both the dominant intellectual traditions and reflects on its own development.

In the pages that follow we begin to develop a methodology for doing feminist research based on the view of a social science outlined above.

WOMEN IN TRANSITION: AN EXAMPLE OF AN ATTEMPT TO DO FEMINIST RESEARCH

We, the authors of this essay, started a research project in 1976 with the intention of doing a study that might contribute to the liberation of women. We tried to apply the principles of feminist research discussed above and, in the process, learned about some of the difficulties with this approach. The following is an account of our research process and the problems we encountered.

The feminist critique of social science and our own commitment to the women's movement led us to select a particular problem. The choice of the problem, together with the critique, dictated a qualitative method of investigation. We chose repeated, unstructured, individual interviews as well as some group interviews. Although this proved to be difficult and we are critical of our work at many points, the choice of a qualitative approach also produced new insights, new for us at least, about some of the issues raised above. As the project is concluding with the writing of a report, we are still convinced of the value of the method.

The Problem and the Method

The problem we chose was the relation between changes in the structural situation of women and changes in consciousness. We decided to look at the experiences of women who had been primarily mothers and wives and were attempting to move into the labor market. This group has participated in one of the major demographic changes in women's lives, their increasing entry into the paid labor force. We believed that these women, involved in a process of changing life circumstances, would come to see themselves differently as women and would reinterpret their problems, particularly in a social context that includes a widely discussed feminist movement.

The question of consciousness was important to us from a political point of view; consciousness-raising is an essential component of the feminist movement and a necessary part of feminist action (Bartky 1975; Westkott 1979). An understanding of how women's consciousness changes or doesn't change might be helpful to other women. Consciousness is important in a framework that views people as actors who intentionally try to affect their own situations. The oppression of women has limited our ability to actively intervene in working out our own destiny, but changing work opportunities and the feminist challenge to a whole range of barriers should have increased the possibilities for purposive action. An examination of whether or not this was occurring was thus relevant to our theories about the relation between individuals and social structure.

We were convinced that middle-aged women who had spent most of their lives as wives and mothers had been ignored by much of the movement and we hoped that we might give voice to some of their perspectives. We were also interested in this group because their long commitment to being housewives and mothers might make them resistant to change in a feminist direction. We also had a theoretical concern about adult life. At the time of the beginning of the research, very little had been written on middle-aged women; collectively as social scientists we knew next to nothing about the middle years of adult life. We were critical of what little literature existed and were skeptical of widely held assumptions about women of this age. For example, we questioned the idea that women suffered from having an "empty nest" syndrome, an assumption that has since been discounted by a number of other researchers such as Lillian Rubin (1979). This was our general theoretical orientation, but consistent with the feminist critique that we, along with others, were working out, we decided not to structure interviews with predetermined definitions of consciousness. Rather, we entered our interviews in an unstructured way, getting women to talk about the changes occurring in their lives, leaving the definition of consciousness as an emergent knowledge that would come out of the discussions. This would allow us to develop a more thorough understanding of the women's own perspectives as well as get unanticipated information about events and problems. The women were interviewed in their own homes by one of the three of us as investigators. We had interviews with sixty-five women and followed a subgroup of thirty women for four to five years. We tried not to impose our ideas about what was important; our intention was to let the concepts, explanations, and interpretations of those participating in the study become the data we would analyze (Glaser and Strauss 1973). While we tried to avoid determining what was to be considered in the content of consciousness, we were still aware of our own theoretical ideas. In our continual process of analysis we had to confront discrepancies between our ideas and interpretations and those of the women we interviewed. As the interview process proceeded, we decided to bring up certain questions if they did not emerge in the interviews. The areas most likely to be unmentioned were the women's movement, feelings about aging, and sexuality. However, in most of the related interviews, the topics that we thought would be important came up spontaneously. Sometimes we did direct the interview. For example, after discussing present life situations and challenges, we asked about past history beginning with adolescence unless the interviewee herself initiated the subject of earlier experiences.

We got accounts of significant childhood experiences, as the women perceived them in the present. We also gathered information on education and work experience; on relationships with parents, husbands, children, and friends; and on aspirations and hopes for the future.

In second and subsequent interviews, we filled out areas not touched on before, but in particular focused on the changes that had taken place since the previous interviews, as well as on the issues that seemed to be paramount at the time of the interview. During the whole period of interviewing, which for some of the participants extended over five years, we in the research group had extensive discussions of the interview process. In these discussions we were in an ongoing process of reformulating our ideas and examining the validity of our assumptions about the change process; about how to conceptualize consciousness; about the connections between changing life circumstances and changing views of self, others, and the larger world; and about how to link analytically these individual lives with the structure of industrial capitalism in the United States in the seventies. Each of us had both formal training and considerable past experience in interviewing. Consequently, although we discussed the interview process, our main focus was on the analysis and integration of the data.

The initial interviews and many of the second interviews were taped and transcribed. Later interviews were treated differently—we took notes during the interview and then wrote, immediately afterward, to the best of our ability, a process account of the interview. Some of the taped interviews were not transcribed. Instead, we listened to the interviews, perhaps several times, noting topic areas and their locations on the tapes so that they could be listened to again when we were working on a particular theme. We then made detailed summaries of each woman's situation that included the main facts about her current life (marital status, number of children, work status, class, age) her perception of her problems, her goals, her consciousness of the women's movement, and the dilemmas or contradictions that we saw in her life. We made similar summaries at later interviews. At the same time, we were trying to identify common themes and also differences in experience. This analysis went on during the whole period of interviewing. We will return to the analysis process later, but here we want to discuss some other issues related to the interview process, in particular the influence of our relationship with our study participants.

The Research Relationship

The idea of neutrality and objectivity in the social sciences has been extensively criticized by those working within the interpretive traditions (Blumer 1969; Hughes 1980) and by some Marxists and critical theorists of the Frankfurt School (Habermas 1971; Bernstein 1978). Taking a women's perspective adds to that critique in some important ways. The ideal of objectivity is to remove the particular point of view of the observer from the research process so that the results will not be biased by the researcher's subjectivity. "Recent versions of this ideal of objectivity have emphasized the importance of the universal application of social science methods as the best guarantee against the bias or subjectivity" (Westkott 1979:425). These methods are designed to separate the knower from the object of study. Rejecting the notion that such a separation is possible, Dorothy Smith (1977) argues that the illusion of this separation can be maintained so long as the knower can be posited as an abstract being and the object can be posited as the Other who cannot reflect back on and affect the knower. "Once women are inserted into sociological sentences as their subjects, however, the appearance of impersonality goes. The knower turns out not to be the 'abstract knower' after all, but a member of a definite social category occupying definite positions within the society" (Smith 1974:16–17). It also turns out that research is embedded in a definite social relationship in which there is a power differential in favor of the knower, who assumes the power to define in the process of the research. Research reports reflect only one side of this social relationship—that of the more powerful "knower."

That there is a relationship between the subject and object of study is more easily made visible when women are researching women. "Women studying women reveals the complex way in which women as objects of knowledge reflect back upon women as subjects of knowledge. Knowledge of the other and knowledge of the self are mutually informing because self and other share a common condition of being women" (Westkott 1979:426). The research process becomes a dialogue between the researcher and the researched, an effort to explore and clarify the topic under discussion, an attempt to clarify and expand understandings; the researcher and the researched are assumed to be individuals who reflect upon their experience and who can communicate those reflections. This is inherent in the situation; neither the subjectivity of the researcher nor the subjectivity of the researched can be eliminated in the process.

Our commitment to reducing so far as we could the unequal power in the research relationship and acknowledging the subjectivity of our study participants took a variety of forms. One strategy was encouraging the interviewee to take the lead in deciding what to talk about. This did not always work; people have ideas about what it is like to be interviewed and they want to be asked questions so that they can give the "right responses." Some women were uneasy with us because we were from the university. Others did not want to set the terms of the discussion because they felt that there couldn't be anything interesting about their lives. However, those with whom we had more than one interview increasingly took the lead in discussions and even took the initiative to get in touch with us to tell us what had been happening to them. Unstructured interviewing and letting the women take an important part in the discussion helped to counter some of the problems other researchers have confronted when using a more standard sociological methodology. Thus we did not have the problems encountered by Diana Woodward and Lynne Chisholm, who used more structured interviews and, as a result, enlarged the gap already existing between them and their subjects of study: "The very nature of our questions about employment and the domestic division of labor served to reveal our pre-occupation with work, marital conflict and women's oppression, rather then with the satisfaction of motherhood and housewifery" (1981:177).

Another part of the attempt to deal with the subject-object problem was to try to establish some reciprocity by offering, at the end of the first interview, to tell the women something about ourselves if we had not done so earlier. Often we didn't have to offer—it was a request made to us. We always responded as honestly as we could, talking about aspects of our lives that were similar to the things we had been discussing about the experience of the interviewee—our marriages, our children, our jobs, our parents. Often this meant also that our relationship was defined as something that existed beyond the limits of the interview situation. We formed friendships with many of the women in the study. We were offered hospitality and were asked to meet husbands, friends, and children. Sometimes we would provide help to one or another woman in the study. For example, one woman became depressed and called the interviewer, who then went to the interviewee's house and spent several hours with her while she talked about her troubles and gradually became less distressed. However, we recognized a usually unarticulated tension between friendships and the goal of research.[3] The researcher's goal is always to gather information; thus the danger always exists of manipulating friendships to that end. Given that the power differences between researcher and researched cannot be completely eliminated, attempting to create a more equal relationship can paradoxically become exploitation and use. We recognized this more as the research progressed and tried to avoid it.

During the interviews we were also often asked for information, which we provided. We viewed this as an additional opportunity to reciprocate for the help these women were giving us by participating in the study. Now, at this stage of the writing, we continue to have feelings of obligation to the women we interviewed—to finish the writing and find a way to publish our—their—material. If we do not do this, we will have failed on our part of our joint project.

A high degree of participation in the research was not established with all interviewees. As we noted above, repeated interviews resulted in more involvement. However, not only the number of interviews but also the experiences women were having at the particular time that we first interviewed them influenced our contact. With those women who experienced this period as a critical period in their lives, we seem to have established the best rapport. Although our lives differed from most of the women we interviewed, with many we shared a sense of uneasiness, an experiencing of dilemmas and contradictions as well as a willingness to acknowledge them.

Another way that we tried to overcome the distance between researchers and researched was to show our written material to the women we wrote about. We did not do this with every woman in the study. We shared most of this material with the women with whom we had the most interviews, who were those who identified themselves as consciously trying to change. Since change was the central issue of the study, there was a theoretical rationale for spending more time with them. And, given the focus on change as well as our limited time and other resources, it made more sense to ask these women to reflect on our written material. They were, as we mentioned above, also women who most shared our worldview; a common frame of reference provided the grounds from which a dialogue could proceed. We have to admit to some reluctance to share our interpretations with those who, we expected, would be upset by them. There was a potential conflict between our feminist frame of reference and their interpretations of their own lives. Our solution to this conflict was not to include them as active participants in the analysis of our research. Whether or not to confront groups or individuals with interpretations of their lives that are radically different from their own is an ethical question faced by anyone attempting critical social research. This is particularly true when the researcher's interpretation is not only different but potentially threatening and disruptive to the subject's view of the world. For example, many of the women who were housewives defined themselves as very independent whereas our perspective defined the conditions of their lives as creating both a structural and personal dependence. These housewives had a stake in their own definition that was also a source of worth and dignity, while we as feminist researchers interpreted their situations differently. At that moment, we were dealing with a tension between the goal of reducing the power differences between the researcher and the researched and the difficulties of carrying this out when there was a lack of agreement on the meaning of experiences. We have not solved this problem; we believe that the solution lies in accepting the dilemmas and maintaining an awareness of when and why we are not able to make the research process a true dialogue, this giving full legitimacy to the subjectivity of the Other as well as to our own. At least then we can articulate the difficult balance between granting respect to the Other's interpretation of her reality, while going beyond that interpretation to comprehend its underlying relations.

Problems of Analysis

As we pointed out, our commitment to minimizing the power differentials of the relationship in the research was further confounded when it came to the analysis. We found that we had to assume the role of the people with the power to define. The act of looking at interviews, summarizing another's life, and placing it within a context is an act of objectification. Indeed, we the researchers took the position that some process of objectification of the self is a necessary part of coming to an awareness of one's own existence; it is not less a part of coming to an understanding of others. Acknowledging that a necessary part of understanding another's experience involves an act or moment of objectification poses further problems and contradictions. The question becomes how to produce an analysis that goes beyond the experience of the researched while still granting them full subjectivity. How do we explain the lives of others without violating their reality? This is part of a larger problem: a critique of objectivity which asserts that there can be no neutral observer who stands outside the social relations she observes can easily become a relativism in which all explanations are subjectively grounded and therefore have equal weight. When all accounts are equally valid, the search for "how it actually works" becomes meaningless. Though we don't claim to have resolved this problem, we tried to avoid it by claiming a validity for our analysis (see discussion below) while not in the process forcing that analysis into categories such as worker, housewife, or mother and divorced or married, which fracture women's experience.[4] However, in the actual task of analysis, we initially found ourselves moving back and forth between letting the data "speak for itself" and using abstracted categories.

Our feminist commitment had led us to collect data that were difficult to analyze and had provided us with so much information that it was difficult to choose what was "essential" at the same time that we tried to give a picture that provided a "totality." Our solution to this series of problems was to present a number of life histories, expressed largely in the women's own words, to typify what we thought were particular patterns of change. We based these patterns on apparently discrete categories such as whether change was occurring and how it was initiated.

This attempt to make sense out of our information by placing the women into categories of "changers" and "nonchangers" obscured the complexities of women's lives. Although it was possible to categorize women using simple and rigid criteria, the boundaries between changers and nonchangers were not at all clear. We at first called all women who were enrolled in school or were looking for a job "changers." But interviews revealed that some of the nonchangers were going through an active process of rethinking their lives while some of the changers (a small minority, but nevertheless bothersome in terms of a neat analysis) were actively resisting all but very superficial changes.[5]

We were pushed to develop our analysis further by women in the study whom we asked to read the manuscript. They were hesitant about being negative, but were clearly critical. What they wanted, they said, was more of our own sociological analysis. They wanted us, the researchers, to interpret their experience to them. Here, once more, we faced incompatibilities between various components of our feminist approach to social research. If we were to fulfill the emancipatory aim for the people we were studying, we had to go beyond the faithful representation of their experience, beyond "letting them talk for themselves," and put those experiences into the theoretical framework with which we started the study, a framework that links women's oppression with the structure of Western capitalist society.

Both the ways in which we were categorizing experience and the kinds of categories we then developed were still somewhat antithetical to our theoretical position. We experimented with dividing our interviewees into housewives and workers for the purpose of analysis. We had tried to only recruit housewives for the study, but—not surprisingly—found that about half the women we interviewed had had considerable work experience. Almost all of them had continued to see themselves as housewives. How should we see them? What is the critical cutting point in work experience that can tell us how to differentiate? We came to the obvious conclusion (Acker 1978) that the stationary concepts of housewife and paid worker are problematic ones. Most women move from unpaid work to paid work during their lifetimes and only a few fit totally within the unpaid work/paid work dichotomy, as quantitative data clearly show (Maret-Havens 1977). Our concepts do not reflect the reality of women's lives; this was demonstrated to us again in our qualitative data. Our initial use of traditional categories, despite our own feminist critique of them, illustrates the power of conventional ways of thinking about the social world and the difficulty of breaking out of its boundaries.

Another difficulty we faced was the difficulty of conceptualizing process. We first tried to solve this and the categorizing problem together by thinking up categories of ways that women engaged in the change process. Thus, we tried talking about those who initiated change in an active way as contrasted with those who were forced into changes by outside events. We soon found that this categorization fell apart as we looked in-depth at the actual processes. We also rejected a life cycle perspective partly because of its biological determinist implications and partly because we could not find a common pattern among the women we interviewed in the time that change began in either the family or the individual life cycle.

We also attempted to categorize feminist consciousness and, to some extent, were successful.[6] However, again, the boundaries were unclear and we felt that the strategy of analysis was not productive. We were not gaining any new insights nor deepening our understanding of the relationship between the individual and social structure and it was in this part of the research process that these connections had to be made explicitly.

At the same time that we were trying to find some fruitful categories in which to group our interviewees, we were analyzing issues or themes in the interviews. The contradictions between our commitment to a dialectical analysis, our aim of reconstructing women's experience in a way that accounts for both their and our explanations of that experience and the relation between the two, and our actual use of rigid categories sent us back to our theoretical beginnings in Marxism, feminism, and critical theory. We saw that the themes of everyday life we were identifying could be understood as manifestations of contradictions or dilemmas inherent in the underlying social relations. We explore the nature of these relations in our account of the research itself (see, e.g., Acker, Barry, and Esseveld 1981). As the analysis proceeded we tried to understand what was changing in these women's lives and whether or not the underlying dilemmas we had identified were being resolved or were reappearing in new ways, as the specific conditions of their lives were altered in a society that was both changing and remaining static. In the process of analysis, we refined and reshaped our initial questions, trying to make the act of objectification analogous to a moment of critical reflection. The concepts and questions that are central in our final report are different from those with which we started. We know that this is the history of many other research projects, although usually it is an unwritten history. We expected to work in this way, but if we understood beforehand how long and difficult the process would become, we might have more consciously and more quickly worked out strategies of analysis.[7]

Problems of Validity

The research perspective outlined in the first section of this essay makes problematic the conventional way of evaluating the products of the research. How shall we decide whether what we have done—the knowledge we develop—is worthwhile? How shall we decide if what we say is true? The first question about the development of worthwhile knowledge has to be answered in terms of an emancipatory goal. We might ask whether our findings contribute to the women's movement in some way or whether they make the struggles of individual women more effective or easier by helping to reveal to them the conditions of their lives. We know that this is the case for some of the women in our study. This is also a historical question that can only be resolved in the future. An emancipatory intent is no guarantee of an emancipatory outcome. Perhaps the best we can do is to guard against our research being used against women, although that also may be difficult.

The second question, how to decide what is true or valid, is one we have in common with all social scientists. We differ, however, with many of them in how we conceive of this truth. We are not interested in prediction, but adequate reconstruction (Schutz 1963). We conceive of this at two levels. The first has to do with adequacy of interpretation and involves selection, organization, and interpretation of our findings with the help of our social theory. The other level of concern is with the adequacy of our findings. We want to know that our research results fairly and accurately reflect the aspects of social life that we claim they represent.

If validity is to be judged by the adequacy of interpretation, we must return to our theoretical orientation to determine the criteria of adequacy. This, as briefly discussed above, is a position that has its origins in feminism, Marxism, and critical theory and that is working toward a sociology *for* women. The first criterion of adequacy in this approach is that the active voice of the subject should be heard in the account. Our interpretations should avoid transforming the acting and thinking human being solely into an object of study, while recognizing that some objectification is inherent in the process of interpretation or reconstruction. Moreover, seeing persons as active agents in their own lives, we will not view them as totally determined or lacking in comprehension of the social world. For example, we consider the concept "false consciousness" inadequate as part of a valid interpretation.

A second criterion for adequacy is that the theoretical reconstruction must be able to account for the investigator as well as the investigated. The interpretation must locate the researcher in the social structure and also provide a reconstruction of the social relations that produce the research itself. For example, what are the social relations that produce this research situation and the enterprise of research itself? What makes it possible to raise the research problem at this time, in this place, in this society? What are the processes that have resulted in the researched and the researchers coming together in a particular kind of social relationship? Such a reconstruction should be possible, in principle, although we do not argue that every research report should spell it out in detail.

Our third criterion for adequacy is that the reconstruction should reveal the underlying social relations that eventuate in the daily lives we are studying. This is the heart of the idea of a sociology *for* women; we want to understand how the underlying organization of actions and practices results in the ordinary daily lives of women. This is a complex task, perhaps an impossible task. For example, to trace back from the daily experience of a working-class mother, getting three or four children ready for school in the morning, unassisted by another adult, packing lunches, buttoning coats, and so forth, to the arrangements and relations that put her there, would be to describe much of the organization of the society. Thus, we need to make decisions and choices; this is part of the process of analysis that we have discussed above.

The adequacy of the interpretation fundamentally depends on the accuracy of our descriptions of the experience we wish to locate within the social relations of the society. Have we told it the way that it actually happens? This is the question we turn to now.

Our research problem demanded that we try to understand reality from the perspective of the people experiencing it. Since we directly asked them about their experience we did not have the problem of developing indicators of concepts. Rather, we wanted to maximize direct communication in their terms. We assumed that our study participants would have a better chance of telling us about their worlds as they saw them if their active participation in defining the dialogue was encouraged. As we have indicated above, we are confident that in most of our interviews the interviewees felt comfortable about stating their own cases.

In qualitative work, the accuracy of listening and hearing may be as important as the openness of telling. The fact that we, the interviewers, were women who have been married, divorced, and had children (one of us had a baby after the study began) increased the validity of our data. We did not have to go through the process of getting to know the special perspectives and nuances of meaning of those we were studying—a process that is often identified as necessary if the qualitative researcher wants to avoid errors that simply come from ignorance (see, e.g., Filstead 1970). We were studying people who had experiences very similar to ours, although of course there were important differences (the most important being our status as researchers) and we were, thus, sensitive to problems and issues that might otherwise have been invisible.[8]

We think that it was also important that we were feminists. Our feminist analysis of women's oppression, which constituted much of the theory informing our work, also increased our sensitivity and awareness in the interview process and contributed to the emergence of an empathetic atmosphere in the interaction process. A faithful account is best pursued, we are arguing, in research such as ours in which changing consciousness is the central question, through the close and sympathetic involvement with the informant rather than through distancing and objectifying. At the same time such closeness may create certain kinds of blindness in the researcher. One protection we developed against this was in the ongoing process of analysis in the research group. Our analytic discussions, of necessity, forced us to distance ourselves from our subjects.

We have confirmation of the accuracy of our findings from those women we interviewed. We received extensive feedback from many of them in both individual and group discussions. Some read their interviews or listened to their tapes. We also discussed our written material with many and in those discussions our findings and our interpretations were confirmed.

Much more difficult problems of validity began to emerge in the interviews that were continued over a period of four years. These problems have to do with how reality is constructed and reconstructed in the process of talking and thinking about it and how the process of research becomes part of the process of change. We will leave the psychological aspects of the reconstruction of reality to the psychotherapeutic professions. Here, we will limit ourselves to specific methodological issues and only discuss the content of the change process in relation to them. Our insights into these issues come from women in our study and in particular from one person whom we asked to participate in a workshop on developing a feminist methodology in social science.[9] Her comments on the experience of being the researched tell us a great deal about the validity of interview or questionnaire data. We will give a brief account of her experience as a background to further comments on validity.

Joanne began the first interview with a positive attitude toward the research. She knew that the objective was to contribute to the goal of women's liberation; she herself had a feminist orientation and was anxious to cooperate. During the interview, she did her best to be open and honest. The interview lasted for three hours and both the interviewer and Joanne thought it was a good interview. However, reflecting on what she had said during the next few days, Joanne realized that she had omitted some very important aspects of her life and had unintentionally misrepresented others. She felt that the account she had given was chaotic, unclear, and disorganized. In the months between the first and second interviews, she thought about her life, tried to clarify events, relationships, and feelings; in the second interview she discussed herself within this altered point of view. Still, reviewing later what she said, she again was dissatisfied with the accuracy of her presentation of her current and past life. Once more, she went through a process of self-examination and rethinking. The third interview was somewhat better, but she was not yet satisfied. Only after the fourth interview did she begin to feel that she was portraying her life as she actually lived it. By the fifth interview she had arrived at a coherent explanation of her experiences. Joanne said that this was the first time in her life that she was able to put together a reasonable account for herself. She believes that her first accounts were chaotic and disorganized because that was the way that her life was, filled with multiple and conflicting demands from her husband, her five children, her jobs, her volunteer work in the community, and her friends. In the research process, between interviews, she spent long hours analyzing those relationships; her work on herself was part of the work on the research. She, as the researched, was constantly checking out the validity of the data she was giving us, the researchers. But, in the process, these data changed in some ways. The facts of the past were not altered, but they were elaborated and important omissions were filled in. Her own definition of what was important also changed in the process. Although it seems the best validity check is to have the study participant determine accuracy, one could also argue that the first interview might have reflected her conscious assessment of the reality of her life at that time, while the fifth interview reflected an equally valid picture at a later time. Are we, thus, getting a more and more valid account or are we getting several accounts that reflect the process of change? Certainly for Joanne, the interviews were part of a change process in which she was trying to deal with fundamental contradictions in her life situation. Her understanding of her present dilemmas became clearer too, clearer in that she was more satisfied with them.

Such problems have been discussed many times by others who have argued that retrospective accounts are suspect in terms of validity. For example, Howard S. Becker and Blanche Geer stated: "Changes in the social environment and in the self inevitably produce transformations of perspectives, and it is characteristic of such transformations that the person finds it difficult or impossible to remember his [*sic*] former actions, outlook or feelings. Reinterpreting things from his [*sic*] new perspective, he [*sic*] cannot give an accurate account of the past, for the concepts in which he [*sic*] thinks about it have changed and with them his [*sic*] perceptions and memories" (1957:31). We take a different position, arguing that both the past and the present accounts are accurate. The first account was, we think, a true representation of Joanne's conscious thoughts about her life at that time, with all the things she forgot, held back, and interpreted in ways she thought would be acceptable. But now that we have her own analysis of the process we cannot take it as adequate "data" about her life history or her present situation. Her interpretations at the first interview were more narrow than the broader perspectives she had during the fifth interview, which was informed by social theory and by the interactions with the researchers. At this moment we have left our discussion of validity in a narrow sense and returned to our view of science in which an emancipatory goal is an essential part (Touraine, Hegedus, Dubet, and Wieniorka 1980). To return to our discussion: we should not take that first interview as filled with "error," although critical omissions may make our interpretations suspect. Especially painful memories or difficult experiences may be obscured—events such as the birth of an illegitimate child put up for adoption, abortion, rape, or an illicit love affair may be clouded over or simply seen as unimportant when from the point of view of the outsider, they are critical to understanding a life. These obscured experiences are central to the systematic devaluation of women in a male-dominated world. A feminist perspective redefines these experiences as part of women's oppression, helping women to see their feelings as legitimate and eroding the taboos against discussing such life events. Moreover, distance and some confidence in the interviewer that has been built up over time may make it possible to reveal such events while altering the ways that they are assessed by the person who experienced them.

Unless a relationship of trust is developed, we can have no confidence that our research on women's lives and consciousness accurately represents what is significant to them in their everyday lives and thus has validity in that sense. This is particularly true if we are trying to understand lives in their totality, as ongoing processes in which the person plays an active part. Certain survey data becomes, then, even more suspect. We have difficulty in assessing the validity of even the most factual data, to say nothing of data about opinions and attitudes. Even "in-depth" interviews present problems of interpretation, as the above discussion indicates. We are probably faced with another unresolvable dilemma: working from a perspective in which we are trained to want to give a reasoned and connected account, we face live material that is constantly in the process of transformation, that is not organized in the way of academic theories. Virginia Woolf, among other novelists, may give a better account of the conscious experiencing of life in all its episodic and unorganized ways than we sociologists can achieve. However, as sociologists we can find representations of such experiences that allow us to build a sociology *for* women, a sociology that connects experience at that level to its structural determination in the wider society. What distinguishes us from those who are not social scientists lies in our method of systematically attempting to reconstruct social reality and to put these systematic reconstructions into a social theory that we share with other social scientists. We are part of a group endeavor to understand society, even though the group is scattered and many of its members remain unknown to us.

SUMMARY

In this essay we have discussed our attempt to use principles of feminist research in a systematic way as we carried out a research project. For us, feminist research should contribute to the liberation of women. We chose our research problem with this goal in mind. The problem was the relation between changes in consciousness and changes in the structural situation of individuals. Women who were at the end of their period of intensive mothering were the ones we chose to study. Our problem dictated qualitative data gathering. This method of data collection forced us to confront issues about the research relationship and influenced our data analysis. It was extremely difficult to analyze process, even though we had at least some relevant data. We still tended to look at our participants at one interview and then at the next, observing the changes but unable to adequately account for the intervening process. Yet, that process may be most important to understand if we are to comprehend the ways the larger structure penetrates the life of individuals, as well as the ways that individuals in their daily lives both reproduce and undermine that structure.

Our commitment to bringing our subjects into the research process as active participants[10] influenced our rethinking of our original categories, strengthened our critique of research methods, and forced us to realize that it is impossible to create a research process that completely erases the contradictions in the relation between researcher and researched.

In the relationship with those women who were actively changing both their life circumstances and their understandings of their lives, we were able to glimpse the research process as consciousness-raising or emancipatory. Many of them told us that they experienced the interviews in this way. However, the emancipatory potential could only be partially attained even with those who were most aware of subjective change. The limits were in the restricted possibilities for satisfying work and financial independence facing all the women in our study. The research process was not consciousness-raising for those whose life situation had not brought them into contact with the movement nor confronted them with the necessity to reflect upon their experiences. These were the women who were not in the process of trying to establish new forms of daily life and those whose interests seemed to be furthest from ours, the researchers. As we evaluate our experiences in interviewing these women, we are led to another dilemma of feminist research—should we do research that is not consciousness-raising for the participants? Is such research an oppressive process that of necessity exploits the subject? If our answers to these questions are yes, we are faced with the possibility of only doing research with people who are very much like us, eliminating most women from our view and limiting the usefulness of our projects. Perhaps this is another necessary tension in the ongoing project of feminist investigation.

We have not solved the problems of doing emancipatory research. By trying to make our hopes and failures explicit, perhaps we have made a contribution toward that end.

AFTERWORD

On rereading this essay, originally written in 1980, our reactions were mixed: much of it still represents our views on problems in doing feminist research. But, at the same time, on some issues our thinking has changed and our different experiences in the intervening years have led us to identify diverse aspects of our earlier argument that we would change if we were rewriting it today. Although we did not always agree with each other, we did agree that this piece should be understood as belonging to a particular historical time and place.

"Objectivity and Truth" was written when the women's movement was still in its exciting days of rising consciousness and expanding possibilities. Our essay reflects this optimistic mood in its emphasis on the goal of emancipation, defined as the end of social and economic conditions that oppress women, and in its belief that a sociology *for* women could contribute to that goal. This essay was part of a process of creating a context of feminist practice and research and claiming legitimacy for such research. While we three have not abandoned these goals, we see the issues as much more complex and difficult to resolve. The years of promotion of competitive capitalism with its lack of concern for human costs and attacks on equality efforts, as well as the ensuing economic depression, have dampened optimism about change. At the same time, the clear relationship that we felt existed between feminist scholars within the university community and the women's movement has become attenuated and, in many ways, transformed. As feminist scholarship has become institutionalized within the academy, increasingly abstract theoretical concerns seem to have less and less to do with practical problems of women's everyday lives. Moreover, feminist arguments have become more complex as women from many different classes, races, and ethnic groups define their own feminist positions and issues. The women's movement is no longer cohesive and easily identified. Increased understanding of these complexities of social reality creates problems for theory and action. Consequently, today we would be more cautious about the possible role of sociology in helping women to change our situations.

We have two criticisms of our essay in this regard. First, although we think our understandings were more complex, our essay could be read as locating the major problem of theory in absence of women and gender from sociological thinking. Now we would emphasize that the issues are who is doing the theorizing, from what standpoint(s), and with what practices and procedures. Second, while in our essay we are critical of theory developed from a universalistic male perspective, we counterpose to this a woman's perspective that also is universal. Our assumptions of a universal, and mostly heterosexual, woman's standpoint pervade the essay. We also assume that we, the researchers, as well as the mostly middle-class, all white interviewees represent this universal perspective. Today, our theoretical beginnings would be much more complex and would attempt to recognize the multiple diversities of women's experience. This would influence our discussions of methodological issues as well, such as the possibilities for the establishment of mutual subjectivity and for erasure of power differences between researcher and researched.

Our discussion of the research relationship, then, would be more complex today. We focused on a relationship in which the researcher has more power than the researched. We wanted to make this relationship as nonexploitative as possible and tried to do this through creating conditions in "which the object of research enters into the process as an active subject." Although we discussed the dilemmas and contradictions in trying to do this, our different intervening experiences have led us to see even more difficulties in dealing with power in the research relationship. Differences in class, race, and age are even more difficult to transcend than we thought. In addition, the very techniques we used to increase the subjects' active participation may have worked in a way opposite to what we intended. For example, establishing reciprocity, even friendship, in the relationship may set up expectations on the part of the interviewee that the researcher cannot possibly meet.

Follow-up interviews conducted after this essay was published reveal another problem. Some of those we interviewed felt that we researchers had expectations of them that they had failed to meet. They had not been successful and they were disappointed. In contrast to them, one of us, Joan Acker, was about the same age as many of the respondents and was, by their definition, a success (a professor). We felt that, for some, reluctance to talk about reversals of fortune were linked with an implicit comparison of themselves with Joan. A more distant, traditional, objectifying research relationship might not have generated these difficulties.

Our essay implies that empathy is a necessary component of a feminist research relationship. Today we would say more emphatically that empathy is not always possible, nor is it a defining quality of feminist research. Feminist researchers may work on topics that require interviews with women and men who have more power or different political aims than the researcher. Such a relationship is different from the ones in our study because the powerful subject has no difficulty in being active and determining the parameters of the interview. Empathy might be impossible in such a relationship. However, a feminist researcher would still need to recognize the researched as an active subject and to comprehend the effects of the social locations of both the researcher and the researched on the process and content of the interview.

We also assumed in our essay that only women who are feminists can do emancipatory research. The three of us had some disagreements on this. Two of us maintained that while we do not propose as a universal principle that only women can interview women, for many feminist research issues women interviewers can establish more productive and less threatening research relationships than can men. There is a potential connection of experience between women and an ability to be self-revelatory about shared life events that is less likely to be present with a male interviewer. One of us thought that, in principle, men can establish as nonexploitative and supportive research relationships as women and can elicit the same information.

We want to point to the parts of our discussion that are still central in all our thinking or that, we believe, are still important contributions to feminist research methodology. The idea of social relations and processes enunciated here still constitute the understanding of individual experience and social structure for all of us. We still "see individuals' activities in daily life as producing their social worlds; yet at the same time we recognize that there is an underlying organization of these activities that results in similar outcomes." We still think that feminist sociology is about explicating the interrelations between daily experience and the social relations that underlie it. This is one reason that the object of research must enter the process as an active subject, for this is the only way to discover what it is we need to understand.

In our view, probably the most substantial contribution of this essay is in our discussion of the problems of analysis and establishing validity. We tried to get away from the procedures of categorization and classification that are often the first moves in an analysis of sociological data. In addition, we continually attempted to reflect upon our own social locations and how those locations influenced the research relationship and the information we elicited.

We defined validity in terms of our feminist research perspective and our theoretical approach. This translated into assessing the adequacy of interpretation and the adequacy of our findings. We tried to spell out the criteria of adequacy in these two meanings, recognizing that the procedures for satisfying the criteria will vary with the research perspective and problem. Today, on the basis of further experience, we might modify what we had to say about procedures. We would not emphasize so much the contributions to accurate description of similarities between the life experiences of the researchers and the research subjects. While similar experience may minimize mistakes from ignorance, they may also lead to untenable assumptions of congruent experience. In addition, sometimes a sympathetic outsider can see patterns that are invisible to those whose daily lives are embedded in such patterns.

In our experience, the issues of how to do feminist research are far from solved. There is still the issue of how to do research that is not exploitative, how to establish research relationships in which there are two active subjects. Can that be done across lines of class, gender, and racial/ethnic differences and what procedures can help?

How we can establish validity is another unfinished issue. Accuracy of description can be partially checked by asking respondents to read their interviews and comment on them. But, as we found, we were not so comfortable asking those we interviewed to assess the adequacy of interpretation, particularly if they were likely to disagree with us. However, if we maintain our commitment to seeing the researched as active and competent subjects, we might ask about the meaning of such disagreement and the social practices that produce it, leading us to more adequate interpretation. As we move more and more from studying women's experiences as oppressed into studying the social relations that organize that oppression, we need to talk with those who have the power to shape some of those relations. Should we take such care with employers, welfare administrators, and the police? And how does gender influence the research relationship when the researcher is a relatively powerless woman and the researched a relatively powerful man? What are the possible effects of this power arrangement on the accuracy of description?

In conclusion, we would like to reiterate that, in our view, postmodernists' objections notwithstanding, our most distinctive contribution in this essay was our attempt to explicate feminist criteria for establishing validity or "truth." Many others are trying to deal with this issue, but it remains unfinished business.

NOTES

This is an updated version of an essay published as "Objectivity and Truth: Problems in Doing Feminist Research" in *Women's Studies International Forum* 6, no. 4 (1983): 423–35. Reprinted with permission from *Women's Studies International*, Elsevier Science Ltd., Pergamon Imprint, Oxford, England. © Pergamon Press.

1. The term *feminist* refers to diverse groups of people who take varying positions on particular issues and who identify with a range of political positions. In our usage here, *feminist* refers to a point of view that sees women as exploited, devalued, and often oppressed; is committed to changing the condition of women; and adopts a critical perspective toward dominant intellectual traditions that have ignored or justified women's oppression. Some people who identify themselves as feminists accept the natural science model of sociology.

2. The term *social relations* here signifies a particular epistemology derived from the Marxist tradition and is not equivalent to the notion of social relationships. We are not referring to interactions between individuals. Rather we see individuals' activities in daily life as producing their social worlds; yet at the same time we recognize that there is an underlying organization of these activities that results in similar outcomes. This organization is what so-

ciologists call social structure, but this is usually conceptualized as a fixed determinate abstract category that is apart from or radically other than individual action. The term *social relation* is a way of overcoming this dichotomy: to give centrality to the organization of social life without positing either "the individual" or "the social structure" as separate and oppositional. See the work of Dorothy Smith (1977, 1979, 1980) for a feminist interpretation of this concept.

3. Daniels (1967) discusses a similar problem.

4. For a perceptive discussion of the need to reconceptualize social structure in ways that do not push women's experience into categories that are no longer reflective of that experience, see Kelly (1979).

5. This attempt to categorize was related also to our initial statement of our problem, the relationship between certain "exterior" changes—going to school or work—and certain "interior" changes—consciousness of self as a woman who exists in a particular world and the interpretations of that world.

6. We used two categories, personal feminism and political feminism. These are explained in Acker, Barry, and Esseveld (1981).

7. Our commitment to doing feminist research and thus the attempt to do away with the hierarchy so often present in research may have prolonged the time the research has taken us as well. We tried to work in a nonhierarchical way as a research team and also tried to do all the necessary work. This included transcribing interviews ourselves, with some positive and negative results.

We three researchers with different theoretical traditions and with specialization in different areas of sociology had the same interests and political goals. By working closely together we developed the central concerns of our research. During the discussions we also developed a common theoretical perspective in which no person attempted to dominate or impose her own views. Differences in interpretation could then be more democratically resolved. This way of working was often a long drawn-out process, but we believe a necessary one for working with the kind of questions in which we were interested. The research process was also prolonged by our decision to do all the work ourselves. This meant that we would do the transcribing, as we believed that to be one of the most oppressive tasks in the research. We did the transcribing during the few extra hours left us after we had taken care of teaching, work loads, and family responsibilities. It was a tedious process, especially since we were not trained transcribers. Eventually we decided to have some of the interviews transcribed or listened to the tapes and noted down topic areas and their locations on the tapes.

Looking back, we may have overemphasized the overcoming of hierarchy and may have lost some of the expert knowledge and differential experience in the group. It might have been better to include a transcriber in our project instead of trying to deal with the oppressiveness of transcribing by doing the work ourselves.

8. Taking the position that the idea of the neutral observer is a false assumption has implications for validity. The researcher does not stand outside social structure. Her location in society enters into the research relationship. To rec-

ognize and take this into account as we did contributes to a better understanding of reality and greater validity.

9. We wish to thank Joanne Ferrero for contributing her perceptive insights to our workshop on feminist methodology and to this essay.

10. The research process affected us as researchers and in our own lives. Our role as researchers was greatly changed because of the more active involvement of the women in our study, something that became especially clear during the analysis when our interpretations were being questioned. During the interviewing, we faced a tension between being expected to take the initiative and wanting more of a dialogue. Personally, it helped us to reflect on our own situations and influenced future personal choices.

REFERENCES

Acker, Joan. 1978. "Issues in the Sociological Study of Women's Work." In *Women Working*, ed. Ann Stromberg and Shirley Harkess. Palo Alto: Mayfield. 134–61.

——— 1973. "Woman and Social Stratification: A Case of Intellectual Sexism." *American Journal of Sociology* 78 (4): 936–45.

Acker, Joan, Kate Barry, and Joke Esseveld. 1981. "Feminism, Female Friends, and the Reconstruction of Intimacy." In *The Interweave of Social Roles*, ed. Helena Z. Lopata. Greenwich, Conn.: J.A.I. Press. 2:75–108.

Bart, Pauline. 1971. "Sexism in Social Science: From the Iron Cage to the Gilded Cage—The Perils of Pauline." *Journal of Marriage and the Family* 33 (4): 734–45.

Bartky, Sandra Lee. 1975. "Toward a Phenomenology of Feminist Consciousness." *Social Theory Practice* 3 (4): 425–39.

Becker, Howard S., and Blanche Geer. 1957. "Participant Observation and Interviewing: A Comparison." *Human Organization* 16 (3): 28–32.

Bernard, Jessie. 1973. "My Four Revolutions: An Autobiographical History of the ASA." In *Changing Women in a Changing Society*, ed. Joan Huber. Chicago: University of Chicago Press. 11–29.

Bernstein, Richard. 1978. *The Restructuring of Social and Political Theory.* Philadelphia: University of Pennsylvania Press.

Blumer, Herbert. 1969. *Symbolic Interactionism.* Englewood Cliffs, N.J.: Prentice Hall.

Daniels, Arlene Kaplan. 1967. "The Low-Caste Stranger in Social Research." In *Ethics, Politics, and Social Research*, ed. Gideon Sjoberg. Cambridge, Mass.: Schenkman.

Esseveld, Joke. 1980. "Critical Social Research: Women's Perspective." In *Kvindeforskning 1980: Rapport Fra Hindegard Seminaret*, ed. Mette Kunde and Bergitta Possing. Alborg universitetsforlag.

Filstead, William J. 1970. *Qualitative Methodology.* Chicago: Markham.

Glaser, Barney G., and Anselm Strauss. 1973. *The Discovery of Grounded Theory: Strategies for Qualitative Research.* Chicago: Aldine.

Habermas, Jürgen. 1971. *Knowledge and Human Interests.* Boston: Beacon.

Hartsock, Nancy. 1981. "Fundamental Feminism: Process and Perspective." In *Building Feminist Theory: Essays from Quest.* New York: Longman. 3–19.

———. 1979. "Feminist Theory and the Development of Revolutionary Strategy." In *Capitalist Patriarchy and the Case for Socialist Feminism,* ed. Zillah Eisenstein. New York: Monthly Review Press. 56–77.

Hughes, John. 1980. *The Philosophy of Social Research.* Essex: Longman House.

Karabel, Jerome. 1976. "Revolutionary Contradictions: Antonio Gramsci and the Problem of Intellectuals." *Politics and Society* 6 (2): 123–72.

Kelly, Joan. 1979. "The Double Vision of Feminist Theory: A Postscript to the 'Women and Power' Conference." *Feminist Studies* 1 (5): 216–27.

McCormack, Thelma. 1975. "Towards a Non-sexist Perspective on Social and Political Changes." In *Another Voice: Feminist Perspectives of Social Life and Social Sciences,* ed. Marcia Millman and Rosabeth Moss Kanter. Garden City, N.Y.: Anchor. 1–33.

Maret-Havens, Elizabeth. 1977. "Developing an Index to Measure Female Labor Force Attachment." *Monthly Labor Review* 199 (5): 35–38.

Roberts, Helen, ed. 1981. *Doing Feminist Research.* London: Routledge and Kegan Paul.

Rubin, Lillian. 1979. *Women of a Certain Age.* New York: Morrow.

Schutz, Albert. 1963. "Concept and Theory Formation in the Social Sciences." In *Philosophy of the Social Sciences,* ed. M. Natanson. New York: Random House. 231–49.

Sherman, Julia A., and Evelyn Torton Beck, eds. 1979. *The Prism of Sex: Essays in the Sociology of Knowledge.* Madison: University of Wisconsin Press.

Smith, Dorothy. 1980. "An Examination of Some Sociological Methods of Thinking from the Standpoint of a Sociology for Women, and an Alternative." Paper presented at the annual meeting of the American Sociological Association. New York.

———. 1979. "A Sociology for Women." In *The Prism of Sex: Essays in the Sociology of Knowledge,* ed. Julia A. Sherman and Evelyn Torton Beck. Madison: University of Wisconsin Press. 135–87.

———. 1977. "Some Implications of a Sociology for Women." In *Woman in a Man-Made World: A Socioeconomic Handbook,* ed. Nona Glazer and Helen Waehrer. 2d ed. Chicago: Rand McNally. 15–29.

———. 1974. "Women's Perspective as a Radical Critique of Sociology." *Sociological Inquiry* 4 (1): 7–13.

Touraine, Alaine, Zsuzsa Hegedus, Francois Dubet, and Michel Wieniorka. 1980. *La Prophete Anti-Nucleaire.* Paris: DuSueil.

Westkott, Marcia. 1979. "Feminist Criticism of the Social Sciences." *Harvard Educational Review* 49 (4): 422–30.

Woodward, Diana, and Lynne Chisholm. 1981. "The Expert's View?: The Sociological Analysis of Graduates' Occupational and Domestic Roles." In *Doing Feminist Research,* ed. Helen Roberts. London: Routledge and Kegan Paul.

CHAPTER 4

JUDITH STACEY

Can There Be a Feminist Ethnography?

Most feminist researchers, committed, at a minimum, to redressing the sexist imbalances of masculinist scholarship, appear to select their research projects on substantive grounds. Personal interests and skills meld, often mysteriously, with collective feminist concerns to determine a particular topic of research, which, in turn, appears to guide the research methods employed in its service. Indeed, in such a fashion, I chose my dissertation project, a study of patriarchy and revolution in China designed to address major theoretical questions about Western feminism and socialism. The nature of this subject, compounded by limitations in my training, necessitated the macrostructural, abstract approach based almost exclusively on library research that I adopted. And, as a consequence, its textual product offered an analysis of socialism and patriarchy that, as several reviewers justly complained, left out stories about actual women or patriarchs (Stacey 1983). My dissatisfaction with that kind of research process and outcome led me to privilege methodological considerations over substantive interests when I selected my next research project, a fieldwork study of family and gender relationships in California's Silicon Valley. I was eager for a "hands on," face-to-face research experience, which I also believed was more compatible with feminist principles.

When I began my Silicon Valley research project in 1984, the dominant conception of feminist research among feminist scholars advocated research on, by, and especially *for* women and drew sharp distinctions between the goals and methods of mainstream and feminist scholarship.[1] Feminist scholars had begun to express widespread disenchantment with the dualisms, abstractions, and detachment of positivism, rejecting the separations between subject and object, thought and feeling, knower and known, and political and personal as well as their reflections in the arbitrary boundaries of traditional academic disciplines. Instead most feminist scholars advocated an integrative, transdisciplinary approach to knowledge that grounds theory contextually in the concrete realm of women's everyday lives. The "actual experience and language of women is the central agenda for feminist social science and scholarship," asserted Barbara Du Bois (1983: 108) in an essay advocating "passionate scholarship," and only a minority of feminist scholars ventured a dissent. Indeed feminists were celebrating "feeling, belief, and experientially based knowledge," which draw upon such traditionally feminine capacities as intuition, empathy, and relationship (Stanley and Wise 1983a). Discussions of feminist methodology generally assaulted the hierarchical, exploitative relations of conventional research, urging feminist researchers to seek instead an egalitarian research process characterized by authenticity, reciprocity, and intersubjectivity between the researcher and her "subjects" (Klein 1983; Mies 1983; Du Bois 1983; Reinharz 1983; Stanley and Wise 1983a, 1983b). "A methodology that allows for women studying women in an interactive process," Renate Duelli Klein argued, "will end the exploitation of women as research objects" (1983:195).

Judged by such criteria, the ethnographic method, by which I mean an intensive participant-observation study that yields a synthetic cultural account, appears ideally suited to feminist research. That is why in "The Missing Feminist Revolution in Sociology," an essay reflecting on the limitations of feminist efforts to transform sociology, Barrie Thorne and I (1985) wondered with disappointment why so few feminist sociologists had turned to the ethnographic tradition of community studies within the discipline, a tradition that seemed to us far more compatible with feminist principles than are the more widely practiced positivist methods. Many other feminist scholars shared the view that ethnography is particularly appropriate to feminist research (Klein 1983; Mies 1983; Reinharz 1983; Stanley and Wise 1983b). Like a good deal of feminism, ethnography emphasizes the experiential. Its approach to knowledge is contextual and interpersonal, attentive like most women, therefore, to the concrete realm of everyday reality and human agency. Moreover, because in ethnographic studies the researcher herself is the primary medium, the "instrument" of research, this method draws on those resources of empathy, connection, and concern that many feminists consider to be women's special strengths and that they argue should be germinal in feminist research. Ethnographic method also appears to provide much greater respect for and power to one's research "subjects," who, some feminists propose, can and should become full collaborators in feminist research (Klein 1983; Mies 1983; Reinharz 1983; Stanley and Wise 1983a).

This, at least, is how ethnography appeared to me as I found myself unintentionally but irresistibly drawn to it in a study originally intended to be based on more conventional interview methods. An ethnographic approach seemed to resolve the "contradiction in terms" involved in interviewing women that Anne Oakley (1981) had identified in her critique of classical sociological interview methods. Oakley rejected the hierarchical, objectifying, and falsely "objective" stance of the neutral, impersonal interviewer as neither possible nor desirable, arguing that meaningful and feminist research depends instead on empathy and mutuality. And I was reassured by Shulamit Reinharz's assertion that the problems of experiential fieldwork methodology "seem minor in comparison with the quality of relations that I develop with people involved in the study and the quality of the understanding that emerges from those relations" (1983:185).

But after two and one-half years of fieldwork experience, I became less sanguine and more focused on the difficult contradictions between feminist principles and ethnographic method I encountered than on their compatibility. Hence the question in my title, which is modeled (but with a twist) on the implicit question in Oakley's "Interviewing Women: A Contradiction in Terms." The twist is that, after conducting feminist ethnographic research, I came to perceive the opposite contradiction between feminist ethics and methods than the one that Oakley discusses. I found myself wondering whether the appearance of greater respect for and equality with research subjects in the ethnographic approach masks a deeper, more dangerous form of exploitation.

There were two major areas of contradiction my efforts at feminist fieldwork exposed. The first involves the ethnographic research process, the second its product. Precisely because ethnographic research depends upon human relationships, engagement, and attachment, it places research subjects at grave risk of manipulation and betrayal by the ethnographer, as the following vignette from my fieldwork illustrates. One of my key informants had been involved in a closeted lesbian relationship immediately prior to the period of my fieldwork research. I first learned of this relationship from her spurned lesbian lover, and this only six months after working in the field. Of course, this immediately placed me in an extremely awkward situation ethically, a situation of triangulation and potential betrayal in relation to these two women and of inauthenticity toward the more secretive one. Several months later (partly, I believe, in response to her perception of my inauthenticity) this informant "came out" to me about this affair, but she asked me to respect the confidentiality of this knowledge when relating to her relatives, friends, and co-workers. Moreover, she and her rejected lover began to compete for my allegiance, sympathy, and ultimately for my view of their shared history.

I could give numerous other examples (such as the case of a secret of paternity, of an illicit affair, and of illicit activities). All placed me in situations of inauthenticity, dissimilitude, and potential, perhaps inevitable, betrayal, situations that I came to understand are inherent in fieldwork research. For no matter how welcome, even enjoyable the fieldworker's presence may appear to "natives," fieldwork represents an intrusion and intervention into a system of relationships, a system of relationships that the researcher is far freer than the researched to leave. The inequality and potential treacherousness of this relationship is inescapable.

So too does the exploitative aspect of ethnographic process seem unavoidable. The lives, loves, and tragedies that fieldwork informants share with a researcher are ultimately data, grist for the ethnographic mill, a mill that has a truly grinding power. More times than I would have liked, my Silicon Valley study placed me in a ghoulish and structurally conflictual relationship to tragedy, a feature of ethnographic process that became particularly graphic during the death of another one of my key "informants." My ethnographic role consigned me to experience this death both as friend and as researcher, and it presented me with numerous delicate, confusing dilemmas, such as whether or not, and to whom, to make a gift of the precious, but potentially hurtful tapes of an oral history I had once conducted with the deceased. I was confronted as well with the discomforting awareness that as researcher I stood to benefit from this tragedy. Not only did the funeral and family grieving process serve as further research "opportunity" but also the death freed me to include more of this family's "truths" in my ethnographic account than would have been possible had he lived. This and other fieldwork experiences forced my recognition that conflicts of interest and emotion between the ethnographer as an engaged, related person (i.e., participant) and as an exploiting researcher (i.e., observer) are also an inescapable feature of ethnographic method.

The second major area of contradiction between feminist principles and ethnographic method involves the dissonance between fieldwork practice and ethnographic product. Despite the aspects of intervention and exploitation I have described, ethnographic method appears to (and often does) place the researcher and her informants in a collaborative, reciprocal quest for understanding, but the research product is ultimately that of the researcher, however modified or influenced by informants. With very rare exceptions it is the researcher who narrates, who "authors" the ethnography. In the last instance an ethnography is a written document structured primarily by a researcher's purposes, offering a researcher's interpretations, registered in a researcher's voice.[2]

Here too, therefore, elements of inequality, exploitation, and even betrayal are endemic to ethnography. Perhaps even more than the ethnographic process, the published ethnography represents an intervention into the lives and relationships of its subjects. As author an ethnographer cannot (and, I believe, should not) escape tasks of interpretation, evaluation, and judgment. It is possible (and most feminists might claim it is crucial) to discuss and negotiate one's final presentation of a narrative with informants, but this does not eliminate the problem of authority and it can raise a host of new contradictions for the feminist ethnographer.[3] For example, after several years involving scores of hours of mutual reflections on the meaning of the lesbian relationship mentioned above, this "research collaborator" asked me to leave this part of her history out of my ethnographic account. What feminist ethical principles could I invoke to guide me here? Principles of respect for research subjects and for a collaborative, egalitarian research relationship demand compliance, but this forced me to collude with the homophobic silencing of lesbian experience, as well as to consciously distort what I considered to be a crucial component of the ethnographic "truth" in my study. Whatever we decided, my ethnography was forced to betray a feminist principle.

Indeed the irony I came to perceive is that ethnographic method can expose subjects to far greater danger and exploitation than do more positivist, abstract, and "masculinist" research methods. And the greater the intimacy, the apparent mutuality of the researcher/researched relationship, the greater the danger.

The account I have just given of the paradoxes of feminist ethnography is falsely innocent. I have presented my methodological/ethical quandaries the way that I first conceptualized them as a feminist researcher, innocent as then I was of relevant literature by ethnographers who long have grappled with related concerns. I am no longer so innocent and ignorant, but I retained this construction to help underscore a curious fact. Until quite recently, there has been surprisingly little cross-fertilization between the discourses of feminist epistemology and methods and those of the critical traditions within anthropology and sociology.[4] Most pertinent has been the dearth of dialogue between feminist scholarship, particularly within feminist sociology, and contemporaneous developments in the literature referred to as the "new" or "postmodern" or "reflexive" ethnography.[5] This is curious, because the new or postmodern ethnography is concerned with quite similar issues as those that concern feminist scholars and, at first glance, it offers a potential resolution to the feminist ethnographic paradox.[6]

Postmodern ethnography is critical and self-reflexive ethnography and a literature of meditation on the inherent, but often unacknowledged hierarchical and power-laden relations of ethnographic *writing*.[7] Like most feminist scholars, critical ethnographers tear the veil from scientific pretensions of neutral observation or description. They attempt to bring to their work an awareness that ethnographic writing is not cultural reportage, but cultural construction, and always a construction of the self as well as of the Other. In James Clifford's words, the "historical predicament of ethnography" is "the fact that it is always caught up in the invention, not the representation of cultures" (1986:2).

The favored postmodern solution to the reflexive anthropological predicament has been to fully acknowledge the dialogic and discursive character of the ethnographic process and product and to deconstruct their own claims to ethnographic authority. Like most feminists, critical ethnographers eschew a detached stance of neutrality, and they perceive their subjects as collaborators in a project the researcher can never control. Moreover, they acknowledge the indispensably intrusive and unequal nature of their participation in the studied culture.

Even more than most feminist scholars, I believe, critical ethnographers have been excruciatingly self-conscious about the distortions and limitations of the textual products of their studies. Here they have attempted first to fully acknowledge and own the interpretive authorial self and second to experiment with dialogic forms of ethnographic representation that place more of the unassimilated perspectives of the researched into the narrative and that more effectively reflect the dissonance and particularity of the ethnographic research process.

Finally, postmodern ethnographers, influenced by deconstructionist fashions, aim only for "partial truths," as James Clifford suggests in his introduction to *Writing Culture,* which, ironically enough, has become the canon-setting collection of this genre: "Ethnographic truths are thus inherently *partial*—committed and incomplete. This point is now widely asserted—and resisted at strategic points by those who fear the collapse of clear standards of verification. But once accepted and built into ethnographic art, a rigorous sense of partiality can be a source of representational tact" (1986:7).

Until quite recently, the reflexivity and self-critique of "postmodern" ethnographic literature seemed to parallel, while keeping surprising distance from, feminist methodological reflections. It seems likely that it unwittingly exploited some of the latter as well, as feminist social scientists had published compatible reflections on matters of the self, commitment, and partiality in research.[8] In fact, there were even rare moments in *Writing Culture* when "postmodern" ethnographers incorporated feminist insights into their reflexive critiques. Vincent Crapanzano, for example, suggested that "interpretation has been understood as a phallic, a phallic-aggressive, a cruel and violent, a destructive act, and as a fertile, a fertilizing, a fruitful, and a creative one," and he self-consciously retained the male pronoun to refer to the ethnographer "despite his or her sexual identity, for I am writing of a stance and not of the person" (1986:52). Yet, few feminist authors or works appeared in the primary texts that came to define postmodern ethnography, and this too-familiar form of exclusion and marginality fueled considerable suspicion, anger, and defensiveness among feminist ethnographers, some of whom nearly advocated a rejection of "the postmodernist turn."[9]

Although there were legitimate grounds for feminist suspicions that many "representations" of postmodern ethnography could serve as coded alibis for the reassertion of male authority, this helped to establish a rivalrous and dichotomous formulation of the relationship between feminism and reflexive ethnography that I find unfortunate and unproductive. For example, the implication that feminist ethnographies have been less experimental than postmodernist texts has either been denied by feminists or defended on the political grounds that we have been too preoccupied with challenging the appalling conditions of women's subordination to indulge in the luxuries of textual innovation.[10]

While I find considerable insight in such feminist rejoinders, I worry that ultimately they both cede and shun more ground than is advisable. Instead of cementing a competitive relationship between feminism and postmodern ethnography, we gain more when we take more seriously the parallel insights from both discourses about partial truth, situated knowledge, and multivocality. All oppositional ethnographic projects could benefit from constructing multiple genealogies of radical reflexivity, rather than insisting upon the priority or superiority of their own. For example, ethnic studies, feminism, gay studies, American studies, and even ethnomethodology each can produce diverse, but overlapping, narratives about the genesis of contemporary interest in reflexive ethnography.[11] These might prepare the grounds for more fruitful dialogue and exchanges among these discourses than has been typical thus far.

The feminist anthropologist Marilyn Strathern (1987) also noted the surprising paucity of constructive engagement between feminism and the new ethnography and, in an important initiation of such dialogue, offered an analysis of the grounds for mutual resistance that undergird what she termed the "awkward relationship" between the two. Feminism and critical anthropology, Strathern claimed, are mutually "vulnerable on the ethical grounds they hold to be so important": "each has a potential for undermining the other" because they rest upon incompatible constructions of the relationship between self and Other (1987:289). Feminism, Strathern argued, presumes an antagonistic relationship to the male Other, a presumption that grounds its acute sensitivity to power inequalities and has the power to undermine those anthropological pretensions of alliance and collaboration with the Other upon which new ethnographic strategies for multiple authorship reside. Anthropology, in turn, from its cross-cultural vantage point, suggests the illusory nature of feminist pretensions of actual separation from men of their own culture.

I view the resistances somewhat differently. Feminism's keen sensitivity to structural inequalities in research and to the irreconcilability of Otherness applies primarily, I believe, to its critique of research by men, particularly to research *by* men but *about* women. The majority of feminist claims about *feminist* ethnographic and other forms of qualitative research, however, continue to presume that such research occurs almost exclusively woman-to-woman.[12] Thus feminist researchers are apt to suffer the delusion of alliance more than the delusion of separateness and to suffer it more, I believe, than do most reflexive ethnographers. Recall the claims about empathy and identification between feminist researchers and the women they study and the calls by feminist scholars for an egalitarian research process, full collaboration, and even multiple authorship with which this essay began. Less defensive engagement with critical ethnographic literature has begun to temper certain feminist celebrations of ethnographic methods with the same salutary note of humility about the limitations of cross-cultural and interpersonal understanding and representation that have been fostered by critiques of white feminist theory leveled by feminists of color.[13] A fruitful dialogue between feminism and critical ethnography would continue to address their complementary sensitivities and naivetés about the inherent inequalities and the possibilities for relationships in the definition, study, and representation of the Other.

With the hope of promoting such a dialogue, I have begun a collaborative project with Judith Newton, a feminist literary critic, that combines textual and ethnographic approaches to a study of the political and intellectual trajectories of male "tenured radicals," a group that includes numerous cultural critics of ethnography. This paradoxical attempt to partially "study up" (white, heterosexual females studying diversely situated males), at the same time we "study across" (as tenured radicals ourselves), is an attempt to conduct ethnography as a dialogic, political intervention. It represents one, unavoidably ambivalent, feminist response to the postmodern ethnographic impasse.[14]

Indeed, I agree with Strathern that the relationship between feminism and ethnography *is* unavoidably ambivalent. I am less convinced than she of the virtues of this awkwardness, but I concur that it can only be mitigated, not effaced. Even an exhaustive, mutually beneficial exchange cannot resolve the ethnographic impasse concerning study of the Other that postcolonial conditions and feminist politics have exposed. Reflexive strategies are inadequate responses to the ethical and political issues endemic to ethnographic process and product that I have encountered and described. They acknowledge, but do little to ameliorate, the problems of intervention, triangulation, or inherently unequal reciprocity with informants; nor can they resolve feminist reporting quandaries. For example, acknowledging partiality and taking responsibility for authorial construction could never reduce my handling of the lesbian affair into a matter of "representational tact."

My response to the question in my title is that while there cannot be a fully feminist ethnography, there can be (indeed there are) ethnographies that are partially feminist, in both senses of the term, that is, accounts of culture enhanced by the application of feminist investments and insights. There also can and should be feminist research that is rigorously, culturally self-aware and therefore humble about the partiality of its ethnographic vision and its capacity to represent self and Other.[15] Moreover, even after my loss of ethnographic innocence, I believe the potential benefits of "partially" feminist ethnography seem worth the serious moral costs involved.

Indeed, as Carole Joffe has suggested to me, my initial assault on the ethical foundations of fieldwork may have been unduly harsh, a fairer measure, perhaps, of my prior illusions about ethnographic virtue than of ethnographic vice.[16] Certainly, as she, Shulamit Reinharz, and many other feminists assert, fieldworkers can and do form valuable relationships with many of those we study, and some of our unsolicited interventions into the lives of our informants are constructive and deeply appreciated. For example, a daughter of the informant whose death I mentioned above later consoled me on the sudden death of my own father and thanked me for having allowed her to repair her hostile relationship with her father before he died by helping her to perceive his pride in and identification with her. Often fieldwork research offers particular research subjects practical and emotional support and a form of loving attention, of comparatively nonjudgmental acceptance, that they come to value deeply.

But then again, beneficiaries of such attention may also come to depend upon it, and this signals another ethical quandary in fieldwork, the potential for, indeed the likelihood of, desertion by the researcher.[17] Although I have maintained contact with the "key informants" in my Silicon Valley study, several presciently feared that the publication of my ethnography about their lives would sunder my interest in its subjects (Stacey 1990). Indeed, they have been, and felt, increasingly displaced in my ethnographic commitments by the male cultural critics featured in my current project.

Of course, rigorous awareness of the ethical and political pitfalls in the method enables one to monitor and then to mitigate some of the dangers to which ethnographers expose their informants, but no research or rhetorical strategy can grant absolution from the power/knowledge nexus. I conclude in this Talmudic fashion to leave the dialogue open, believing that an uneasy fusion of feminist and critical ethnographic consciousness may allow us to construct cultural accounts that, however partial, can achieve the contextuality, nuance, and insight I consider to be unattainable through less dangerous, but more remote research methods.

NOTES

This is an updated version of an essay published as "Can There Be a Feminist Ethnography" in *Women's Studies International Forum* 11, no. 1 (1988): 21–27. Reprinted with permission from *Women's Studies International,* Elsevier Science Ltd., Pergamon Imprint, Oxford, England. I thank Gloria Bowles, Mary Frank Fox, Carole Joffe, Suad Joseph, and Barrie Thorne for comments on a draft of the original essay and Marilyn Strathern for responses to the published version.

1. Perhaps the most comprehensive summary of the characteristic distinctions between these approaches that feminists draw appears in several pages of tables detailing contrasts between the two in Reinharz (1983:168–72).

2. For just this reason Klein, Mies, and, to a lesser extent, Stanley and Wise argue against this approach and for fuller collaboration between researcher and subjects, particularly for activist research in the tradition of Paulo Freire generated by and accountable to grass-roots women's movement projects. But, as Smart (n.d.) as well as Stanley and Wise (1983a, 1983b) recognize, such an approach places severe restraints on who and what can be studied and on what could be written, restraints that could seriously harm feminist interests.

3. Smart (n.d.) offers important reflections on the adverse implications of this ethical principle when feminists study, as she believes we should, the powerful and the agents of social control rather than their targets.

4. Critical reflections on the ethics and politics of fieldwork have a long history in both disciplines, and by now the literature is vast. For important examples from the past two decades, see Asad (1973); Emerson (1983); Haan, Bellah, Rabinow, and Sullivan (1983); Hymes (1974); and Thorne (1978, 1980).

5. Becker (1987) makes a similar point about the unfortunate paucity of exchange between critical traditions in sociology and post-structuralist anthropology in a review of Clifford and Marcus (1986).

6. A few feminist essays published after I first published this essay indicate that feminists, at least, have begun to engage the postmodernist ethnographic literature. I discuss and cite these developments below. Thus far there is less evidence of engagement with feminist literature by male anthropologists engaged in the postmodernist discourse.

7. A good sampler and bibliography of postmodern ethnographic criticism appears in Clifford and Marcus (1985). Other important texts include Clifford (1983), Crapanzano (1977), Marcus and Cushman (1982), and Marcus and Fischer (1986).

8. For examples of parallel feminist works, see Krieger (1985), Mies (1983), Rosaldo (1983), Smith (1987), and Stanley and Wise (1983b).

9. For feminist critiques of the appropriation and exclusion of experimental feminist ethnographic literature by male critical ethnographers see Gordon (1988); Mascia-Lees, Sharpe, and Cohen (1989); R. Chabram (1990); and hooks (1990:123–33).

10. Mascia-Lees, Sharpe, and Cohen challenged the definition of *experimental* by which feminists were excluded from the Clifford and Marcus collection (1985) and from the Marcus and Fischer bibliography (1986). Abu-Lughod (1990) developed the analysis of feminist political priorities in an essay with the same title as this one.

11. See, for example, A. Chabram (1990), Newton and Stacey (1992–93), R. Chabram (1990), and Pollner (1991). For a particularly thorough, constructive exploration of the intersecting genealogies of feminism and reflexive ethnography, see especially Strathern (1991:part 1).

12. Recent examples of this premise appear in the title and many of the essays in Gluck and Patai (1991). See, for example, Anderson and Jack (1991) and Minister (1991).

13. Strathern (1991) is the most explicit analytical engagement of these discourses (Minh-ha 1989; Visveswaren 1994). Behar and Gordon (forthcoming) promises to advance this project further.

14. I have described the personal, political, and theoretical antecedents to this project (1993). Newton and Stacey (1992–93) is the first publication from this project. We discuss some of the paradoxical fieldwork dynamics (forthcoming).

15. Strathern provides a provocative discussion of an earlier version of this essay and helpfully advances my notion of a "partially feminist" ethnography (1987:34–36).

16. Personal communication with author, 1986.

17. In her inimicably witty style, Arlene Kaplan Daniels (1983) discusses the etiquette of abandoning one's research subjects as well as other ethical questions in fieldwork. Because of the intensity and depth of the relationships formed, the problem of desertion seems more serious in long-term ethnographic studies than in those based on the more limited contact characteristic of other forms of qualitative research.

REFERENCES

Abu-Lughod, Lila. 1990. "Can There Be a Feminist Ethnography?" *Women and Performance: A Journal of Feminist Theory* 9:1–24.

Anderson, Kathryn, and Dana C. Jack. 1991. "Learning to Listen: Interview Techniques and Analyses." In *Women's Words: The Feminist Practice of Oral History,* ed. Sherna Berger Gluck and Daphne Patai. New York: Routledge. 11–26.

Asad, Talal. 1973. *Anthropology and the Colonial Encounter.* Atlantic Highlands, N.J.: Humanities Press.

Becker, Howard. 1987. "The Writing of Science." *Contemporary Sociology* 16 (1): 25–27.

Behar, Ruth, and Deborah Gordon, eds. Forthcoming. *Women Writing Culture/ Culture Writing Women.* Berkeley: University of California Press.

Chabram, Angie. 1990. "Chicana/o Studies as Oppositional Ethnography." *Cultural Studies* 4 (3): 228–47.

Chabram, Richard. 1990. "Culture and Truth: The Encounter between Rhetorical Anthropology and Chicano Studies." Paper presented at the conference "Chicano Cultural Studies: New Directions." University of California at Santa Barbara.

Clifford, James. 1986. "Introduction: Partial Truths." In *Writing Culture: The Poetics and Politics of Ethnography,* ed. James Clifford and George Marcus. Berkeley: University of California Press. 1–26.

———. 1983. "On Ethnographic Authority." *Representations* 1 (2): 118–46.

Clifford, James, and George Marcus, eds. 1986. *Writing Culture: The Poetics and Politics of Ethnography.* Berkeley: University of California Press.

Crapanzano, Vincent. 1986. "Hermes' Dilemma: The Masking of Subversion in Ethnographic Description." In *Writing Culture: The Poetics and Politics of Ethnography,* ed. James Clifford and George Marcus. Berkeley: University of California Press. 51–76.

———. 1977. "The Writing of Ethnography." *Dialectical Anthropology* 2:69–73.

Daniels, Arlene Kaplan. 1983. "Self-Deception and Self-Discovery in Fieldwork." *Qualitative Sociology* 6 (3): 195–214.

Du Bois, Barbara. 1983. "Passionate Scholarship: Notes on Values, Knowing, and Method in Feminist Social Science." In *Theories of Women's Studies,* ed. Gloria Bowles and Renate Duelli Klein. London: Routledge and Kegan Paul. 105–16.

Emerson, Robert M. 1983. *Contemporary Field Research: A Collection of Readings.* Boston: Little Brown.

Freire, Paulo. 1970. *Pedagogy of the Oppressed.* New York: Seabury Press.
Gluck, Sherna Berger, and Daphne Patai, eds. 1991. *Women's Words: The Feminist Practice of Oral History.* New York: Routledge.
Gordon, Deborah. 1988. "Writing Culture, Writing Feminism: the Poetics and Politics of Experimental Ethnography." *Inscriptions* (3/4): 7–24.
———. Forthcoming. *Gender in the Field: The Politics of Cultural Description, 1967–1990.* Ann Arbor: University of Michigan Press.
Haan, Norma, Robert N. Bellah, Paul Rabinow, and William M. Sullivan, eds. 1983. *Social Science as Moral Inquiry.* New York: Columbia University Press.
hooks, bell. 1990. "Culture to Culture: Ethnography and Cultural Studies as Critical Intervention." In *Yearning: Race, Gender, and Cultural Politics.* Boston: South End Press. 123–33.
Hymes, Dell, ed. 1974. *Reinventing Anthropology.* New York: Vintage.
Klein, Renate Duelli. 1983. "How to Do What We Want to Do: Thoughts about Feminist Methodology." In *Theories of Women's Studies,* ed. Gloria Bowles and Renate Duelli Klein. London: Routledge and Kegan Paul. 88–104.
Krieger, Susan. 1985. "Beyond 'Subjectivity': The Use of the Self in Social Science." *Qualitative Sociology* 8 (4): 309–24.
Marcus, George E., and Dick Cushman. 1982. "Ethnographies as Texts." *Annual Reviews of Anthropology* 11:25–69.
Marcus, George, and Michael M. J. Fischer. 1986. *Anthropology as Cultural Critique.* Chicago: University of Chicago Press.
Mascia-Lees, Frances E., Patricia Sharpe, and Colleen Ballerino Cohen. 1989. "The Postmodernist Turn in Anthropology: Cautions from a Feminist Perspective." *Signs* 15 (1): 7–33.
Mies, Maria. 1983. "Towards a Methodology for Feminist Research." In *Theories of Women's Studies,* ed. Gloria Bowles and Renate Duelli Klein. London: Routledge and Kegan Paul. 117–39.
Minh-ha, Trinh T. 1989. *Woman, Native, Other.* Bloomington: Indiana University Press.
Minister, Kristina. 1991. "A Feminist Frame for the Oral History Interview." In *Women's Words: The Feminist Practice of Oral History,* ed. Sherna Berger Gluck and Daphne Patai. New York: Routledge. 27–41.
Newton, Judith, and Judith Stacey. 1992–93. "Learning Not to Curse; or, Feminist Predicaments in Cultural Criticism by Men: Our Movie Date with James Clifford and Stephen Greenblatt." *Cultural Critique* 23 (Winter): 51–82.
———. Forthcoming. "Ms.representations: Feminist Dilemmas in Studying Academic Men." In *Women Writing Culture/Culture Writing Women,* ed. Ruth Behar and Deborah Gordon. Berkeley: University of California Press.
Oakley, Anne. 1981. "Interviewing Women: A Contradiction in Terms." In *Doing Feminist Research,* ed. Helen Roberts. London: Routledge and Kegan Paul. 30–61.
Pollner, Melvin. 1991. "Left of Ethnomethodology: The Rise and Decline of Radical Reflexivity." *American Sociological Review* 56 (3): 370–80.
Reinharz, Shulamit. 1983. "Experiential Analysis: A Contribution to Feminist

Research." In *Theories of Women's Studies,* ed. Gloria Bowles and Renate Duelli Klein. London: Routledge and Kegan Paul. 162–91.

Rosaldo, Michelle Z. 1983. "Moral/Analytic Dilemmas Posed by the Intersection of Feminism and Social Science." In *Social Science as Moral Inquiry,* ed. Norma Haan, Robert N. Bellah, Paul Rabinow, and William M. Sullivan. New York: Columbia University Press.

Smart, Carol. N.d. "Researching Prostitution: Some Problems for Feminist Research." Ms. Institute of Psychiatry, London.

Smith, Dorothy. 1987. *The Everyday World as Problematic: A Feminist Sociology.* Boston: Northeastern University Press.

Stacey, Judith. 1993. "Disloyal to the Disciplines: A Feminist Trajectory on the Borderlands." Paper presented at the conference "The Missing Feminist Revolution, Revisited." Berkeley, Calif.

———. 1990. *Brave New Families: Stories of Domestic Upheaval in Late Twentieth Century America.* New York: Basic Books.

———. 1983. *Patriarchy and Socialist Revolution in China.* Berkeley: University of California Press.

Stacey, Judith, and Barrie Thorne. 1985. "The Missing Feminist Revolution in Sociology." *Social Problems* 32 (4): 301–16.

Stanley, Liz, and Sue Wise. 1983a. "'Back into the Personal'; or, Our Attempt to Construct 'Feminist Research.'" In *Theories of Women's Studies,* ed. Gloria Bowles and Renate Duelli Klein. London: Routledge and Kegan Paul. 192–209.

———. 1983b. *Breaking Out: Feminist Consciousness and Feminist Research.* London: Routledge and Kegan Paul.

Strathern, Marilyn. 1991. *Partial Connections.* Savage, Md.: Rowman and Littlefield.

———. 1987. "An Awkward Relationship: The Case of Feminism and Anthropology." *Signs* 12 (2): 276–92.

Thorne, Barrie. 1980. "'You Still Takin' Notes?': Fieldwork and Problems of Informed Consent." *Social Problems* 27 (3): 284–97.

———. 1978. "Political Activist as Participant Observer: Conflicts of Commitment in a Study of the Draft Resistance Movement of the 1960s." *Symbolic Interaction* 2 (1): 73–88.

Visweswaren, Kamala. 1994. "Refusing the Subject." In *Fictions of Feminist Ethnography.* Minneapolis: University of Minnesota Press.

PART 2

The Outsider Within

CHAPTER 5

PIERRETTE HONDAGNEU-SOTELO

Immigrant Women and Paid Domestic Work: Research, Theory, and Activism

Many commentators refer to paid domestic work as the "invisible occupation." The work occurs in private households; it is generally performed in isolation, without the company of co-workers or managers; and in the United States, it has historically been the province of marginalized women, of women of color and immigrant women. The occupation did achieve national visibility for a moment in 1993 with the revelation that two female nominees for attorney general had hired undocumented immigrant workers to care for their children in their homes. Yet even as national attention focused on nannies as domestic workers, the objections raised by the Senate inquisitors, the media, and the constituents centered on the "illegality" of hiring unauthorized immigrant workers and in particular on Zoe Baird's failure to pay the requisite taxes and make social security payments. This focus obscured issues that have to do with basic work rights of domestic workers. In fact, the media attention ignored the voices and concerns of the domestic workers themselves.

Who performs paid domestic work in the United States today? While domestic employees are a diverse group that include European au pairs, college students, and laid-off aerospace workers, the principal entrants into the occupation are Latina and Caribbean immigrant women. They represent a group of workers who, due to their class, race, gender, and legal status, are among the most disenfranchised and vulnerable in our society. Little wonder, then, that their needs and concerns remained largely "invisible," even when highlighted in a national controversy labeled by some pundits as "nannie-gate."

Paid domestic work encompasses multiple tasks—cleaning, serving, child care, gardening, and so forth—and is currently organized in various ways.[1] In this chapter, I will discuss only the employment of immigrant women who do housecleaning according to job work arrangements, where they maintain a weekly or bi-weekly route of employers. Under job work, domestic workers are able to position themselves as "experts" to sell their labor services in much the same way a vendor sells a product to various customers, and since they work for different employers on different days, they are less likely to become involved in deeply personal employer-employee relations than are live-in domestics or those who work for the same employer on a daily basis (Romero 1988).

While job work holds the potential to provide better working conditions and pay than those encountered by live-in domestic workers, it is still problematic. Job terms and pay are generally negotiated without the benefit of guidelines established by government, unions, employment agencies, or private firms, and domestic workers must locate and secure multiple sources of employment to survive. My research in a San Francisco Bay area community examined how immigrant women domestic workers devised ways to improve their employment in job work, and some of these findings were utilized in an innovative information and outreach project in Los Angeles that seeks to upgrade the occupation for Latina immigrant women. In both the research process and the dissemination of the research findings, I attempted to incorporate cultural models resonant with Latino communities. As I gathered research materials, I often acted as a *servidora,* an informal social worker, and later in the outreach project, some of the research findings were disseminated through *novelas,* a popular form of Latin American print media.

This chapter addresses research, theory, and activism in the context of immigrant women who do paid domestic work. I will argue that interaction between sociological research and activism informed by feminism can yield new theoretical insights and understandings. First I will discuss and reflect on how a research process informed by feminism shaped a particular set of findings. Feminist principles shaped the research process by first encouraging me to see immigrant women as experts in defining their most urgent concerns, thus restraining me from imposing my own preconceived research agenda, and second by inspiring me to rely on reciprocity. In particular, feminist concerns with reciprocity in fieldwork relationships inspired me to act as a *servidora,* and this revealed aspects of the occupation that may have otherwise remained concealed. Next, I will discuss how I utilized these research findings in an information and outreach project aimed at Mexican and

Central American immigrant women who do paid domestic work in Los Angeles. Finally, I reflect on how this process stimulated further theoretical insights for me. When I returned to ask women in the original community of study for suggestions on some of the materials I had prepared for use in the Los Angeles outreach project, the comments revealed new insights.

Discussion of theory and praxis often privilege the manner in which research and theory inform or direct political practices and activities. In this chapter, I will suggest a less unilinear relationship between research and theory on the one hand and political activism on the other. In the instance discussed here, the dissemination of the research findings in an advocacy project led to a new understanding and theoretical interpretations of the research. Research, theory, and activism run on a feedback loop.

RESEARCH AND RECIPROCITY

My research on domestic employment comprises part of a larger study on migration patterns and changing gender relations among Mexican undocumented immigrant women and men that I conducted in a Mexican immigrant community located in the San Francisco Bay area. I chose qualitative methods—in-depth interviews and participant observation—in order to develop an explanation of processes as they unfold at the microstructural level. The materials discussed in this chapter draw mainly from observation and informal conversations that occurred in various public and private locales and is supplemented by interviews with seventeen women who were working as non-live-in domestic housecleaners or had done so in the recent past. All interactions and interviews were conducted in Spanish and research began in November 1986, just as the Immigration Reform and Control Act[2] was passed, and continued for eighteen months.

I had not initially entered the field with the intention of examining how women organize paid domestic work. As I became immersed in many activities and groups in this community, I learned that the undocumented immigrant women there were concentrated in jobs as paid domestic workers in private households, usually working for different employers on different days. In many settings, everywhere, it seemed, I saw women talking about how they managed paid domestic work; I began to focus part of my research on these issues, and as I did, I read books such as Judith Rollins's *Between Women: Domestics and Their Employers* (1985) and Evelyn Nakano Glenn's *Issei, Nisei, Warbride: Three Generations of Japanese Women in Domestic Service* (1986). The ideas and approaches used in these studies prompted new questions for me, and so my ethnographic and interview research emerged in dialogue with some of this literature.

To date, most studies of domestics are largely based on information gathered from interviews and historical materials (Dudden 1983; Glenn 1986; Katzman 1981; Romero 1988, 1992). An exception is Rollins's study (1985), which is based on interviews with domestic employers and employees and on participant-observation material gathered by Rollins when she went "undercover" as a domestic worker, a method that provided a wealth of insights. The novelty and strength of participant-observation in this study is that it occurred in multiple settings. I did not seek employment as a paid domestic worker, but I interacted on a regular basis with the women who do the work and I gathered information at parties, church and community events, and in their homes. Observing paid domestic workers in their daily social life reveals that many social connections and exchanges undergird what appears to be a privatized economic relationship.

Ethnographic research involves constant face-to-face interaction over a prolonged period of time, and playing different roles offers the researcher different perspectives on social reality. The vantage point from which the researcher interacts and observes constitutes an important part of the research strategy; it structures the investigation's findings and shapes the parameters of the investigator's research roles and findings (Hondagneu-Sotelo 1988). My different roles, besides student/researcher, included activist and community organizer, friend, nosy person, and *servidora*. Reciprocity was a central component to all of these roles, but here I wish to focus on how this played out as I assumed elements of what appears to be an autochthonous woman's role in Latino immigrant communities.

Servidoras are Latina women who act as informal purveyors of information and who provide referrals and personal services to immigrant families. Two Chicana women and two immigrant women, one Mexican and the other Guatemalan, served a large number of families as community brokers, and I used them both as role models and sources of information.[3] Although I worked in legal services and in a bilingual education program in this particular community seven years prior, it was not my old contacts so much as my English language and literacy skills, and my concurrent involvement in community organizations, that were valuable. I regularly accompanied individuals and families to collection agencies and doctor's and lawyer's offices, translated bank statements and insurance policies, provided updated information on amnesty-legalization provisions, and so forth. My activities as a *servi-*

dora opened windows to immigrant lives that would have otherwise remained closed to me. These activities also opened the windows to a series of ethical issues.

The Ethics of Reciprocity

Ethics in field research generally refers to either covert research, where the true identity and purpose of the investigator remains unknown to those who are studied, or to the protection of human subjects (Bulmer 1982). The practice of reciprocity, a practice consonant with feminist principles, also raises several ethical issues.

Why use reciprocity in the first place? Reciprocity offers a way to lessen the asymmetry of doing research among people lacking basic resources, rights, and power in society. For me, reciprocity was a way to avoid a more colonialist way of doing research or just entering the field to pillage "raw data" for export. It allowed me to engage in more of a mutual exchange, whereby people's time, efforts, and energy in helping me with my research project were compensated by some of the resources to which I had access.

But was it less exploitative? In some cases, reciprocity served as an informal quid pro quo, as an IOU for participation in research. In several instances, people—most often men—offered to pay me cash for my assistance with filling out forms, translations, or transportation and instead I negotiated their participation in a formal interview (to which they had already agreed, but were procrastinating). Some of the women with whom I spent a good deal of time often thanked me for being such a good friend, such a ready and patient listener. One older woman compared me to a public health nurse she had known, and another referred to me as a "saint" for helping poor people in the community. Although initially flattered, I grew uncomfortable with these rituals of deference. The results of my assistance were minimal, and more importantly, these same people helped me too. Often when I was praised I would interject something to the effect of, "Well I'm a student and I appreciate the help you give me with my project too." Although it seemed cold and calculated, I tried to remind them of my research interest, as it more adequately reflected the exchange.

Some of the most revealing information I collected came not from the in-depth interviews but was disclosed to me in the context of being a friend. People enmeshed in explosive family conflicts or problematic decisions often produced unedited, but reflective outpourings of emotions, motives, and private incidents. Like the best letters and the best diary entries, these outpourings resulted from personal crises.

People offer some of the most revealing details of their lives when they are not relating to one as a researcher. This is double-edged, for although all of the respondents consented to serve as "human subjects" in the research project, it was when I served in capacities other than "questioning researcher" that I obtained some of the most telling information. Acting as a *servidora,* I gained detailed knowledge of personal finances, marital intimacies, and conflicts. With regard to paid domestic work, I sometimes wrote letters or made phone calls on the women's behalf when they asked for pay raises, I observed the women complain about particular employers or other domestic workers, and I listened very carefully when they discussed their strategies for dealing with these problems.

Although all of the women knew I was conducting research, my reciprocity obscured my research intent and availed more information to me. Yet rather than seeing reciprocity as constituting unbridled coercion or deceit, I believe it made the research process more egalitarian. Although my primary goals were clearly different than the respondents' interests, our interests did not necessarily conflict. Reciprocity allowed me to exchange a service for what the subjects were giving to me.

Judith Stacey (1988) has argued that researchers acting as friends or advocates leave subjects open to betrayal, exploitation, and abandonment. While research relationships are problematic, I maintain that reciprocity in field research can represent an instance where the means justify the means. The traditional appeal to nonexploitative research generally argues that the ends, or the finished research product, justifies the means. In this scheme, the dangers and risks assumed by research participants are outweighed by the potential benefits, such as a cure for a disease. This justification for the effects of research on people's lives derives from the physical sciences, and human subjects protocol in the social sciences generally mimics this approach, in spite of how poorly the protective clauses translate from the physical to the social sciences (Duster, Matza, and Wellman 1979).

The standard human subjects protocol informs respondents that the end product might shape policies that may ultimately benefit people like themselves. As I read a formatted statement to research participants, I placed little conviction in those words, and I believe that the study participants interpreted those words as empty promises as well. People engaged in the research less in expectation that by doing so they would help formulate more just immigration policies but more, I believe, in the expectation that their research relationship with me could be a nonthreatening and even a personally beneficial, advantageous one. Rarely did subjects or others in the community inquire about the potential benefits that they might derive from the finished research product.

RESEARCH FINDINGS

In various social settings—at picnics, baby showers, at parish legalization clinic, and in peoples' homes—I observed immigrant women engaged in lively conversation about paid domestic work. Women traded cleaning tips; tactics about how best to negotiate pay, how to geographically arrange jobs so as to minimize daily travel, how to interact (or more often avoid interaction) with clients, and how to leave undesirable jobs; remedies for physical ailments caused by the work; and cleaning strategies to lessen these ailments. The women were quick to voice disapproval of one another's strategies and to eagerly recommend alternatives.

The ongoing activities and interactions among the undocumented Mexican immigrant women led me to develop the organizing concept of "domestics' networks," immigrant women's social ties among family, friends, and acquaintances that intersect with housecleaning employment. These social networks are based on kinship, friendship, ethnicity, place of origin, and current residential locale, and they function on the basis of reciprocity, as there is an implicit obligation to repay favors of advice, information, and job contacts. In some cases these exchanges are monetized, as when women sell "jobs" (i.e., leads for customers or clients) for a fee. Information shared and transmitted through the informal social networks was critical to domestic workers' abilities to improve their jobs. These informational resources transformed the occupation from one single employee dealing with a single employer to one in which employees were informed by the collective experience of other domestic workers.

The Job Search and Contracting

Although the domestics' networks played an important role in informally regulating the occupation, jobs were most often located through employers' informal networks. Employers typically recommended a particular housecleaner among friends, neighbors, and co-workers. Although immigrant women helped one another sustain domestic employment, they were not always forthcoming with job referrals precisely because of the scarcity of well-paid domestic jobs. Competition for a scarce number of jobs prevented the women from sharing job leads among themselves, but often male kin who worked as gardeners or as horse stable hands provided initial connections. Many undocumented immigrant women were constantly searching for more housecleaning jobs and for jobs with better working conditions and pay.

Since securing that first job is difficult, many newly arrived immigrant women first find themselves subcontracting their services to other more experienced and well-established immigrant women who have steady customers. This provides an important apprenticeship and a potential springboard to independent contracting (Romero 1987). Subcontracting arrangements can be beneficial to both parties, but the relationship is not characterized by altruism or harmony of interests. In this study, immigrant women domestics who took on a helper did so in order to lighten their own workload and sometimes to accommodate newly arrived kin.

For the new apprentice, the arrangement minimizes the difficulty of finding employment and securing transportation, facilitates learning expected tasks and cleansers, and serves as an important training ground for interaction with employers. Employee strategies were learned in the new social context. Women sometimes offered protective advice, such as not to work too fast or be overly concerned with all crevices and hidden corners when first taking on a new job.

A subcontracted arrangement is informative and convenient for an immigrant woman who lacks her own transportation or possesses minimal English-language skills, but it also has the potential to be a very oppressive labor relationship. The pay is much lower than what a woman might earn on her own. In some instances, the subcontracted domestics may not be paid at all. These asymmetrical partnerships between domestic workers continue for relatively long periods of time. Although subcontracting arrangements may help domestics secure employment with multiple employers, the relationship established between the experienced, senior domestic and the newcomer apprentice is often a very exploitable one for the apprentice.

The Pay

Undocumented immigrant women in this study averaged $35 to $50 for a full day of domestic work performed on a job basis, although some earned less and others double that amount. What determines the pay scale for housecleaning work? There are no government regulations, corporate guidelines, management policy, or union to set wages. Instead, the pay for housecleaning work is generally informally negotiated between two women, the domestic and the employer. The pay scale that domestics attempt to negotiate for is influenced by the information that they share among one another and by their ability to sustain a sufficient number of jobs, which is in turn also shaped by their English-language skills, legal status, and access to private transportation. Although the pay scale remains unregulated by state mechanisms, social interactions among the domestics themselves serve to informally regulate pay standards.

Unlike employees in middle-class professions, most of the domestic workers that I observed talked quite openly with one another about their level of pay. At informal gatherings, such as a child's birthday party or community event, the women revealed what they earned with particular employers and how they had achieved or been relegated to that particular level of pay. Working for low-level pay was typically met with murmurs of disapproval or pity, but no stronger sanctions were applied. Conversely, those women who earned at the high end were admired.

As live-out, day workers, these immigrant women were paid either on an hourly or "job work" basis, and most women preferred the latter. Being paid *por trabajo,* or by the job, allowed the women greater flexibility in caring for their own families' needs. And with regard to income, being paid by the job instead of an hourly rate increased the potential for higher earnings. Women who were able to work relatively fast could substantially increase their average earnings by receiving a set fee for cleaning a particular house. If they could schedule two houses a day in the same neighborhood, or if they had their own car, they could clean two and sometimes even three houses in one day.

USING ETHNOGRAPHIC FINDINGS FOR ADVOCACY

In every major U.S. city with a large immigrant population, large umbrella coalitions that include community, church, legal, and labor groups are now working to establish and defend civil rights and workplace rights for immigrants and refugees. Two key features distinguish these efforts. First, the claims are typically made outside the traditional and exclusive category of U.S. citizenship. Second, until recently many of these efforts were aimed only at male immigrants. For various reasons, among them the "invisibility" of immigrant women's employment, immigrant rights advocates have been slower to defend immigrant women's labor rights. But this is changing.

A year and a half after completing the research, I began meeting with a group of lawyers and community activists associated with the Coalition for Humane Immigrant Rights in Los Angeles to plan an information and outreach program for paid domestic workers, the majority of whom in Los Angeles are Latina immigrant women. It was in this context that I utilized some of the research findings on immigrant women and domestic employment.

The newly formed committee met for one year before launching an innovative informational outreach program. The planning stage was long because of the obstacles that this occupation poses for organizing strategies and because the group was not working from an existing blueprint. How to organize paid domestic workers who work in isolated, private households is neither easy nor obvious. There are no factory gates through which all employees pass, and instead of confronting only one employer, one finds that the employers are nearly as numerous as the employees. Traditional organizing strategies with paid domestic workers encompass both trade unions and job cooperatives (see Chaney and Castro 1989; Salzinger 1991), but both models necessarily build in numerical limitations. Our group decided that reaching workers isolated within multiple residential workplaces could best be accomplished through mass media and through distribution of materials at places where paid domestic workers are likely to congregate, such as on city buses and in public parks. The key materials in our program were *novelas*.

Novelas are booklets with captioned photographs that tell a story, and they are typically aimed at working-class men and women.[4] In recent years immigration rights advocates in California have successfully disseminated information regarding legalization application procedures, legal services, and basic civil rights to Latino immigrants using this method, and in southern California, even the Red Cross has developed a *novela* on AIDS awareness. Our group developed the text for several didactic *novelas*, and in lieu of photographs, we hired an artist to draw the corresponding caricatures. One *novela* centers on hour and wage claims, and another was designed as an emergency measure to alert domestic workers that a rapist was getting women into his car by offering domestic work jobs to women waiting at bus stops. Based on the research with paid domestic workers, I prepared a two-sided *novela* sheet that cautions women about the abuses in informal subcontracting relations, underlines that payment by the "job" or house yields higher earnings than hourly arrangements, and recommends that domestic workers share cleaning strategies and employment negotiation strategies with their friends. The text also reminds women of their entitlement to receive minimum wage ($4.25).

With a small grant, the advocacy group hired four Latina immigrant outreach workers, two Salvadoran women and two Mexican women,

TRABAJADORA DOMESTICA:

Si Ud. es recien llegada, cuidado con desconocidos que prometan presentarte supuestos empleadores

Mantenga en mente estos tres consejos

1 Si Ud. puede trabajar rapidamente le conviene cobrar por casa en vez de cobrar por hora.

2 mantengase bién informada con amigas, comadres y vecinas que también hacen trabajo doméstico, sobre problemas y soluciones.

3 Siempre comunique al patrón o la patrona, los productos que se necesitan para hacer la limpieza.

Recuerde: Ud. tiene derecho a recibir el sueldo mínimo de $4.25 por hora, aunque esté entrenando.

Comparta sus problemas de trabajo con sus amistades, para aprender más.

to distribute these materials to Latina immigrant domestic workers. Posters were printed up and placed on over four hundred municipal buses that run along east-west routes. In large black print written across a red background the text reads (in Spanish): "Domestic Worker: Do You Have a Problem at Work? For Help or Free Information, Call the Labor Defense Network"; an accompanying illustration shows a domestic worker with octopuslike arms, with one hand balancing a crying baby while the other hands hold a feather duster, an iron, a baby bottle, a stirring spoon, and a soapy sponge. The posters also included tear-off sheets with information on where to solicit legal counsel for domestic work issues, such as salary disputes or sexual harassment. As they distributed the materials, the outreach workers advised domestic workers on their employment rights and provided resource information on where to obtain legal assistance for job-related problems. The outreach workers also distributed small notebooks and encouraged domestic workers to record daily all work hours, tasks performed, and pay received, so that if a labor dispute should arise, they would have documentation to present in court.

RESEARCH, ACTIVISM, THEORY

After I had prepared the text for the *novela*, I sent the Spanish-language text to several of the immigrant women respondents in my study so that I might elicit their feedback. Most of them had little to say, and when I spoke with them, they agreed that the project and the materials were useful, but they did not offer recommendations or suggestions. There was, however, one exception. The woman who had been most active in using the domestics' network resources and successful in accumulating an enviable list of jobs, Maria Alicia N., did voice strong views on the *novela* text. She expressed these views in the form of a lengthy tape-recorded "letter." Verbal letters recorded on cassettes are sometimes used by some Mexican immigrants to communicate with their family back home, and Maria Alicia favored this form of communication as she was trying to control her already steep phone bills. In the cassette she sent me, she spoke of the recent challenges she had faced as a single working mother, of her worries about her twelve-year-old son's affinity with a local gang, and her disappointment in discovering that her boyfriend of seven years was still married to another woman in Mexico. But on the upside, her work was going well, as she still maintained a steady route of employers and was earning more than ever before. On the subject of the text, she offered many insightful remarks on the subcontracting relationship that are worth quoting:

> You asked for my opinion on these *novelas* that you're making. Look, with my sister it took me a lot of work to make her independent, and little by little she got out on her own with her own houses [to clean], right. Now she works for herself, but it took me a lot of work because at the beginning she didn't like to be left alone. She didn't want to drive, she didn't want to do this or that, but now she realized that she is independent and it would be terrible if she was working for me. Perhaps something would have happened, we probably would have broken off our association.
>
> There have been other occasions. Once I tried to help a woman, and I told her I would leave her a house. I showed her the house, I took her there, and I told the señora that she was my sister. I wanted to give her that house [to clean] and do you believe it? She didn't go the day that she was supposed to do so! So then I looked bad with the señora. So I say how is it possible that one can have such great need and not have the desire to work? They are asking god for work, but they don't want to work. I mean, they are looking for work and praying to god that they don't find it!
>
> So then a cousin, no a sister, of Amador also came here. I told her it was a good business with houses, "Little by little I'll leave you a few, little by little because now it's really slow." I told her, "You'll make a lot of money very fast, because this is a good job, you earn well." So we went to do some houses, and in one of them it seemed to her that I charged too little, and in another, it seemed to her that I did too much work, that I should only do this and do that. What happens is that people are not conscious that they must make merits. . . . And people just don't want to make that kind of sacrifice.

Maria Alicia responded defensively to the materials I had sent for her commentary. Rather than recalling her experiences as a "helper" hired to assist another paid domestic worker, she cited three more recent examples in which her own hired "helpers" had not performed up to the standard she set. In the above quote she blames her sister for being too dependent, her friend for being irresponsible and lazy, and her boyfriend's sister for being unwilling to work hard and accept a low level of pay initially.

The subcontracting relationship embodies and reproduces inequality among paid domestic workers. Maria Alicia responded defensively to the text warning women of the abuses that occur among Latina domestics themselves because the position that Maria Alicia identified with was as a moderately successful paid domestic worker who occasionally took on her own helpers. But in fact, she herself had entered the occupation by working as a subcontracted helper for virtually nothing and living rent free with another Mexican immigrant woman domestic worker. That relationship seemed too distant for her to even recall, but when I had interviewed her several years earlier, she had complained about it. At that time, she related disappointment and anger with her experiences as a "helper" subcontracted by another domestic worker who exploited her labor and her situation: "I helped her to work a lot, and she did not pay me. Nothing, nothing. I would help her to do three or four houses a day. No, no, no, no, they were giving me nothing! It would have been better if I had never accepted such an arrangement."

Maria Alicia's divergent responses in the interview, and then in reaction to the research findings in the form of the *novela* text, prompted me to see the dual nature of the domestic workers' networks. Although the subcontracting relationship is just one facet of the network relations, it provides an important means of entry into the occupation for women who lack sufficient contacts with employers. For domestic workers who hire their own helpers, the subcontracting relationship is a way to yield enough labor to cover an increasing number of lucrative jobs. I began to see Maria Alicia's comments as reflections of different positions in the network, and I began to conceptualize paid domestic work as a career where movement is governed in part by the domestic worker's networks (Hondagneu-Sotelo 1994).

This revelation allowed me to see that there is mobility within an occupation that is generally held to be either static or, alternately, the route to upward mobility by changing occupation. Paid domestic work has typically been seen either as a "bridging occupation" that facilitates acculturation and mobility into industrial employment for rural-urban migrant or immigrant women (Broom and Smith 1963; McBride 1976) or, alternately, as an "occupational ghetto" for women of color (Glenn 1986; Romero 1987, 1988). For women such as Maria Alicia, paid domestic work is neither a static position nor the route to jobs in the formal sector of the economy. Even in paid domestic work conducted outside the purview of formal regulations, some immigrant women can move up the ranks and obtain better employers who offer higher pay and better working conditions, more houses to clean, and, eventually, their own "hired help."

Are Feminist Sociology and Activism Compatible?

In her essay in this volume Francesca M. Cancian discusses some of the ways that mainstream academic power structures and careerism dissuade sociologists from incorporating social change into their research agendas, and she correctly, I think, emphasizes that vast structural changes in universities and academic publishing are necessary to change traditional approaches to scholarship. These broad, structural changes are necessary and will require a concerted, organized effort on the part of feminist sociologists, especially those in relatively senior, decision-making positions. But in the interim, or simultaneously perhaps, more limited, circumscribed innovations might be pursued by individuals.

The interactions between research, activism, and theory related in this chapter suggest that feminists with academic careers can combine traditional academic scholarship with social change activism. In fact, feminists working within academic careers may find a double pay-off, as I did, to integrating social research and activism. On the one hand, there is the satisfaction of having an impact, however modest, on enhancing the social conditions of the people one has studied. This advances the notion of reciprocity to another level, and, if one is predisposed to asking existential "so what?" questions about the social significance of one's research, it may provide some answers. On the other hand, the experience of seeking outlets in which to implement research findings may also advance previous interpretations and theoretical implications drawn from the original research. The prospects for sociologists who wish to apply their findings toward women's equality would seem to have increased with the proliferation of new feminist research. In the instance I have discussed here, research and theory informed activism, but it was the dissemination and advocacy work that in turn allowed me to gain new insights from my findings and interpretations.

NOTES

1. The dominant form of organization in domestic work has historically shifted from live-in employment, where there is no separation between place of residence and employment, to day work, where employees work for the same employer on a daily basis but reside with their own families and communities, and, ultimately, to job work (Romero 1988). These various arrangements, however, continue to coexist.

2. The Immigration Reform and Control Act (IRCA), enacted in November 1986, included major provisions in the areas of employment restrictions and legalization for undocumented immigrants in the United States.

3. Cornelius (1982) suggests using women who serve as community brokers as a means to generate snowball samples. I did this to a very limited ex-

tent, but they proved to be more useful to me as role models, facilitating my ethnographic research.

4. In Latin America, paid domestic workers constitute a substantial part of the audience for these magazines and are also portrayed in the narrative stories. For an analysis of how images of paid domestic workers in Latin America are represented in *novelas,* see Flora (1989).

REFERENCES

Broom L., and J. H. Smith. 1963. "Bridging Occupations." *British Journal of Sociology* 14:321–34.

Bulmer, Martin, ed. 1982. *Social Research Ethics.* New York: Holmes and Meier.

Chaney, Elsa M., and Mary Garcia Castro, eds. 1989. *Muchachas No More: Household Workers in Latin America and the Caribbean.* Philadelphia: Temple University Press.

Cornelius, Wayne A. 1982. "Interviewing Undocumented Immigrants: Methodological Reflections Based on Fieldwork in Mexico and the U.S." *International Migration Review* 16:378–411.

Dudden, Faye. 1983. *Serving Women: Household Service in Nineteenth-Century America.* Middletown, Conn.: Wesleyan University Press.

Duster, Troy, David Matza, and David Wellman. 1979. "Fieldwork and the Protection of Human Subjects." *American Sociologist* 14:136–42.

Flora, Cornelia Butler. 1989. "Domestic Service in the Latin American *Fotonovela.*" In *Muchachas No More: Household Workers in Latin America and the Caribbean,* ed. Elsa M. Chaney and Mary Garcia Castro. Philadelphia: Temple University Press. 143–59.

Glenn, Evelyn Nakano. 1986. *Issei, Nisei, Warbride: Three Generations of Japanese American Women in Domestic Service.* Philadelphia: Temple University Press.

Hondagneu-Sotelo, Pierrette. 1994. "Regulating the Unregulated: Domestic Workers' Social Networks." *Social Problems* 41 (1): 201–15.

———. 1988. "Gender and Fieldwork." *Women's Studies International Forum* 11 (6): 611–18.

Katzman, David M. 1981. *Seven Days a Week: Women and Domestic Service in Industrializing America.* Urbana: University of Illinois Press.

McBride, Theresa. 1976. *The Domestic Revolution.* New York: Holmes.

Rollins, Judith. 1985. *Between Women: Domestics and Their Employers.* Philadelphia: Temple University Press.

Romero, Mary. 1992. *Maid in the U.S.A.* New York: Routledge.

———. 1988. "Chicanas Modernize Domestic Service." *Qualitative Sociology* 11 (4): 319–34.

———. 1987. "Domestic Service in the Transition from Rural to Urban Life: The Case of La Chicana." *Women's Studies* 13:199–222.

Salzinger, Leslie. 1991. "A Maid by Any Other Name: The Transformation of 'Dirty Work' by Central American Immigrants." In *Ethnography Unbound: Power and Resistance in the Modern Metropolis,* ed. Michael Burawoy, Alice

Burton, Ann Arnett Ferguson, Kathryn J. Fox, Joshua Gamson, Nadine Gartrell, Leslie Hurst, Charles Kurzman, Leslie Salzinger, Josepha Schiffman, and Shiori Ui. Berkeley: University of California Press. 139–60.

Stacey, Judith. 1988. "Can There Be a Feminist Ethnography?" *Women's Studies International Forum* 11 (1): 21–27.

CHAPTER 6

LINDA CARTY

Seeing through the Eye of Difference: A Reflection on Three Research Journeys

> The truth is, well, truth is not important at one end of a hemisphere where a bird dives close to you in an ocean for a mouth full of fish, an ocean you come to swim in every two years, you, a slave to your leaping retina, capture the look of it. It is like saying you are dead. This place so full of your absence, this place you come to swim like habit, to taste like habit. . . . Our nostalgia was a lie and the passage on that six hour flight to ourselves is wide and like another world, and then another one inside and is so separate and fast to the skin but voiceless, never born, or born and stilled . . . hush.
>
> —Dionne Brand

As a woman born and raised in the Caribbean who migrated to North America by parental choice, I always had yearnings for "home." The opportunity to carry out research in the region was my big chance. I had promised myself that returning to the Caribbean for a considerable period of time, more than the two-week trip every four or five years, would provide me with a long escape from my struggle with feelings of being a perpetual outsider in my adopted society. I was going "home." My first fieldwork trip to the Caribbean, however, taught me painfully and regrettably that the place I longed for never really existed. It was a creation of my nostalgia, a nostalgia that assuaged alienation I frequently experienced as an immigrant in Canada.

This chapter examines my experiences doing fieldwork both in the

Caribbean and among Caribbean populations in Canada and the United States. Even when working among people with whom I shared cultural patterns and understandings, I frequently found myself an outsider, a stranger, with as much fear and trepidation as that status entails. Being born and raised in the Caribbean did not give me authenticity in the eyes of my research participants. Hence, I was positioned as insider and outsider simultaneously.

The insider/outsider/stranger status does not require foreignness as an inherent feature, just as the element of familiarity is not extrinsic to it. One can indeed experience the foreign within the familiar. According to the sociologist Georg Simmel (1921:322–27), there is some sociological significance to this status of outsider within.[1] It provides a unique window on "objectivity" because of the peculiar position of nearness and remoteness, concern and indifference, that one occupies. One becomes the stranger when one is not grounded in the traditions or does not share the attitudes and biases of the group to which one belongs.

In my own case, while some of my experiences in the field amounted to erasures and exclusions,[2] leaving me a stranger, I was also able to make important connections and acquire valuable information because of my privileged insider status. Yet I often found myself with few intellectual tools to help me negotiate a very difficult research terrain. This was due, in some part, to my training in a sociology that conveyed deep epistemological and ontological misunderstandings of Third World peoples.[3] Initially, I attempted to apply qualitative research methods that reflect the dominant ideology and culture of the advanced industrialized countries. However, such methods, like the discourse from which they evolved, reproduce the misconceptions of Third World peoples held by Western scholars and therefore become glaring failures in Third World community settings, being incompatible with their social reality. Inevitably, the researcher is left to improvise research procedures. The following three research "episodes" highlight the difficulties I experienced in trying to apply the "objective" methods I was taught to doing research among "my own" people. These illustrate the ways in which the environment shaped the research.

EPISODE I: AN OUTSIDER'S VIEW FROM THE INSIDE

In 1986, I embarked on an extended research trip to the English-speaking Caribbean to investigate the social relations of gender at a prominent institution of higher education. I had left the Caribbean as a teenager. My family rode the wave of immigration that colonialism, and later imperialism, had forced out of the region to make a living. In returning to carry out research, I realized that others might see me as being *from* the Caribbean but not *of* it. Therefore, I could not assume immediate acceptance by research participants based on cultural familiarity. At the same time, my origins gave me an advantage, enabling me to understand cultural nuances that could either help or hinder my research. With grave trepidation, I set out on this journey.

Almost two decades had passed since I had lived in the Caribbean. The affinity I felt with the region as my "homeland" became more poignant, I later realized, with my immigrant sense of "not belonging" in Canada. Such feelings of "home" reside only in the immigrant's imagination and serve the purpose of comforting nostalgic reflection. The immigrant lives with this perpetual contradiction. My new knowledge of adulthood in another country made me aware that I would never feel at home there, yet this knowledge created the yearning for "home." These feelings shaped my decision to study the Caribbean. My decision was also fueled by the absence of "experts" on the Caribbean in my graduate program. I felt the need (almost a responsibility) to help fill the void.

There is a general perception, a mixture of resentment and hesitation, among Caribbean academicians toward scholars who come from North America and Europe "to study Caribbean people." Such perceptions and feelings stem from the legacies of slavery, which afforded more respect to whites than to Blacks, and are particularly strong among women, who face the realities of patriarchal privilege accorded to men. These attitudes also relate to practices of some white researchers in the past. For example, according to many of my research participants, some white scholars have published elaborate articles based on their brief tourist research, which amounted to a single two-week visit. They view such work as inherently colonialist in its perspective.

My position as a Black woman researcher in this milieu, struggling to minimize the impact of gender, race, and class legacies, inscribed me as an outsider. I represented one of those "coming to study Caribbean people." This must have conjured up questions of whether I was going to be "the native informant" (Minh-ha 1989). I had been schooled and remained entrenched in the colonizer's world. Further, it was the outsider's view (i.e., the North American feminist view) that shaped my research questions, which suggested that women deserved special attention. Finally, I was in a privileged position relative to most of the population and to some of my research participants. Most Caribbean academicians are also foreign-trained, but they hold fast to the notion that being Caribbean means residing there.

Prior to going to the region, I sampled women and men in each department to ensure representation. I then wrote letters to the one hundred academics and staff in my sample, seeking their participation. I informed them of the purpose and goals of the study and the research design. I further provided what I perceived to be relevant information about myself and assured them confidentiality and anonymity. Subsequently, I made a short "get acquainted" visit to the region to meet those who had responded (less than 20 percent) and to seek, in person, a response from the others. The actual participation rate in the study came close to 100 percent.

On this initial visit, I gained some insight into the future fieldwork experience. The standard criteria for interviewing that I had been taught suggested that the interviews have no personal significance, that the setting and the relations between parties are of no importance. The interviewer's role is to evoke and collect but never to give information. This ultimately reduces the interviewee to mere data. Feminist research methods in the social sciences challenged these conventions (Roberts 1981; Stanley and Wise 1983) but those available at the time I did my first fieldwork offered little guidance for work in a context where race and culture are primary factors.

On the preliminary research trip I realized that holding on to the conventions of sociological research methods would create major obstacles. For example, trying to remain neutral in discussions in which a reciprocal relationship was clearly a condition of getting information would have been foolhardy. To remain silent in conversations, or simply to gesture understanding with a nod or a smile, being overly concerned with what I came to understand as the biased notion of "learned neutrality" and "objectivity," would engender mistrust and in rare cases even hostility. These were the conventions of the administrators' world, that is, the white masculinist thought that constitutes the core of sociology. They had nothing to do with the experienced world in which most of the participants, particularly the women, and I lived. Their world resembled mine. In both cases, as Black women, our contributions in academe had been rendered less than that of men, in specific ways, *because* we are Black women. These conventions were meant to force me to substitute the concerns of the administrators' world with the world as experienced by me and my research participants.[4] The two are incongruous. To enter this conceptual mode would have meant disassociating from what I was doing, from what I understood all too well because I lived it daily.

This essay elaborates on the extent to which context can seriously impact, if not determine, research outcomes. Perhaps more importantly, the fieldwork taught me that method could not be divorced from context and that conventional methods were not applicable. From this experience I concluded that normative research criteria, which have had a long history of excluding certain groups, for example, Blacks, women, and peoples and cultures of the Third World, cannot then be the definitive characteristic of so-called "objective knowledge." Such "situated knowledge" (Haraway 1988; also see Collins 1990:233–35) offers only a privileged particularistic perspective of social reality masquerading as universal.

As Black women, we have been objectified by this form of "objective" knowledge, the discursive imperialism that constitutively locates us as part of the ruled, whose role is to learn, accept, and apply the methods that sustain those relations of ruling. While white sociologists have recognized the distinctiveness of Black society and culture, whether African, African American, British, or Caribbean, they often separate the societies from the larger socioeconomic and political environment. Hence, the dialectic of how the subjects negotiate the larger society, the strategies they apply to survive, how they resist oppression while at the same time being victimized by it, in short, how they impact the social world, is lost (Dill 1987).

This revelation came to me vividly during my first fieldwork experience. I realized then that my work could/would not reproduce these social relations of oppression. I had been schooled in a system of higher education that had excluded me as a person and people of African descent as having no historical relevance. Moreover, while some of the most renowned North American feminist scholars were teachers in my graduate program, they taught me by their racialist patterns of omission in their theories and praxis why my feminism had to differ.

Recently, Third World social scientists have begun to examine the inherent biases in the methodologies and philosophies of Western social science, which always assumes a universal character. They view Western social science, both as it has developed in the advanced industrialized countries and in its influence on the development of social sciences in the Third World, as a significant tool in the maintenance of Western capitalist hegemony. Of more specific relevance to this argument, however, is the *nakedness* one feels in the field when applying one's Western training, even as (or perhaps because) one tries to study one's own culture. An excellent analysis of fieldwork by a group of Arab women scholars (all Western trained) gets to the heart of this dilemma. The authors discuss the multiplicity of problems they encountered trying to study their own non-Western societies (Altorki and El-Solh 1988). As in my own situation, the context often determined the shape of their research. They had to immerse themselves in the daily lives of their research subjects and frequently, because the latter considered them "one of their own," they shared information that they would not have with non-Arabs. These Arab women researchers too were sometimes treated as outsiders, but all acknowledged the many advantages that their insider status afforded them.

As I left the Caribbean after the initial research trip, I contemplated my return. It became clear that the women's participation in my study hinged on making *connections* with them. But recognizing the problems with my academic training, and understanding that fundamental differences of feminism and nationalism divided us, the crucial question for me was, On what basis could I make genuine connections that would bear fruit for my research?

The male participants questioned the study, specifically its "legitimacy," because I was "looking at this woman thing," which, they claimed, had little relevance in the Caribbean because, after all, "men and women academics get paid the same." Their security as the dominant partners in the immediate relations of rule, however, created no hesitation on their part to participate. Even those who had little respect for the type of research I was doing (i.e., feminist) agreed to participate. They wanted to make sure that I got "both sides of the story." Their concerns about legitimacy emanated from their deeply entrenched sexism. At the same time, it became clear that the methods I was attempting to force onto my research were racialist and sex-biased. Both of these issues intensified my worries.

The research methods I had been taught emphasized the advanced capitalist world over Third World cultures and peoples, implying that the latter were consumers and not producers of knowledge and thus, the research methods should be applied without alteration. The male participants in my research, like their female counterparts, most of whom were trained in North American and European universities, understood the limitations of my training. They too tested me, and again I found myself negotiating my outsider/insider status. To them I was an outsider, meaning feminist, and the label with its pejorative meaning was invoked not only to challenge me but also to silence me.

Making Connections

When I returned to the region some three months later to carry out the research, I knew I would not be able to merely plunge in and begin interviewing. It was necessary to meet with many of the women individually, and sometimes in groups, to become involved in certain activities in their colleges and to interact with them outside of the university. I sometimes went to dinner at their homes, was invited on more than one occasion to attend department faculty meetings, and sometimes socialized with some of them on weekends.

I often went to meetings of the Women's Studies Group and listened to debates and discussions about the newly developing gender studies program. One of the more significant debates was about how the program got its name and why it was necessary to debate whether it should be called women or gender studies. Central to the argument was that the women did not want to alienate the men in the university who were supportive of the program. Another issue, which had not been settled by the time I left, was about whether the program should be developed as an independent discipline or as a program dispersed throughout the colleges with courses in different departments. The feasibility of an independent program versus the possible ineffectiveness of the so-called interdisciplinary approach were not primary concerns. Instead, the focus seemed to be on how the administrators (the institution's male hierarchy) would view the push for women's studies as a discipline, since they were already hesitant about all proposals from the group and saw women's studies as a marginal area of study. The women voiced concern that their program would eventually go the way of black studies in American universities.

While listening intently to these discussions, being weary with what I viewed as the women's lack of feminist consciousness and reluctance to challenge the institutional male hegemony and being very cognizant that my views would hardly be understood or appreciated in this environment, I was asked for my opinion. In my struggle to be diplomatic, I suggested that perhaps it would be useful to consider the ultimate goals for the program and then try to determine if these could be accomplished through a program that had, at best, a marginal status and that was without a solid base. I was promptly told that women faculty in the Caribbean who research such issues engender more respect than their counterparts in the United States and Canada, because they can accomplish their goals without approaching the administration with a "feminist baseball bat." I remember thinking, "So much for our shared cultural understanding." This encounter was another instance when my authenticity as a Caribbean woman was questioned.

The terms upon which I came to feminist consciousness differed from those of my Caribbean sisters. As a Black woman in North America, my struggle, along with all other women of color, was directed against the combined effects of sexism and racism. For Caribbean women, on a local level the women's struggle is primarily about sexism, while on an international level racism tends to supersede sexism. Many in the Caribbean perceive North American feminism (a perception cultivated through distorted media reports) as equivalent to anti-male antagonism with an exclusive focus on patriarchy. The reference to the "feminist baseball bat" therefore meant that what I was negotiating at that point was feminism with a North American media face. Our experiences with North American feminism differed dramatically. I, for example, knew of the many faces of that feminism. Nevertheless, the perceptions of these women served to further compound my problem of fitting in.

Although no one openly criticized my research, I felt that, for the most part, I was being tested on my "Caribbeanness" and on my "womanness" to earn their trust. Like them, I was a Caribbean woman, which meant that I understood women's position in this particular society. Thus, I could share the jokes and understand the rage about certain experiences, yet it did not translate into full acceptance and trust. Constantly being tested was quite stressful and heightened my awareness of the missing emotional and psychological anchors that I needed to navigate my terrain.

I had spent more than half of my life in North America. I returned as a feminist who considered herself a national of the region more than a national of any one country in the region. I did not share the "big and small island" syndrome that typified most of the people of the region, i.e., the staunch masculinist nationalism that I see as regionally divisive. As a feminist, even though I knew better than to use the term during my stay there, my political commitment to end unequal relations between women and men belied the role that women in the region are expected to play. This meant that the social relations of gender often offended me. I had come to feminism after witnessing the acute failures of the struggle against racism that did not address sexism. These factors, together with the color and class legacies of slavery and indentured labor, engendered in fair complexion privilege,[5] produced cultural alienation: I was now the outsider within.

Factors such as feminism and nationalism deeply affected the relationships I developed. There is a strong women's movement in the Caribbean, but "feminist" is not its operative definition. In general, the term is seen as a white, North American import. While many women are politically astute about women's secondary status and are committed to working to create change, most eschew "outsiders'" opinions, including returning Caribbean nationals. At times, I understood their doubts and fears, as they recalled bad experiences with North American (= white) researchers. While my philosophies and those of my respondents differed greatly, I apparently succeeded in letting my behavior speak to my sincerity.

The Status of Experience in Methodology

As I started the interview process, it became more evident to me that the merger of experience and method was not only relevant but indispensable in order to adequately represent the research participants' experiences. I refused to enter the conceptual mode of abstraction and indifference as they recounted their experiences in the academy. Although our experiences differed when the ruling dynamic was that of race, we shared many common experiences as women. While I was the researcher, we shared the same critical space as the subjects of the research. I found myself confronting the dilemma of how and where to draw the line to define my involvement with my research participants. There was no easy resolution to this problem; the women's decision to share the truth of their experiences depended, in a large part, on my interaction and relationship with them. This does not mean that experience is the sole category of truth. Experience is itself mediated; it cannot be dismissed as merely "the subjective."

The women participants in my research had, what I now perceive to be, a healthy skepticism, much of it born out of experience. They prefigured the objectives of my research. Many of them insisted that I acknowledge the problems of always being researched. Also, the very subject of my research added to their hesitation. After all, I was investigating their experiences with the male administrative hierarchy of the institution. I wanted to know what kind of support (if any) they received for their work, what their experiences were in applying for tenure, what level of collegiality existed between men and women. Such issues address the institution in which they all still worked. Indeed, many of the women expressed the fear that even with anonymity, if I included their own words in the study, some readers might discover their identity. Understandably, many of them believed that criticism of the structure would affect them emotionally and perhaps catastrophically. None of the men expressed hesitation, or even interest, in the particular methodology I was using.

Some of the concerns the women participants had about me were strongly influenced by their notions of North American feminism as narrowly focused and racist. Either during their training periods or in frequent travels to North America, many of them had become familiar with the primary concerns of the mainstream women's movement in both the United States and Canada. They claimed that the prioritizing of abortion rights, lesbian rights, and equal pay for work of equal value were of greater significance to white women. They felt that such issues overlooked the more pressing concerns of widespread poverty, the ability for most poor people to find jobs, and racism, all of which presented numerous obstacles in the everyday lives of women who were poor and nonwhite.

EPISODES 2 AND 3: DIFFERENT, YET THE SAME

After the Caribbean research encounter, I began a study investigating the work experiences of Caribbean domestic workers in the metropolitan Toronto area. Domestic work in Canada, as in many other advanced capitalist societies, is not only a gender-specific occupation but also a race-bound one. Among other things, I wanted to understand how women who did this type of work saw themselves in relation to their employers, primarily upper- and middle-class white women, how and why they entered the field, and if they intended to remain in domestic work. A colleague and I conducted the interviews.

Initially, many of the women hesitated to meet with us. They all knew about numerous instances of harassment of Caribbean women domestics by Canadian immigration officials. They perceived the state as a body of racist institutions and saw themselves as powerless relative to other workers. Because these women enjoyed no legal protection, they were reticent about telling their stories even to other Caribbean women. As researchers, we represented a privileged category to many of the domestics and this carried with it the assumption that we were incapable of understanding their situation. Yet, some of the women with either college or vocational training in the Caribbean resisted less, and in some instances viewed us as an inspiration to accomplishing their ultimate goals to which domestic work was merely the initial stepping stone.

Much of the hesitation on the part of the interviewees to sit and have a taped discussion with us revolved around past experiences with either researchers or authority personnel who had violated their trust. Because of these situations, they felt powerless to protect their interests. Also, many stood in a very tenuous immigration status. Some had a "live-in" arrangement with their employer, which made that house their primary place of residence. They had Saturdays and Sundays off to go "home," which was often the residence of a friend or relative. None had permanent residency status, and in fact, achieving such status depended on their relationship with their employers and a history of consistent employment. They perceived discussing their work experiences as revealing the horror stories of their lives in Canada. Work for them was more than the place where they earned a wage.

In many respects, we were outsiders, strangers to their experiences. To some degree we understood what it meant to interview women who were positioned in a particular hierarchy of race, class, and labor relations. We understood why they felt that disclosure could result in severe repercussions. As one woman told us: "It would be stupid to bite the hand that feeds you." Occasionally, some of them conveyed resentment toward us. Much of the context of this research paralleled my earlier experiences in the Caribbean. On one level, as Caribbean women, we had an instant rapport with the interviewees, yet as domestics in an extremely vulnerable position with little autonomy over their work or personal lives, there was little reason for them to confide in us.

We had to earn their trust. We promised to share our findings with them (and did). For some of them who were taking high school or college courses at night, we often helped them with assignments. On three occasions we made the difficult decision to attend church with some of them. In more than a few cases, we put them in touch with supportive and affordable legal experts to work on their behalf with the state.

We were "insiders" in that we shared ethnicity and culture. We too were often victims of racism or sexism and frequently of racist sexism. Even though our insider status had afforded us the privilege of getting much more detailed and graphic information than white researchers, we were also aware that our position of relative privilege denied us the ability to fully appreciate their experiences. At the same time, however, because the Caribbean community (indeed, the entire Black population) in Toronto is relatively small, we shared the experience of vulnerability as "outsiders" with our interviewees.

The Toronto research project has been expanded to include New York City for comparison. Though not yet completed, it is already evident that there are numerous similarities and differences. Because of the relatively large Black population in New York, Caribbean women who work as domestics do not feel the same kinds of vulnerability and fear's of being exposed as their counterparts in Canada. However, trust is equally as important. For example, one woman initially agreed to participate in the project, and in numerous telephone conversations trying to work out a convenient time and place (since she worked four jobs), she assured me that she felt comfortable about it. When I showed up, however, she apologized:

> I'm sorry, you know, but I changed my mind. I was talking it over last night with my husband, who is still in Jamaica, and he reminded me of a terrible thing that happened to us in Jamaica a few years ago with a white woman who was doing something like you. She was working in our town for a while talking to people and taking pictures, doing research she said. We trusted her and took her into our home and everything. We told her that we did not want to be in her movie even though we were talking to her and answering many of her questions. Next thing, after she leave, one of my cousins in Canada called us and told us that they saw us on TV making a fool of ourselves telling this white woman about our poor lives in Jamaica. We were so mad but what could we do? I know you're not going to do that, and I know you understand a lot coming from the Caribbean too, but I'm still afraid 'cause I don't understand what this research thing is all about. It seems to mean that you people doing the work have all the rights and we who take part don't have any.

Other factors compound trust and frequently become temporary impediments to completing a project. Many of the domestic workers in New York City are illegal immigrants whose employers, some of whom are city and state officials, know of their illegal status. As workers, they have no rights and no legal avenues through which to redress their employers' exploitation. Explaining to them my depth of understanding of their plight does little to resolve their personal dilemma or reduce their emotional pain. Yet my position as an insider comes with advantages. Some women have been more than willing to share their experiences with me, specifically because of the solidarity we share as immigrants from the Caribbean, in the hopes that I could at least expose their exploitation and the state's complicity in it. Like many of the women in Toronto, what some of my interviewees recount as past experiences, everything from being terminated without wages to sexual assault by employers, no worker should have to tolerate.

In Toronto, helping people to negotiate the bureaucracies that created difficulties in their lives facilitated the development of trust at a much quicker pace than it has in New York. Because I do not reside in New York City, I am denied any similar privilege. There are numerous telephone conversations with my New York subjects prior to interviews because there is no other avenue through which a relationship emphasizing my sincerity to earn their trust is possible. For many of the women, the telephone calls become a virtual precondition to granting an interview. This has delayed my New York research.

My Training as a Sociologist: The Experience/Method Dichotomy

There have been numerous debates over the past decade by feminist sociologists examining the social construction of a patriarchal sociology from the standpoint of women and questioning the notion of value neutrality and objectivity in sociological research (Reinharz 1992; Ramazanoglu 1990; Smith 1987a; Stacey and Thorne 1985). Building on a long history of interdisciplinary critiques of the male ways of seeing in the social sciences, feminist sociologists question the assumptions in the discipline regarding what constitutes convincing and therefore acceptable knowledge. The assumptions have been predicated on the privileging of a masculinist view of social reality. Some of the feminist critiques have questioned more than the patriarchal appropriative properties of the discipline; they have also examined the racial dimensions and implications of this white male standpoint. Specifically, they explore the privileges it affords, the responses of those it oppresses to maintain itself, and the result of research that employs paradigms that are incapable of explaining or understanding the lived experiences of its subjects, people of color (Collins 1990; Dill and Zinn 1990; Andersen 1988).

In this essay, I have addressed some of these issues with specific reference to my own research. By focusing on my experiences in the field, I have pointed to how mainstream sociological research paradigms, and to a lesser extent certain elements of feminist research methods, handicapped my own work. The reasons traditional methodologies have been less than adequate include adapting to my simultaneous status of insider/outsider in the field as a researcher, recognizing the limitations of the learned methods, and having to learn "on the spot" how to navigate the research terrain.

The study of women and gender in sociology is a recently established field of inquiry. Though the areas of race and class have long been a part of the fields of race relations and social stratification, the study of gender, race, and class as inextricable analytic categories in the examination of the lived experiences of women of color, and indeed, as complex categories that fundamentally impact all human social behavior, is very new. I learned in my sociological training to treat race and class as discrete, though crucial categories with particular significance in the study of inequality. These categories become mere variables for analysis and therefore interchangeable with Blacks, Latinos, native peoples, Asians, the ruling class, the working class, and the poor. Later, the category of gender was merely "added" to the existing analysis. Both the relevance and significance of race and class within the category of gender, and vice versa, and the fact that women of color experience the social world differently, were taken up as a feminist body of scholarship (gender, class, and race studies) that gained prominence, while remaining peripheral, in the field of women studies. It is still not widely acknowledged in sociology. The generally accepted notion remains that "good methodology" can explain experiences, but to start with experience weakens method.

Even in mainstream feminist sociology, there has been no place for analyses addressing the intersection of colonialism, imperialism, and gender. There continues to be an apparent lack of understanding (or an unwillingness to acknowledge) that the narrative of gender in the discipline must extend beyond relations of inequality between women and men. Rescripting sociology requires more than an assault on its patriarchal heritage and its intransigence to change. This is most urgent at this historical juncture in the evolution of the social sciences in the academy and women's place in both. At a time when 30 percent of Ph.D.'s in the United States are being earned by women and well over 50 percent of those are in the social sciences but less than 2 percent are being earned by women of color, it is necessary to examine why this is the case.

To have any meaningful structural impact gender analyses must take seriously and deal directly, rather than tangentially, with the issues of race, social class, and ethnicity (Williams and Sjoberg 1993). Claims of knowledge reconstruction by most feminist sociologists, creating a sociology of (presumably all) women's standpoint, ring hollow when the subject of analysis again and again privileges white women's lives. Ultimately, this replicates the old hegemonic tradition with the exception of women at the center. As Patricia Hill Collins (1990:222) argues, it is necessary to reconceptualize the hegemonic knowledge frameworks, in sociology and feminism, by embracing a paradigm of race, class, and gender as interlocking systems of oppression.

THE FAILURE OF SOCIOLOGY'S HEGEMONIC TRADITION: ERASING EXPERIENCE WITH METHOD

In studying sociological methods of inquiry, I learned from the omissions what topics were deemed relevant and salient. Among those rendered unimportant were the issues that I wanted to investigate: the experiences of people of color (particularly women) as subjects objectified in an abstract and culturally alien world. They rarely showed up in the annals of sociology.

Sociology argues against researchers placing ourselves in any "personal" relation to our "subject" of study. To do so supposedly nullifies *objectivity* that is critical to the legitimacy of our work. In other words, we are to separate ourselves from what we know and what we investigate if we wish to produce legitimate sociology. The fundamental principle of *objectivity* in the discipline is based on the separation of what is known from the interests of the knowers and the separation of the knowers from what is known (Smith 1990:16). Accordingly, the principle of *objectivity* as defined and authorized by the discipline allows sociologists to study some unknown subject and then claim coming to know it through an objectified, unbiased route called value-free inquiry. Conversely, the pursuit of knowledge of a subject with which one may have some relation of knowing is believed to lack *objectivity.* One must always find ways to transform one's knowing into a neutral form.

Because investigations of the experiences of women, particularly women of color, are yet to be taken seriously in the discipline, and the methodological precedent for such work is to be found primarily in feminist research, which has been criticized for its sociological perspective (Hammersley 1992; Hawkesworth 1992), any attempts at such research run the risk of being labeled methodologically weak.

The debate over experience versus method is quite old,[6] but it has become a particular challenge to sociology, and the social sciences in general, only since feminist research began to gain prominence. Male sociologists struggle to explain it away, arguing that experience is an unstructured method and is therefore an inefficient and unreliable methodological tool of data collection (Hammersley 1992:192). On the other hand, female sociologists, including women of color, painstakingly exert and reinforce the compelling significance of experience. The point is that the definitional criteria for "acceptable structured methods" in sociology, as in all the social sciences, have been informed by the hegemony of a white masculinist social thought construction. This is a definition that, historically, has allowed limited acknowledgment of white women's research but continues to exclude women of color.

For women of color, specifically Black women in academe, creating a separation between experience and method is to compartmentalize the world in which these two are inextricable and which function as such to maintain our distinct oppression. As a Caribbean-born woman who came to a new kind of adulthood in Canada as an immigrant, part of which involved the painful experience of receiving higher education that excluded all people of color, I am, indeed, obliged to examine the consciousness that emerged from that experience. Now as a U.S. resident, traversing the boundaries and limitations of race and gender experiences in both countries and finding more similarities than differences, I see it as a natural compulsion to examine the experiences of women of color in these two settings. How women of color are constructed, even by exclusion, in social thought formation is critical to understanding their/my experiences.

The racial formation of the U.S. social structure did more than merely influence social thought in the United States. It defined it as one of its inherent features. The denial of the contributions of women of color to the construction of American social thought is therefore not accidental. Recently, many of these women have been asserting the different standpoint of their own work and this has served to identify the stark limitations of white masculinist and, I might add, white feminist social thought. Patricia Hill Collins defines a Black women's standpoint and argues for the necessity of a distinct view:

> [It] rejects either/or dichotomous thinking that claims that *either* thought *or* concrete action is desirable and that merging the two limits the efficacy of both. . . . Very different kinds of "thought" and "theories" emerge when abstract thought is joined with concrete action. Denied positions as scholars and writers which allow us to emphasize purely theoretical concerns, the work of most Black women intellectuals is influenced by the merger of action and theory. (1990:28–29)

White masculinist, as well as white feminist, standpoint and method have produced discourse grounded in white male and white female experience, though that experience remains concealed while being used as the criteria by which all else is judged. The schizophrenic split between experience and method has much of the same effect as the separation between theory and action to which Collins points.

Understanding how theory and action intersect to formulate a Black women's standpoint is essential to understanding how crucial we deem the connection between method and experience. For the Black woman researcher, studying an issue that emanates from specific race, class, gender, and cultural biases held by the dominant society toward the Black community, biases that construct that community as relevant only at particular moments in history, and having the knowledge of the interrelatedness of method and experience informs the very environment and defines the terrain in which she must etch out her space as researcher. In this environment, though one may not be *from* the particular community, it is only by understanding the culture, and what it means to be *of* the community, that one is allowed entry into the community and the research is even possible.

In the case of my own research in the Caribbean, though I could rely on some elements of cultural and historical familiarity many of the cultural anchors were no longer present for me. Further, I had no precedent for this kind of research in the region from which to gain advantage. Indeed, there is little, if any, research in the region on professional women's work lives. However, women academicians in the region who have done any kind of fieldwork with women subjects have had access to stronger cultural ties, all of which are obtained by residency in the region. The sense of individual country nationalism, for example, is shared and respected. Such anchors afford a stronger sense of familiarity (Massiah 1988; French and Mohammed 1988).

CONCLUSION

My conviction of the absolute necessity for the integration of method and experience, my refusal as an intellectual to separate theory from social reality, was informed by my experiences in these three episodes of sociological fieldwork. In each case, I realized that as a Black feminist sociologist, nothing in my training provided me with the tools that were necessary to negotiate the terrain. I was simultaneously negotiating the critical issue of *objectivity* and my insider/outsider status in the field. In these research projects, the "subjects" of my research were women with whom I shared a similar cultural background, but this did not create an atmosphere of automatic trust and understanding.

Being from the Caribbean was not enough. Because I had spent most of my life in North America, I had to fight the erroneous assumptions that I could only examine the society through imperialistic lenses and also that I had taken on the distorted white, middle-class feminist notions of what the emancipation struggle for the majority of the world's women meant. Each step of the way I fought the ideological power of neocolonialism and imperialism. Ironically, a white woman researcher would not necessarily have had the same negative perceptions applied against her. Certainly, she would not have experienced any overt expressions; whiteness would have somehow given her more privilege, if not legitimacy.

In my three research cases, the research involved the lives of other people, but because it resonates with much of my own historical, racial, gender, and often class experiences, epistemologically I view it as "situated knowledge." My view cannot be as the sociological discipline claims it should be, that of a purportedly anonymous perspective. Feminist epistemology grants us the legitimacy to claim all the identities we have been taught to deny as real knowledge, and we have since learned that the impersonal, so-called objective approach is incapable of doing justice to this kind of work. In my own research, however, like sociological theory and methodology, feminist epistemology also had its limitations.

NOTES

I am especially grateful to Jacqui Alexander for her encouragement and astute comments on earlier versions of this essay. I also wish to thank Sarah Hurley for her editorial suggestions. My research on Caribbean domestic workers in New York City is supported in part by a Faculty Development Grant from the University of Michigan–Flint.

1. Others have questioned the sociological significance of the insider/outsider concept within the discipline itself in its relations with certain groups (Collins 1990).

2. For example, some people, in their interactions with me, refused to acknowledge my Caribbean heritage. They felt that people who had left the Caribbean a long time ago and had not lived there since simply could not understand the current situation. For such people, I was merely another foreigner, a privileged one, who came to study them and with whom they felt no obligation to be particularly nice, and certainly with whom they shared no familiarity.

3. The term *Third World* is used here to denote countries caught in a web of geopolitical hegemonic relations with advanced capitalist countries that, historically, have designated the former as enclaves of people of color from whom the world's cheapest labor has been extracted. The concept, therefore, captures this historical process.

4. Dorothy Smith (1987b) provides an excellent critique of a patriarchal sociology, but her standpoint is that of relatively privileged middle-class white women. For a critique of this top-down approach see Williams and Sjoberg (1993). This problem of erasures and exclusions is not unique to sociology but is common throughout the social sciences. Anthropologists, for example, affected by anti-imperialist struggles around the world, developed critiques of their Western-dominated and gender-biased discipline even before sociologists (Asad 1982, 1973; Reiter 1975).

5. There is a close and somewhat unique relationship between class and color in the Caribbean. Historically, the ruling and middle classes rarely comprised people of African descent, since throughout slavery and indentureship they were not allowed to occupy any other role than that of laborers. Class, then, had a status based in color, and color gradations became an important feature of Caribbean sociality. It was precisely this color status that afforded people of lighter-skinned complexions greater privilege even when they did not have the material trappings of class. In the early 1970s, with the effect of the Black Power movement in the United States, there were serious challenges to the injustices of the color/class dynamic in the Caribbean. Political lead-

ers and society in general were sensitized to this issue. In the aftermath of social unrest, some changes were legislated, while others were adopted. However, old habits die hard, and the societies soon reverted to many of the old patterns. Today, though less overtly than in the past, skin color in the Caribbean is still closely tied to privilege.

6. The debate never considered the issue of women and the impact of patriarchy on the assumed "ways of knowing" in the social sciences, yet the issue of experience was the unmentioned question if only for the reader (Weber 1949; Bulmer 1982).

REFERENCES

Altorki, Soraya, and Camillia Fawzi El-Solh, eds. 1988. *Arab Women in the Field: Studying Your Own Society.* New York: Syracuse University Press.

Andersen, Margaret. 1988. *Thinking about Women.* New York: MacMillan.

Asad, T. 1982. "A Comment on the Idea of Non-Western Anthropology." In *Indigenous Anthropology in Non-Western Countries,* ed. H. Fahim. Durham: Carolina Academic Press. 284–87.

———. 1973. *Anthropology and the Colonial Encounter.* Atlantic Highlands, N.J.: Humanities Press.

Brand, Dionne. 1990. *No Language Is Neutral.* Toronto: Coach House Press.

Bulmer, Martin, ed. 1982. *Social Research Ethics.* New York: Holmes and Meier.

Collins, Patricia Hill. 1990. *Black Feminist Thought: Knowledge, Consciousness, and the Politics of Empowerment.* Boston: Unwin Hyman. Reprint. New York: Routledge, 1991.

Dill, Bonnie Thornton. 1987. "The Dialectics of Black Womanhood." In *Feminism and Methodology: Social Science Issues,* ed. Sandra Harding. Bloomington: Indiana University Press. 97–108.

Dill, Bonnie Thornton, and Maxine Baca Zinn. 1990. *Race and Gender: Revisioning Social Relations.* Research Paper no. 11. Memphis: Memphis State University Center for Research on Women.

French, Joan, and Patricia Mohammed. 1988. "Women and Health: A Sistren Participatory Workshop." In *Gender in Caribbean Development,* eds. Patricia Mohammed and Catherine Shepherd. Jamaica: University of the West Indies. 342–52.

Hammersley, Martyn. 1992. "On Feminist Methodology." *Sociology* 26 (2): 187–206.

Haraway, Donna. 1988. "Situated Knowledges: The Science Question in Feminism and the Privilege of Partial Perspective." *Feminist Studies* 14 (3): 575–99.

Hawkesworth, M. E. 1992. "Knowers, Knowing, and Known: Feminist Theory and Claims of Truth." *Signs* 14 (3): 553–55.

Massiah, Joycelyn. 1988. "Researching Women's Work: 1985 and Beyond." In *Gender in Caribbean Development,* ed. Patricia Mohammed and Catherine Shepherd. Jamaica: University of the West Indies. 206–31.

Minh-ha, Trinh T. 1989. *Woman, Native, Other.* Bloomington: Indiana University Press.

Ramazanoglu, Caroline. 1990. "Improving on Sociology." *Sociology* 23 (4): 427–44.

Reinharz, Shulamit. 1992. *Feminist Methods in Social Research.* New York: Oxford University Press.

Reiter, Rayna. 1975. *Towards an Anthropology of Women.* New York: Monthly Review Press.

Roberts, Helen, ed. 1981. *Doing Feminist Research.* London: Routledge and Kegan Paul.

Simmel, Georg. 1921. "The Sociological Significance of 'Stranger.'" In *Introduction to the Science of Sociology,* ed. Robert Park and Ernest W. Burgess. Chicago: University of Chicago Press. 322–31.

Smith, Dorothy. 1990. *The Conceptual Practices of Power: A Feminist Sociology of Knowledge.* Toronto: University of Toronto Press.

———. 1987a. *The Everyday World as Problematic: A Feminist Sociology.* Boston: Northeastern University Press.

———. 1987b. "Women's Perspective as a Radical Critique of Sociology." In *Feminism and Methodology: Social Science Issues,* ed. Sandra Harding. Bloomington: Indiana University Press. 84–96.

Stacey, Judith, and Barrie Thorne. 1985. "The Missing Feminist Revolution in Sociology." *Social Problems* 32 (4): 301–16.

Stanley, Liz, ed. 1990. *Feminist Praxis: Research, Theory, and Epistemology in Feminist Sociology.* London: Routledge and Kegan Paul.

Stanley, Liz, and Sue Wise. 1983. *Breaking Out: Feminist Consciousness and Feminist Research.* London: Routledge and Kegan Paul.

Weber, Max. 1949. *The Methodology of the Social Sciences.* New York: Free Press.

Williams, Norma, and Andrée F. Sjoberg. 1993. "Ethnicity and Gender: The View from Above versus the View from Below." In *A Critique of Contemporary American Sociology,* ed. Ted R. Vaughan, Gideon Sjoberg, and Larry T. Reynolds. New York: General Hall. 160–202.

CHAPTER 7

VERTA TAYLOR AND LEILA J. RUPP

Lesbian Existence and the Women's Movement: Researching the "Lavender Herring"

In 1970, in response to Betty Friedan's fear that the rising tide of lesbian feminism represented a "lavender menace" to the respectable women's rights movement, Susan Brownmiller reassured readers of the *New York Times Magazine* that lesbians were no more than a "lavender herring" (Echols 1989). In our research on two very different phases of the women's movement, we have come to see this image of the "lavender herring" as all too evocative of scholarly and popular treatment of the role of lesbianism in the women's movement. For periods before the resurgence of the movement in the 1960s, the questions of how we define "lesbianism" and whether or not such a concept is relevant arise. With regard to the contemporary movement, in which lesbian participation is widely recognized, the question is whether or not lesbians constitute, as Friedan intimated, a "menace" to mobilization and political activism. In researching these questions, we have come to see lesbianism—or, in recognition of the sticky question of identity, what Adrienne Rich (1980) calls "lesbian existence"—as a powerful force helping to sustain feminist activism historically and in the present. In this essay, we discuss the process of making lesbian existence central in two very different research projects.

By training, one of us is a sociologist and the other a historian, and we are lesbians and feminists in a partnered relationship. We began doing collaborative interdisciplinary work on the U.S. women's rights movement in the period from 1945 to the 1960s and have continued to write together on the women's movement, most recently on contemporary American "women's communities." In the first project, the question of lesbianism was somewhat oblique, since none of the women's rights advocates we studied, as far as we could ascertain, identified themselves as lesbians. In the second, lesbianism was central. Yet in both we grappled, in different ways, with the problem of confronting the "lavender herring."

RESEARCHING THE WOMEN'S RIGHTS MOVEMENT

We undertook our research on the women's rights movement of the forties and fifties (Rupp and Taylor 1987) knowing that both the scholarly and popular literature assumed that the women's movement died in 1920, or shortly thereafter, and was not resurrected until the mid-sixties. Our research originated in curiosity about the fate of women who had, during World War II, worked for what they termed "full citizenship" for women. Although we suspected that these women had not been converted or overwhelmed by "the feminine mystique" in the fifties, we did not set out to prove that a women's rights movement existed. We did, however, find the period between the end of the war and what we have come to call the "resurgence" of the women's movement a particularly fascinating one. The fifties followed on the heels of a war that had brought women into areas previously reserved for men and preceded the emergence of a large and active women's movement, yet are traditionally characterized as years of extreme domesticity for American women.

What we found ultimately was not the kind of movement that contemporary feminists are eager to claim. We discovered an abeyance phase (Taylor 1989b) of the women's movement that we termed "elite-sustained." This was not a broadly based grass-roots movement, but a small movement of elite women: primarily white, middle- or upper-class, well-educated, professional women who had developed a commitment to feminism in the early decades of the twentieth century. They did not attempt to mobilize diverse groups of women, nor did they seek alliances with other movements for social change. Some used McCarthyite tactics to try to win support for their goals, and the movement as a whole saw labor as an enemy and the civil rights movement as a competitor. Feminists developed strategies and pursued goals consistent with their interests and with the structure of their movement. Their three primary objectives were passage of the Equal Rights Amendment, increased representation of women in policy-making positions, and recognition of women's history.

The nature of this phase of activism raised some conceptual problems for us. In the contemporary U.S. women's movement, women of color, working-class women, and Jewish women have initiated a critique of the race, class, and cultural bias of a movement that defines only a limited set of goals, those that have traditionally been defined by the interests of white, middle-class, Christian women, as appropriate for a movement focusing on gender inequality. We are entirely in sympathy with this critique, but this did not lead us to broaden our definition of the women's rights movement in the fifties.

There are two ways, we think, in which the contemporary criticism of the Eurocentric, racist, bourgeois, and heterosexist elements in feminism can apply to the conceptualization of the women's movement in the past. One is to recognize a wide variety of struggles to improve women's inferior conditions as part of the women's movement, whether or not the women engaging in them saw themselves as feminists. The other is to stick to women's own self-identification in defining the boundaries of the movement but to recognize the way that the movement's class, race, national, and ethnic composition shaped its definition of interests and goals, recruitment strategies, levels of commitment, and mobilized resources (Rupp 1992). Both have merit, but it is the latter that we chose to use. Rather than explore the activities of women involved in such causes as civil rights, birth control, peace, and social justice, we sought to portray the history of a relatively encapsulated stage of the women's rights movement and to uncover the dynamics that made it that way. We envisaged our study as helping to understand the impact of the preoccupations of white, economically advantaged, heterosexual, Western women on the thinking and practices of feminism, preoccupations that contemporary feminists seek to decenter (A. Davis 1987; Giddings 1984; hooks 1984; Hewitt 1985; Spelman 1988; Nicholson 1990; Harding 1991).

This research revealed that the women's rights movement was able to survive, and feminists were able to sustain their commitment to feminism, by building a supportive community that valued feminist analysis, required high levels of commitment, was held together by intimate personal relationships, and was based to a large extent on ties from the days of the suffrage movement. All of these characteristics helped to create a close-knit world in which participation in the campaign for women's rights was possible, but they also meant that women not already drawn to the feminist cause would be unlikely to be recruited to the movement. In other words, organizational maintenance worked against mass mobilization.

Women's relationships, we came to believe, played a critical role in holding the movement together but also in limiting recruitment to a homogeneous group of women. Women formed a variety of bonds, from friendships to mother-daughter or sororal relationships to couple relationships. In considering the latter, the question of lesbianism—or the "lavender herring"—arose. In the papers of organizations and individuals, we found evidence of women who lived together in marriagelike relationships and formed communities with similar couples. For example, former Vassar College roommates and National Woman's Party members Alma Lutz and Marguerite Smith shared a Boston apartment and summer home, Highmeadow, in the Berkshires from 1918 until Smith's death in 1959. Mabel Vernon, a militant suffragist and worker for peace, and her "devoted companion" Consuelo Reyes, who had met through the Inter-American Commission of Women, spent every summer at Highmeadow with them. Woman's Party members and animal rights activists Alice Morgan Wright and Edith Goode, described as "always together," visited on occasion.

Further evidence suggested that at least some members viewed some relationships between women as lesbian or lesbianlike. One woman who broke away from the National Woman's Party in the forties recorded in her diary "that there was 'talk'"[1] about members Jeannette Marks and Mary Woolley, who lived together for almost fifty years and made "a mutual declaration of ardent and exclusive love" and "exchanged tokens, a ring and a jeweled pin, with pledges of lifelong fidelity" (Wells 1978). The same diarist reported a conversation in which an informant, grown disillusioned with Woman's Party founder and leading light Alice Paul, related "weird goings on at Wash. hedquts. wherein it was clear she thought Paul a devotee of Lesbos & afflicted with Jeanne d'Arc identification."[2] Along the same lines, the daughter of a woman who had left the Woman's Party complained that Alice Paul and another member sent her mother a telegram that "anybody with sense" would think "was from two people who were adolesant or from two who had imbied too much or else Lesbians to a Lesbian."[3]

Were these women lesbians? Does it matter? These are questions with which we had to grapple in the course of our research. None of the women we studied identified as lesbians in a time during which working-class women had created a public bar culture and the female homophile movement had begun to publish an openly lesbian periodical, *The Ladder* (Nestle 1981; Faderman 1991; Kennedy and Davis 1993). Furthermore, we found indications that some of them, at least, disapproved of lesbians. Alice Paul, for example, who attracted intense devotion from women followers and formed close relationships with a number of women, spoke scornfully in the seventies of *Ms.* magazine as "all about homosexuality and so on."[4] We interviewed another Woman's Party member living with a woman friend who, while we talked, went about the house doing the laundry, cooking dinner, and bringing us drinks. Yet this interviewee made it clear that she disapproved of the "lesbians and bra-burners" of the contemporary movement, whom she contrasted to the "respectable" women involved in the ERA struggle in the old days.[5]

So even when we knew that women had chosen women for their life partners, we hesitated to call them "lesbians." Nor, in our interviews, did we tell women that we were lesbians or ask them explicitly about lesbianism in the movement. The women we interviewed ranged in age from their midsixties to their early eighties, and in many cases the interview became a kind of social event, involving food and general conversation. We thought that bringing up lesbianism—even in a general rather than a personal way—would have been imposing contemporary conceptions and violating the atmosphere of the interaction. Barbara Levy Simon, in her book *Never Married Women* (1987), describes a similar dilemma. In fact, her attempt to initiate questions about sexual activity with her older women interviewees broke their rapport and, in at least one case, led to a request that she leave the house.

Ultimately we relied on a woman who is now a lesbian feminist scholar and had had some contact with the women's movement in earlier decades for perceptions about women's relationships in the movement.[6] Our experience with this aspect of the interviewing process represented one of the contradictions embedded in a feminist approach to research. Our own feminist perspectives, and particularly our lesbian feminist standpoint, led to an interest in the role of women's relationships during an earlier stage of activism.[7] But a feminist approach to interviewing—especially the call to validate women's subjective experiences and to learn about interviewees' worlds in their terms—did not allow us to impose our own definitions in framing questions about lesbians and the women's movement (Oakley 1981; Fonow and Cook 1991; Mies 1991). We recognize, however, that the decisions we made could contribute to the invisibility of lesbian lives.

To answer directly the questions of whether or not women's rights activists in couple relationships were lesbians and whether or not it matters for the history of the women's movement, we would say that yes, it matters. But no, we cannot call them lesbians despite their life partnerships or emotional commitment to women. We believe that it is important to pay attention to women's relationships, to describe carefully and sensitively what we do know about them, keeping in mind both the historical development of a lesbian identity and the individual process that we now identify as "coming out." Did such a thing as a lesbian identity exist? Was there a lesbian culture? Did a woman express love or passion for other women? Did she choose a woman for a life partner? Did she recognize the existence of other women with the same kind of commitments? Did she express solidarity with such women? Did she identify as a lesbian? In a world in which some women claimed a lesbian identity and built lesbian communities, the choice to reject that identification has a meaning of its own (Rupp 1989).

RESEARCHING LESBIAN FEMINIST COMMUNITIES

Our research on contemporary lesbian feminist communities might seem worlds apart from our work on the women's rights movement, but we came to both because we saw similarities in the external environment of the two phases of movement activity (Rupp and Taylor 1991). Feminists in both periods confronted a particularly antifeminist social climate that thwarted their efforts to mobilize. After 1945, the escalation of the cold war and the rise of domestic anti-communism stifled social protest, and the cultural ideal of the "feminine mystique" affirmed the restoration of family life and discredited women who protested gender inequality.

Lesbian feminists in the eighties faced a similarly inhospitable social milieu (Chafetz and Dworkin 1987; Echols 1989; Taylor 1989a; Buechler 1990; Castro 1990; F. Davis 1991; Faludi 1991; Ryan 1992; Taylor and Whittier 1993; Ferree and Hess 1994; Ransdell 1995). The other social movements of the sixties, which gave birth to the radical branch of the women's movement, began to ebb in the late seventies. Explicit antifeminism emerged as a major foundation of the New Right, and the election of Ronald Reagan reflected the power of that movement. With the defeat of the Equal Rights Amendment and increasing challenges to reproductive freedom, on the one hand, and complacency among some young women who saw no further need for feminism, on the other, the media gleefully proclaimed the death of feminism. The heyday of the contemporary women's movement gave way by the late seventies to a period of abeyance. Lesbian feminists, like the earlier women's rights advocates, hung on in a climate of declining opportunities.

When we first began to talk in our classes and to community groups about our research on postwar women's rights activists, we felt compelled to explain that feminism in the forties and fifties seemed anachronistic and old-fashioned in contrast to feminism in more recent years. But by about 1985, we realized that feminism as an anachronism no longer needed explaining to the student-age population: they, too, thought of feminism as out of date, the province of women in their thirties or forties. We began to worry about the costs of survival, the dangers of insularity. At the same time, we began to puzzle over the fact that women's culture and intimate bonds between women have, by and large, played a benevolent role in the historiography of the women's movement, yet what had come to be called "cultural feminism" was increasingly blamed for the death of radical feminism ([Williams] 1975; Atkinson 1984; hooks 1984; Ringelheim 1985; Alcoff 1988; Echols 1989; Young 1990). This led us to a reconsideration of cultural feminism (Taylor and Rupp 1993).

Cultural feminism, according to its critics, emphasizes essential differences between women and men, advocates separatism, and focuses on the creation of alternative institutions, thus beating a retreat from politics to "lifestyle." What struck us was the fact that cultural feminism is so closely identified with lesbianism, for essentialism, separatism, and institution building are all strongly associated with lesbian communities. Early on, Redstockings member Brooke Williams (1975), herself a lesbian, identified the development of cultural feminism with the rise of lesbianism as an issue within the women's movement. Alice Echols (1989), also a lesbian and the most influential critic of cultural feminism, sees the tendency as growing out of but modifying lesbian feminism. In the context of the "sex wars" of the eighties—the debate within the movement over whether sexuality for women is more closely associated with pleasure or danger—cultural feminism came to stand for "anti-sex" lesbian feminism (Snitow, Stansell, and Thompson 1983; Vance 1984). In fact, the attack on cultural feminism seemed to us a disguised attack on lesbian feminism.

So we decided to explore "women's culture" in order to evaluate its impact on feminist activism. Has "women's culture" brought about the depoliticization of the women's movement? Or has it helped feminism to survive? In order to understand "women's culture," we focused on the lesbian feminist communities in which it is produced. We used the term "lesbian feminist communities" rather than the euphemistic "women's community" in order to make explicit the role of lesbians in creating and sustaining "women's culture," by which we mean not only music, literature, and art but also alternative institutions such as rape crisis centers, battered women's shelters, bookstores, newspapers, publishing and recording companies, recovery and other self-help groups, spirituality groups, restaurants and coffeehouses, and other women-owned businesses. Our analysis was based on books, periodicals, and narratives by community members; newsletters, position papers, and other documents from lesbian feminist organizations; formal and informal interviews with members of a variety of communities; and participant observation in Columbus, Ohio, and at national women's events over the last fifteen years. We identified four elements of lesbian feminist culture that we think promoted the survival of the women's movement in a period in which new recruits were not flocking to the women's movement: female values, separatism, the primacy of women's relationships, and feminist ritual. We argued that far from leading to the demise of feminism, the culture of lesbian feminist communities both serves as a base of mobilization for women involved in a wide range of protest activities aimed at political and institutional change and, throughout the eighties and into the nineties, provides continuity from earlier stages of the women's movement to the signs of a new flowering of feminism.

With regard to the question of lesbianism, the standpoint we took on lesbian lives in this contemporary research was quite different from the standpoint that framed our earlier study of the women's rights movement. Not only were we explicitly studying lesbians but we also made many of our observations as participants in a lesbian feminist community, and we ourselves came out as lesbian feminists in the article we wrote. To be honest, the fact that we were both by this time tenured and out in almost every aspect of our personal and professional lives, despite the risks ("Report" 1982; Taylor and Raeburn 1995), had some impact on these decisions. But we simply would not have been able to do this research without being involved over a long period of time in the lesbian feminist community. It is not that insider status gave us a privileged vantage point on some "true" story of the community, but rather that we had knowledge of ephemeral developments that might not appear in any written sources or oral histories and were able to interview women who were willing to speak with us because they knew that we were lesbians and trusted that we would generate our analysis from a lesbian feminist standpoint. Outsiders to the community might have taken notice of elements we took for granted, but they would probably have had trouble getting access. But our position as insiders did not eliminate all dilemmas with regard to the "lavender herring." The crucial question was not so much "Is she a lesbian?" although that is often a complex question, as it was "Is she a lesbian feminist?" In other words, as feminism has increasingly become itself a contested zone—that is, there is no single set of claims that can be agreed on among feminists—the critical issue is defining the boundaries and characteristics of lesbian feminist communities.

What does it mean to be a lesbian feminist? Some members of the lesbian feminist community define lesbianism as woman-identification and resistance to patriarchy rather than by sexual attraction to or involvement with women. As one woman put it, lesbianism is "an attempt to stop doing what you were taught—hating women."[8] Adrienne Rich's classic article "Compulsory Heterosexuality and Lesbian Existence" (1980) introduced the notion of the "lesbian continuum," which embraces women who resist male control but are not sexual with women. In the same vein, Marilyn Frye (1990), in an address to the 1990 National Women's Studies Association conference entitled "Do You Have to Be a Lesbian to Be a Feminist?" equated lesbianism with rebellion against patriarchal institutions.

In fact, lesbian feminist communities contain some women who are oriented toward women emotionally and politically but not sexually; they are sometimes referred to as "political dykes" or "heterodykes" (Clausen 1990; Smeller n.d.). Some are women in the process of coming out and some are "going in," or moving from lesbian to heterosexual relationships (Bart 1993). For example, Holly Near (1990) explains in her autobiography that she continues to call herself a lesbian even though she is heterosexually active because of the importance of such a political identity. Expressing the same commitment, a feminist support group sprang up at Ohio State University called "Lesbians Who Just Happen To Be in Relationships with Politically-Correct Men." Lesbian identity is so salient to involvement in the "women's community" that even some women who are not, or not yet, or no longer involved sexually with women claim it.

Most lesbians are, of course, erotically attracted to other women, and there is a strong current within the community critical of the downplaying of sexuality. The popularity of lesbian sex expert JoAnn Loulan (1990), who was brought to Columbus in 1991 by a women's recovery group, indicates that the erotic aspects of lesbian relationships have not been completely submerged. The "sex wars" of the early eighties have spawned or reaffirmed an assertively sexual style on the part of some members of the lesbian feminist community. Advocates of sexual expressiveness, including champions of butch-fem roles and sadomasochism, challenge the less sexual style of what SM practitioners call "vanilla lesbians" and denounce the notion of "politically correct" sex (Califia 1981; Dimen 1984). The lines are explicitly drawn by the very titles of the periodicals associated with each camp: *off our backs*, the classic radical feminist paper, now confronts *On Our Backs* with its sexual "bad girl" style. And the deliberate—and tongue-in-cheek—revision of that title by the founders of *On Our Backs* indicates how much the two publications are in dialogue.

Lesbian feminist communities may be riven by conflict over the nature and proper expression of lesbian sexuality, but sexual relationships are the glue that hold communities together. Highly committed activists tend to form partnerships with each other because, as one woman notes, otherwise "there's too much political conflict."[9] Political organizing, meetings, and conferences become occasions for meeting lovers or spending time with a partner. Women's relationships often structure their entire social worlds. Within the community, lesbian couples or groups of single and paired lesbians construct familylike ties with one another, celebrating holidays, birthdays, commitment ceremonies, birthings, and anniversaries with other lesbians.

We argued, then, that what has been called "cultural feminism"—and it is significant that this is not a label that any women, as far as we know, apply to themselves—is only one ideological strand in the complex culture of lesbian feminist communities, which are made up of women with diverse views and experiences. The lesbian feminist community encompasses cultural feminists and their critics, "anti-sex" and "pro-sex" feminists, separatists and antiseparatists. For us, what is important is that debate over essentialism, separatism, sexuality, and so on takes place *within* the lesbian feminist community. So we defined "lesbian feminists" not so much through their association with an ideological position as through their involvement in a concrete social movement community.

We concluded that lesbian feminist communities both sustain the women involved in them and also are having consequences for what we see as a resurgence of support for feminism among young women. Belief in female difference, limited or total separatism, the primacy of women's relationships, and feminist ritual create a world apart from the mainstream in which women can claim feminism as a political identity. Some young women drawn to the movement are themselves lesbians, but even for those who are not, the link in public discourse between lesbianism and feminism has an impact (Dill "Intersection"). In addition, lesbian feminist communities influence other struggles for social justice (Cavin 1990; Whittier 1995). Beginning with opposition to nuclear power and spreading to the issues of peace, nonintervention, ecological preservation, and gay and lesbian liberation, the direct action movement has adopted from the lesbian feminist community a view of revolution as an ongoing process of personal and social transformation, an emphasis on egalitarianism and consensus decision-making, an orientation toward spirituality, and a commitment to shaping present action according to the values desired in an ideal future world (Epstein 1991; Lichterman n.d.). Similarly, the ongoing dialogue in the lesbian feminist community about diversity has carried over into the gaylesbian movement, and the radical feminist analysis of rape shapes the struggle against anti-gay-lesbian violence (Vaid 1991). Further, the AIDS movement has been driven by the radical feminist definition of control of one's body and access to health care as political issues ("Women" 1991). And lesbians have played a leading role in the development of the recovery movement for survivors of incest (Galst 1991). In short, lesbian feminist cultures of resistance have had political impact not only by sheltering battle-weary feminists but also by influencing the course of other social movements.

CONCLUSION

These two research projects, although quite different, led us to two general conclusions. First, we found that "lesbian existence" is an important topic—not a lavender herring—in analyzing the internal dynamics of the women's movement in different phases. Our experience with this research convinced us of the need to deal sensitively with the question of women's relationships, keeping in mind the historical context.

Recognizing the importance of woman-bonding raises the specter of admitting that, although lesbianism and feminism are not synonymous, they are linked historically. Within the women's movement, feminists fear that this linkage is largely responsible for the tendency of young women to distance themselves from feminism. "I'm not a feminist, but . . ." often prefaces support for feminist goals, and the unacknowledged message is that "I'm not a lesbian, but I am a feminist" (Schneider 1988, n.d.; Kamen 1991; Dill "Qualified"). Such anxiety about the impact of lesbian participation in the women's movement on recruitment of young women has, we think, too often led to the downplaying of lesbian contributions. For example, at an academic feminist conference at which one of us raised a question about lesbian involvement in a particular phase of activism, a noted scholar of the women's movement reacted defensively, assuming that lesbian participation would discredit the movement, until she learned that the question came from a lesbian. She then discussed the central role of lesbians in the organizations she had studied and admitted glossing over the question of sexual identity in her published work in order to protect the women involved. This suggests how important it is to give lesbians and other "woman-identified women" their rightful places in the history of the women's movement.

Second, the similarities between these two quite different cases suggested to us that women's relationships are especially crucial to the maintenance of the movement when mass support for feminism ebbs, for such bonds tie together groups of women who are unlikely to find acceptance for their relationships outside the movement. In fact, the women's movement seems to provide a sort of "cover," albeit in a transparent closet, for women not ready to assume public lesbian identities. The connection between activism and woman-bonding (lesbian or otherwise) is a symbiotic one: women with primary commitments to other women find support within the women's movement and in turn pour their energies into it. Thus we came to argue that women's relationships (of various sorts) have historically played a critical role in the survival of feminism in a hostile social environment.

This does not mean that there are no costs associated with insular survival. As we have seen, the women's rights activists in the forties and fifties sustained their vision in a homogeneous community that did not and could not attract women of color, working-class women, or young women. In the same way, the ideas and practices of lesbian feminist communities can exclude potential participants. Most obviously, the majority of heterosexual feminists may not find the lesbian world congenial. In recognition of lesbian preponderance and potential difficulty for heterosexual women, the 1992 Bloomington Women's Music Festival offered the workshop "Networking for Straight Women in a Lesbian World."[10] Equally as important, the dominance of white, middle-class, Christian women, despite the ongoing dialogue in the lesbian feminist community about race, class, ethnic, and other differences, creates barriers to the achievement of a truly multicultural environment.

But we remain optimistic about the future. In our research on women's rights activists in the post-1945 period, we found these women decrying the lack of "young blood" but unwilling to accept the new ideas and new strategies that young women might bring with them. An aging generation of feminists may always long for fresh recruits who will be drawn to their cause but will not change anything about the movement. The round of the women's movement that seems to be blossoming is likely to take a different course, but it will not be untouched by the collective processes, consciousness, and practices of lesbian feminism. As an indication of how far we have come from the days when the National Organization for Women forbade lesbian banners in pro-ERA demonstrations (Mansbridge 1986), lesbian and gay rights are to become a focus of NOW action for the midnineties.[11] Rather than squelching mobilization, we see lesbian feminist communities as bequeathing a legacy, however imperfect, to the "third wave" of the movement. Lesbians and other woman-identified women of the past do not represent, then, a "lavender herring" or "lavender menace," but constitute an important force for the survival of the women's movement across time.

NOTES

We are full coauthors and have listed our names in reverse alphabetical order. This essay is based on our experience researching *Survival in the Doldrums* and "Women's Culture and Lesbian Feminist Activism: A Reconsideration of Cultural Feminism." We earlier wrote about the process of researching *Survival in the Doldrums* in "Researching the Women's Movement: We Make Our Own History, but Not Just as We Please."

1. Doris Stevens, diary entry, Feb. 4, 1946, Doris Stevens papers, Schlesinger Library, Radcliffe College.
2. Doris Stevens, diary entry, Dec. 1, 1945, Doris Stevens papers.
3. Katharine Callery to Doris Stevens, Aug. 17, 1944, Doris Stevens papers.
4. Alice Paul, "Conversations with Alice Paul: Woman Suffrage and the Equal Rights Amendment," an oral history conducted in 1972 and 1973 by Amelia R. Fry, Regional Oral History Office, University of California, 1976, 195–96.
5. Interview conducted by Verta Taylor and Leila Rupp, 1979.
6. Interview with Monika Kehoe, conducted by Verta Taylor and Leila Rupp, 1982.
7. Our use of "standpoint" here follows Harding (1991), who identifies seven contributions to feminist thought from "thinking from the perspective of lesbian lives": seeing women in relation to other women; seeing and imagining communities that do not need or want men socially; conceptualizing heterosexuality as socially constructed; centering female sexuality as constructed by women; perceiving a link between the oppression of women and the oppression of deviant sexualities; seeing the ways that gynophobia supports racism; and suggesting that the lesbian is a central figure in traditional male discourses.
8. Interview conducted by Nancy Whittier, 1987.
9. Interview conducted by Verta Taylor, 1987.
10. Correspondence with Suzanne Staggenborg, 1992.
11. Interview conducted by Jo Reger, 1992.

REFERENCES

Alcoff, Linda. 1988. "Cultural Feminism versus Post-structuralism: The Identity Crisis in Feminist Theory." *Signs* 13 (3): 405–36.

Atkinson, Ti-Grace. 1984. "Le Nationalisme feminin." *Nouvelles questions feministes* 6–7:35–54.

Bart, Pauline B. 1993. "Protean Woman: The Liquidity of Female Sexuality and the Tenaciousness of Lesbian Identity." In *Heterosexuality: A Feminism and Psychology Reader,* ed. Sue Wilkinson and Celia Kitzinger. London: Sage. 246–52.

Buechler, Steven M. 1990. *Women's Movements in the United States.* New Brunswick, N.J.: Rutgers University Press.
Califia, Pat. 1981. "Feminism and Sadomasochism." *Heresies* 12:30–34.
Castro, Ginette. 1990. *American Feminism: A Contemporary History.* New York: New York University Press.
Cavin, Susan. 1990. "The Invisible Army of Women: Lesbian Social Protests, 1969–1988." In *Women and Social Protest,* ed. Guida West and Rhoda Lois Blumberg. New York: Oxford University Press. 321–32.
Chafetz, Janet Saltzman, and A. Gary Dworkin. 1987. "In the Face of Threat: Organized Antifeminism in Comparative Perspective." *Gender and Society* 1 (1): 33–60.
Clausen, Jan. 1990. "My Interesting Condition." *OutLook* 7 (Winter): 10–21.
Davis, Angela Y. 1987. *Women, Race, and Class.* New York: Random House.
Davis, Flora. 1991. *Moving the Mountain: The Women's Movement in America since 1960.* New York: Simon and Schuster.
Dill, Kim. N.d. "The Intersection of Lesbian and Feminist Identity." Ms.
———. N.d. "Qualified Feminism and Its Influence on College Women's Identification with the Women's Movement." Ms.
Dimen, Muriel. 1984. "Politically Correct? Politically Incorrect?" In *Pleasure and Danger: Exploring Female Sexuality,* ed. Carole Vance. Boston: Routledge and Kegan Paul. 138–48.
Echols, Alice. 1989. *Daring to Be Bad: Radical Feminism in America, 1967–1975.* Minneapolis: University of Minnesota Press.
Epstein, Barbara. 1991. *Political Protest and Cultural Revolution: Nonviolent Direct Action in the 1970s and 1980s.* Berkeley: University of California Press.
Faderman, Lillian. 1991. *Odd Girls and Twilight Lovers: A History of Lesbian Life in Twentieth-Century America.* New York: Columbia University Press.
Faludi, Susan. 1991. *Backlash: The Undeclared War against American Women.* New York: Crown.
Ferree, Myra Marx, and Beth B. Hess. 1994. *Controversy and Coalition: The New Feminist Movement.* Rev. ed. Boston: Twayne.
Fonow, Mary Margaret, and Judith A. Cook. 1991. "Back to the Future: A Look at the Second Wave of Feminist Epistemology and Methodology." In *Beyond Methodology: Feminist Scholarship as Lived Research,* ed. Mary Margaret Fonow and Judith A. Cook. Bloomington: Indiana University Press. 1–15.
Frye, Marilyn. 1990. "Do You Have to Be a Lesbian to Be a Feminist?" *off our backs* 20 (Aug.): 21–23.
Giddings, Paula. 1984. *When and Where I Enter: The Impact of Black Women on Race and Sex in America.* New York: William Morrow.
Galst, Liz. 1991. "Overcoming Silence." *Advocate* (Dec. 3): 60–63.
Harding, Sandra. 1991. *Whose Science? Whose Knowledge?: Thinking from Women's Lives.* Ithaca: Cornell University Press.
Hewitt, Nancy A. 1985. "Beyond the Search for Sisterhood: American Women's History in the 1980s." *Social History* 10 (3): 299–321.
hooks, bell. 1984. *Feminist Theory: From Margin to Center.* Boston: South End Press.

Jaggar, Alison M. 1983. *Feminist Politics and Human Nature.* Totowa, N.J.: Rowman and Allanheld.

Kamen, Paula. 1991. *Feminist Fatale: Voices from the "Twentysomething" Generation Explore the Future of the "Women's Movement."* New York: Donald I. Fine.

Kennedy, Elizabeth Lapovsky and Madeline Davis. 1993. *Boots of Leather, Slippers of Gold: The History of a Lesbian Community.* New York: Routledge.

Lichterman, Paul. N.d. "When Is the Personal Political?: Class, Culture, and Political Style in U.S. Grassroots Environmentalism." Ms.

Loulan, JoAnn Gardner. 1990. *The Lesbian Erotic Dance: Butch, Femme, Androgyny, and Other Rhythms.* San Francisco: Spinsters Book Company.

Mansbridge, Jane. 1986. *Why We Lost the ERA.* Chicago: University of Chicago Press.

Mies, Maria. 1991. "Women's Research or Feminist Research?: The Debate Surrounding Feminist Science and Methodology." In *Beyond Methodology: Feminist Scholarship as Lived Research,* ed. Mary Margaret Fonow and Judith A. Cook. Bloomington: Indiana University Press. 60–84.

Oakley, Ann. 1981. "Interviewing Women: A Contradiction in Terms." In *Doing Feminist Research,* ed. Helen Roberts. London: Routledge and Kegan Paul. 30–61.

Near, Holly. 1990. *Fire in the Rain, Singer in the Storm.* New York: William Morrow.

Nestle, Joan. 1981. "Butch-Fem Relationships: Sexual Courage in the 1950s." *Heresies* 12 (Sex Issue): 21–24.

Nicholson, Linda J. 1990. *FeminismPostmodernism.* New York: Routledge.

Ransdell, Lisa. 1995. "Lesbian Feminism and the Feminist Movement." In *Women: A Feminist Perspective,* ed. Jo Freeman. 5th ed. Palo Alto, Calif.: Mayfield. 641–53.

"Report of the American Sociological Association's Task Group on Homosexuality." 1982. *American Sociologist* 17 (Aug.): 164–80.

Rich, Adrienne. 1980. "Compulsory Heterosexuality and Lesbian Existence." *Signs* 5 (4): 631–60.

Ringelheim, Joan. 1985. "Women and the Holocaust: A Reconsideration of Research." *Signs* 10 (4): 741–61.

Rupp, Leila J. 1992. "Eleanor Flexner's *Century of Struggle:* Women's History and the Women's Movement." *NWSA Journal* 4 (2): 157–69.

———. 1989. "'Imagine My Surprise': Women's Relationships in Mid-Twentieth Century America." In *Hidden from History: Reclaiming the Gay and Lesbian Past,* ed. Martin Bauml Duberman, Martha Vicinus, and George Chauncey, Jr. New York: New American Library. 395–410.

Rupp, Leila J., and Verta Taylor. 1991. "Women's Culture and the Continuity of the Women's Movement." In *Moving On: New Perspectives on the Women's Movement,* ed. Tayo Andreasen, Anette Borchorst, Drude Dahlevup, Eva Lous, and Hanne Rimmen Nielsen. Aarhus, Denmark: Aarhus University Press. 68–89.

———. 1987. *Survival in the Doldrums: The American Women's Rights Movement, 1945 to the 1960s.* New York: Oxford University Press.

Ryan, Barbara. 1992. *Feminism and the Women's Movement: Dynamics of Change in Social Movement, Ideology, and Activism.* New York: Routledge.

Schneider, Beth. 1988. "Political Generations in the Contemporary Women's Movement." *Sociological Inquiry* 58 (1): 4–21.

———. N.d. "The Feminist Disclaimer, Stigma, and the Contemporary Women's Movement." Ms.

Simon, Barbara Levy. 1987. *Never Married Women.* Philadelphia: Temple University Press.

Smeller, Michele M. N.d. "Crossing Over: The Negotiation of Sexual Identity in a Social Movement Community." Ms.

Snitow, Ann, Christine Stansell, and Sharon Thompson. 1983. *Powers of Desire: The Politics of Sexuality.* New York: Monthly Review Press.

Spelman, Elizabeth V. 1988. *Inessential Woman: Problems of Exclusion in Feminist Thought.* Boston: Beacon Press.

Taylor, Verta. 1989a. "The Future of Feminism: A Social Movement Analysis." In *Feminist Frontiers II: Rethinking Sex, Gender, and Society,* ed. Laurel Richardson and Verta Taylor. New York: Random House. 473–90.

———. 1989b. "Social Movement Continuity: The Women's Movement in Abeyance." *American Sociological Review* 54 (Oct.): 761–75.

Taylor, Verta, and Nicole C. Raeburn. 1995. "Identity Politics as High-Risk Activism: Consequences for Lesbian, Gay, and Bisexual Sociologists." *Social Problems* 42 (3): 101–23.

Taylor, Verta, and Leila J. Rupp. 1993. "Women's Culture and Lesbian Feminist Activism: A Reconsideration of Cultural Feminism." *Signs* 19 (1): 32–61.

———. 1991. "Researching the Women's Movement: We Make Our Own History, but Not Just as We Please." In *Beyond Methodology: Feminist Scholarship as Lived Research,* ed. Mary Margaret Fonow and Judith A. Cook. Bloomington: Indiana University Press. 119–32.

Taylor, Verta, and Nancy E. Whittier. 1993. "The New Feminist Movement." In *Feminist Frontiers III: Rethinking Sex, Gender, and Society,* ed. Laurel Richardson and Verta Taylor. New York: Random House. 533–48.

———. 1992. "Collective Identity in Social Movement Communities: Lesbian Feminist Mobilization." In *Frontiers of Social Movement Theory,* ed. Aldon Morris and Carol Mueller. New Haven: Yale University Press. 104–29.

Vaid, Urvashi. 1991. "Let's Put Our Own House in Order." *OutLook* 14 (Fall): 55–57.

Vance, Carole S., ed. 1984. *Pleasure and Danger: Exploring Female Sexuality.* Boston: Routledge and Kegan Paul.

Wells, Anna Mary. 1978. *Miss Marks and Miss Woolley.* Boston: Houghton Mifflin.

Whittier, Nancy E. 1995. *Feminist Generations: The Persistence of the Radical Women's Movement.* Philadelphia: Temple University Press.

[Williams], Brooke. 1975. "The Retreat to Cultural Feminism." In *Feminist Revolution,* ed. Redstockings. New Paltz: Redstockings. 79–83.

"Women in A.I.D.S. Activism." 1991. *off our backs* 21 (Nov.): 4–5.

Young, Iris Marion. 1990. "The Ideal of Community and the Politics of Difference." In *FeminismPostmodernism,* ed. Linda J. Nicholson. New York: Routledge. 300–323.

CHAPTER 8

NANCY A. NAPLES, WITH EMILY CLARK

Feminist Participatory Research and Empowerment: Going Public as Survivors of Childhood Sexual Abuse

Too often our attempts to bridge theory and practice occur at the level of theory rather than of practice. This study starts and ends with activism in order to contextualize the dilemmas of feminist praxis. The analysis is based on a dialogue between Emily Clark and myself, who are "going public" with our experiences of childhood sexual assault in an effort to challenge the medical/psychiatric discourse on treatment of adult survivors. We began our work together with activist goals but without a shared research methodology. This chapter centers my attempt to introduce feminist methodology to our work and to generate participatory research strategies. After a brief introduction, I present background on the broader activist project, summarize Emily's experiences of going public, then describe her influence on my own process. I next profile Emily's reluctance to articulate our work with feminist research strategies and chronicle my efforts to explain the relevance of feminist theories for our activist project. Here I center the attempt to develop a more egalitarian and participatory activist project through personal narrative and dialogue. Finally, I explore how to keep the link between activism and feminist theorizing alive.

Feminists argue for a methodology designed to break the false separation between the subject of research and the researcher (see, for example, Gergen 1988). The objectification of research subjects limits our understanding of the social construction of meaning and experience as well as the process by which the "relations of ruling" organize consciousness and daily life (see Smith 1987). However, what if we turn the problem on its head and start from the perspective of those whose lives we wish to understand. How do we present ourselves and our relationship to them? How do we remain credible to the identified "community"? How do we explain feminist theory and research and its significance for activist goals and objectives? In other words, what if we as researchers become the object of those we research? In this chapter I present the difficulties I encountered in trying to articulate what I believe should be a mutually reinforcing relationship between feminist theories and activism. I show the limits of such an endeavor and reveal the difficulty faced when we open our research agenda to comment and criticism from those we study. I also explore the tension between my own situated perspectives as a survivor of childhood sexual abuse and activist researcher.

Activist researchers enter "the field" in a variety of ways. Each point of entry influences our relationship to the "community," the strategies that we adopt, and the context for the participation of community members. Some activist researchers search for a community-based site through which they might assist in the political agendas defined by community members (see Maguire 1987; Whyte 1991). A second avenue develops when a group, community, or organization seeks outside assistance to generate research for social change (see Light and Kleiber 1988). Another avenue to activist research occurs when we enter "the field" as participants who are personally affected by the issue that is the focus of our work. Many of us who choose to use our personal and community-based struggles as sites for activist research did not begin the work with a research agenda in mind (for example, see Haywoode 1992). Since most personal and community-based problems are politically constituted, activists in the course of struggles against institutionalized relations of ruling inevitably discover the value of social science research to support social change efforts.

For those of us with a foot in each world, the process of negotiation between activism and research is fraught with a complex set of dilemmas. I attempt to negotiate these dilemmas by drawing upon participatory research strategies informed by feminist theories. While such approaches enhance the knowledge and relevance of data gathered to challenge oppression, they do not eliminate the tension between our shifting insider and outsider locations. As a survivor of childhood sexual abuse, I share a great deal with other survivors. However, my white, Irish-American, urban, working-class background, lesbian identity, education, profession, and political perspective (especially my feminist orientation) distance me from other survivors who do not share my sexual orientation, background, or perspective. This chapter illustrates the challenge of and limits to bridging theory and practice with particular focus on developing feminist participatory research.[1] It also chronicles my journey from survivor of childhood sexual abuse to activist "going public" with my experiences and finally to activist researcher in this arena. While not always a linear process, this reconstructed journey illustrates the value of feminist theory as well as friendship and self-reflective dialogue for enhancing participatory research.

BUILDING THE BRIDGE

On April 13, 1991, Emily Clark, at my invitation, addressed a large room of sociologists who attended a session entitled "Feminist Research Agendas: Conflicts and Dilemmas" held at the annual meeting of the Midwest Sociological Society (MSS). For Emily, the presentation was part of her overall goal to help adult survivors by breaking the denial of professionals who may be working with survivors of sexual abuse. For me, it was part of an ongoing effort to bridge the activist/researcher role. I set the stage, gave some background about our project, and then turned the floor over to Emily, who was to briefly tell her story and describe her experience of "going public." In the course of her talk she commented on the limited vision of academics who sit in their offices away from "real people" and make up theories that have nothing to do with people's lives. She used as an example her experience with a psychology professor who taught the one and only college course she attended.[2] The professor was teaching a section on abuse and Emily felt she "had it all wrong" so she went to see her during office hours. She experienced the professor as very set in her ways and, as Emily explained to the room full of professors, "Well, you know how they are, these professors who teach the same things year after year from worn-out notes." The room burst out in laughter and many of us walked away with the knowledge that Emily had objectified us in much the same way we objectify those we study in similar forums. It was a sobering experience yet it also illustrated the irony in the feminist call to break down the barriers between ourselves and those we study. We rarely develop sites in which those we study participate equally in the research enterprise or in conceptualizing the dilemmas in such an undertaking. My own journey illustrates another challenging dilemma: How do we incorporate our position as indigenous to the community we study with our outsider position as feminist researchers?

I met Emily through the Satori Healing Collective in Des Moines, a group formed in the spring of 1989 by survivors and supporters who were dissatisfied with the lack of treatment alternatives available for adult survivors of childhood sexual abuse. The group included a survivor who counsels adult survivors and several women who had been in counseling with her. I was introduced to the group by one of my students who was a member of the Collective and who knew of my work with adult survivors. At that time, my work with adult survivors was personal rather than professional. Upon moving to Iowa from New York City, I helped organize three mutual aid support groups that met weekly, with some breaks between groups, from September 1989 to December 1992. Emily, a native Iowan, was one of the original members of the collective. The collective last met formally in May 1990. Its future remains uncertain; however, individual members are pursuing separate projects that grew out of our group discussions.

Together Emily and I recognized a mutual interest in developing an activist research project designed to assess the prevalence of childhood sexual abuse in Iowa and raise the consciousness of social service providers and health professionals about the effects of childhood sexual abuse.[3] The evidence gathered in the course of our research will be used to advocate treatment alternatives designed from the point of view of survivors themselves. Mental health workers are not immune from the societal pressure to deny the prevalence of childhood sexual abuse. As a consequence, many of us who turn to mental health professionals for help do not receive the acceptance, safety, and trust needed for recovery. On the other hand, there is growing evidence that a disproportionate number of health professionals and social service workers are themselves survivors of childhood sexual abuse (Rew 1989; Williams 1990). Therefore, the broader activist research project includes the complicated goal of raising the consciousness of mental health workers as well as reaching out to other survivors.

We began with the belief that healing from childhood sexual abuse occurs most effectively through collective group processes and mutual aid support from other survivors coupled with supportive counseling.[4] Both of us have benefited from the support of other survivors and supportive counselors who helped us "name" the problem and examine how it affected all areas of our lives. Both of us are now committed to transforming the treatment available for adult survivors through sharing our experiences with mental health professionals, students, and other community members. While we agreed on the overall purpose of our work for and with other survivors, each of us had a different conceptualization of the specific focuses for the project and the methodologies we would employ. The difference can be understood in terms of our contrasting personal histories and social locations.

The dialogue that became the backdrop for this chapter took place on numerous occasions from the winter of 1989 to the fall of 1992. During that time, I was a faculty member at Iowa State University. Emily, a mother of three boys, worked full-time in the business she owns with her husband. While we both were born in the early fifties, we grew up in different social milieus and had differing political histories. I am a native New Yorker and became politically active in the anti–Vietnam War movement and, later, the women's movement. I define myself as a feminist and view my recovery through my feminist identity. By contrast, Emily, a native of Iowa, regards both the women's movement and feminism as peripheral, if not irrelevant, to her work for and with adult survivors. Despite our different views on feminism, we both placed finding our voices and speaking out as central to our survival. It is this commonality in our survival strategies that made our dialogue possible.

The material generated through this dialogic process ranged from discussions of our personal histories that included the stories of our abuse and recovery to reflections on contemporary events and dreams for the future. This chapter focuses on my attempts to bridge our activist goals with the feminist methodological call to break the subject/object dichotomy and remain self-reflective throughout the research process. I am the primary author. Emily shaped the dialogue and commented on the numerous drafts. Through our ongoing dialogue, we made self-conscious the narrative by which we explored our process of "going public" as survivors of childhood sexual assault. Our specific goal for this dialogue was to generate situated knowledge about the coming out process that will, in turn, inform us as we continue to "go public."

GOING PUBLIC: EXCERPTS FROM A SURVIVORS' DIALOGUE

Before I met Emily I resisted "going public" with my experiences as a survivor of childhood sexual abuse. Emily modeled for me the benefits and politics of going public. It is through her example and with her support that I moved from the personal to political stance I now hold as a survivor. Emily believes that by telling her story directly to mental health professionals she could help break their denial of the extent to which childhood sexual abuse occurs. When Emily first spoke out it was at the invitation of her therapist, who asked if she would share her experiences with other health care professionals. Emily agreed and recalled how she felt when she addressed the public forum of two hundred medical doctors and other health professionals:

> I was very nervous, but proud that I was able to stand in front of a crowd with all eyes focused on me. I chose to be there to share my experiences. No one was forcing me or taking anything away from me. I was afraid I would be too nervous to get across what I intended to, but it went OK for my first time. I was nervous both times [I spoke in public about the incest], but the two audiences were different so what I chose to share was a little different in content. Speaking the truth gave me confidence and trust in myself to go on.

She remembered that when she spoke to the physicians and nurses "one physician in the middle row was sitting there [with a look on his face that said] 'Give me a break.'" Yet after finishing her story, she saw his face soften and she concluded that some of his denial had lifted. In this way, Emily believed that by going public in this professional medical forum she had made a difference for the adult survivors who would seek help from this physician in the future. She hoped that others present at the forum were similarly affected. Emily is especially concerned about the extent to which mental health workers themselves may be survivors of childhood sexual assault. If they have not worked to heal from the abuse, "how can they be effective if they are triggered," she said. Finally, Emily hopes to "break through to those sensitive people with the ability to care," thus expanding the network of support that exists for survivors.

Emily defines her desire to speak out as a natural extension of the "caretaker" role she assumed in her family of origin. She recalled: "I was the 'caretaker' of the family. My brothers and sister obviously choose to survive in a quieter way. I took it upon myself to go looking for my parents when I didn't know where they were [to see if they were abusing any of my siblings]. I guess it was a need to know, to gather the truth. I hated our ugly secrets and being kept quiet with threats. I wanted to be big [so] that when I got big I would tell. And I wanted to help my brothers and sisters." Emily's outspokenness was evident early. At the age of eight she told her aunt about the abuse occurring in her household. The aunt confronted her mother, who convinced the aunt "to keep the secret to save my mother from public embarrassment." Emily was further abused by her mother for speaking the truth. She recollected: "My mother slapped me and said she would kill me if I ever told again. Those kinds of threats and intimidation are what keep victims quiet. It's very effective and long lasting." Emily recognized when she was ten years old that speaking out was one of the most powerful weapons she had for fighting her abusers: "When I was ten years old, following a particularly brutal attack, I had a fierce desire to stick a knife in my father's back. But within minutes I decided that what would hurt him the most would be to live among people who knew what he truly was. I would live and he would live to hear the truth be told. The belief that I would *someday* be free to speak of the horrors we survived kept me going day after day." But it was not until years had passed and she was fighting to save her marriage that she sought therapy, which subsequently helped her find her voice again. She explained: "But through my strong desire to be happy I fought the fear that kept me silent and sought a therapist to safely guide me once again through the hidden memories of my past. In the beginning, fighting the repression was a real battle. I felt it in the physical sense. At times I would catch myself saying, 'Yes,' 'No,' 'Yes,' 'No,' until finally the 'Yes' won." Once she faced the pain of her childhood, she quickly confronted her father and spoke out to other family members.

> Within the first few months of my therapy I confronted my parents with the emerging knowledge of my [previously] concealed childhood. And I visited each of my brothers and [my] sister, telling them that we were all sexually abused by our parents. Then towards the end of my therapy I realized that it only mattered that I know the truth. I no longer desired to publish the facts in my parents' city newspaper or enlighten their neighbors and friends about their secret lives. I had let go of a ten-year-old child's thirst for that kind of self-destructive revenge. I began to sense that the focus of my desire to "tell" was shifting from my family of origin. My attention and concern was spreading to all the families out there who, behind closed doors, are suffering similar secretive existences.

The process of her recovery led Emily to reaffirm the power of her voice as a tool to dispute those who deny the existence or the extent of childhood sexual abuse. She asserts: "I know I have knowledge, through victimization and through healing, that is valuable to others. I want to share what I have learned. Maybe a small part of the caretaker is still in me. Maybe it needs to be there for the welfare and education of others. And for my continued growth."

For me, the decision to go public as a political act was less clear-cut and fraught with fears that it would compromise my legitimacy as a "professional." As I explained to Emily:

> When I first began my healing process, I was adamant that I wanted to keep my personal and professional lives separate; that I didn't want to threaten my recovery by bringing it into the unfriendly, alienating

> "professional" realm. I said to myself: "This is something that's about me and it's personal" and that I was sure that I didn't want to turn it into work. At the time, I thought that so much of my past was lost to the abuse that I didn't want to give my work life over to it as well.

However, my interactions with colleagues in social work and women's studies forced me to recognize the hypocrisy in encouraging them to see their personal issues as political when I continued to resist doing so myself. The lesson was brought home to me in one particularly painful meeting with six psychologists and sociologists, all men, who were in the process of designing a research project to assess the needs of adult survivors. I found that it was impossible to keep the worlds separate. I recalled that "I felt torn between my professional identity, the desire to establish legitimacy, and finding my voice to say: 'But it's about me too.' I have some really deeply personal interest in this issue. And that goes against the 'professional discourse' which emphasizes that we keep a 'safe' distance from the issues we study." But I still wasn't comfortable telling, going public in my classes, or speaking out in other more professional contexts until I had the opportunity to witness the effect that Emily and Leslie, another survivor who was also a member of the Satori Healing Collective, had when they told their story to social work students at Iowa State University.

I invited Emily and Leslie to share their experiences as survivors of childhood sexual assault with undergraduate social work students enrolled in a senior practicum seminar. I was impressed with their powerful presentation and kept thinking: "Yes, this is the way to teach, to share." They were both so open and honest that the students were moved to share their own experiences and fears in working with victims of sexual assault. I remembered thinking that my own reluctance to share my experiences inhibited the learning process as well as my own effectiveness as an educator. When Emily and Leslie finished and left the classroom, the professor in charge asked me to stay because he was unsure how to handle any additional questions. I facilitated the discussion with the students and used the word *we*, as in "we as survivors," and I felt much more powerful in myself as well as in my role as teacher. I didn't share any personal details, just the word *we*. It was the first time I ever really owned it in a forum like that. I did share with individual students who came to talk with me about their struggles as survivors or who wanted information about sexual abuse, but I never shared it in a forum in which the point of view of the audience was unknown. This event marks the turning point in my own process of "going public."

Over the course of our meetings and conversations, it became clear to me that for Emily speaking out was an inevitable and logical outcome of her personal history and healing process. I shared with her my fears about going public and we explored why I had more difficulty. We both agreed that my resistance may relate in part to the shame that remains. But it also relates to a fear that it would compromise my legitimacy as a professional. I continue to grapple with this tension even as I write these words. Ironically, I found myself making sense of my desire to go public in terms of feminist theory, which forms the basis for my professional work. I also recognized it as an opportunity to begin to challenge the separation between activist/researcher and personal/political that so haunted me. It is at this point that Emily and I began to grapple with our different standpoints on the research project.

During this phase of our work together, I found myself pushed by Emily's incisive questioning to explain and justify the relevance of theories of feminist methodology for the activist project. My first attempts were more or less successful in that Emily agreed to proceed with the discussions of feminist methodology. I was later to realize that her assent was more an act of friendship than of mutual agreement on the centrality of feminist methodology to our work.

BRIDGING THEORY AND ACTIVISM THROUGH FRIENDSHIP

Emily had modeled for me a way to make my personal experiences part of my political actions. I learned a great deal about the effect of speaking out for one's personal healing and politics. Yet I incorporated these lessons through a deep belief in and commitment to feminist praxis. For me this meant remaining self-conscious about my social location and political commitment and consistently reflecting upon the work itself. I came to see my work with Emily through this process. As my fears about keeping my personal experiences as a survivor separate from my professional identity eased, I began to articulate the links between feminist theories about the research process and the ongoing dialogue that formed the basis for our activist project. The first phase of this articulation resulted in our presentation at the MSS meeting in 1991. Emily agreed to participate in this effort because she saw it as another opportunity to reach professional educators who might be in the position to identify and support adult survivors. She was less enthusiastic about the implications of feminist methodology for our work.

I argued to myself and Emily that it was important to explore how to break these divisions down so that feminist researchers can be more effective in our work and that the outcome of the work would be more relevant to women's lives. In seeking Emily's support in exploring the relevance of feminist methodology for our project, I argued that through our ongoing dialogue we can address three issues that are significant to feminist inquiry. First, we could contest the limits placed on notions of what are legitimate kinds of research. Second, we could contest the top-down and hierarchical ways in which research typically proceeds. Third, we could further demonstrate the value of knowledge generated from the point of view of those whose lives are shaped by social phenomenon, in this case childhood sexual abuse. I explained to Emily that the dominant way to conduct research in sociology is one that stresses objectification, random sampling, control groups, standardized measurement, and large sample sizes. This is why I believe that the feminist critiques of social science are so important—especially the assertion that who we are personally affects how we go about our work. Whether we want to own that or not, whether we are self-conscious about this fact or not our standpoint shapes the way we proceed to gather information and draw conclusions from that information. And as healers, as caretakers, as health care workers, or as researchers, if you have not dealt with your own issues then they get played out in other ways that can further damage victims and inhibit your understanding of their lives.

Emily did not need convincing that one's standpoint "affects how you see the world" as she put it, but was less interested in the implications of this formulation for our research process. I further explained that my goal was to understand the consequences of speaking from our own standpoint, our own experience, and having that form the questions we raise. If we have a research concern that grows out of personal experiences, how do we develop a way of working in terms of the research process that keeps us connected to that personal concern rather than turning it into an objective, alienated study? For example, I did not want to conduct this research by sending questionnaires out to incest survivors. I believe it alienates people and objectifies their lives. I do not even know what questions to ask. Rather, for me, the more effective way is to have the research evolve out of dialogue, out of people coming together and creating a new understanding of the healing process in order to define effective strategies for recovery and, hopefully, to design more effective political strategies so that we can break through the denial that surrounds childhood sexual abuse.

Despite my best efforts, Emily remained unconvinced about the relevance of feminist theory for the activist project. She did not identify with feminism nor did she have much patience for self-reflexive discussions about the research process. Further, when I approached Emily with the idea of documenting our ongoing conversations about "going public" for the MSS session, she felt that I had a very set idea of what I wanted to come out of the so-called "joint venture." At first Emily felt frustrated and "a little angry" with my focus on feminist methodology. Although she did not see how it would directly help adult survivors she agreed to "help" me with *my* project.

Despite her willingness to "help," Emily continued to question the significance of the feminist methodology project. After the MSS session, when I proposed revising the paper we presented for submission to a book entitled *Feminism and Social Change: Bridging Theory and Practice,* she thought: "How will this help adult survivors? Isn't it just mental gymnastics?[5] and Why do I want to do this? Why bother?" While the conference offered her an opportunity to talk with professional educators who may meet adult survivors in the course of their work, a chapter in a book that did not target mental health providers or survivors themselves seemed frivolous. But over time two important shifts occurred. First, Emily reports, I "lightened" up. In the course of our conversations, Emily noticed that I loosened my "set ideas" and increasingly opened up to her. She also noticed the declining speed and increasing clarification in my speech from initial meetings when I was "going so fast, talking too fast," and using language that was unfamiliar to her. Emily challenged me to explain my terms and why feminist methodology was so important to me. This helped her better understand what I had in mind while it forced me to question my concepts as well as my motives and to rethink the overall project. In other words, the dialogic process changed each of us, enhanced our mutual understanding, and helped reshape the project itself. Second, Emily said she began to "realize the significance and need for what *you* are doing." The operative word here is *you*. She did not say *we*. Not surprisingly, the specific project that has resulted in this chapter was not jointly conceived nor evenly shaped despite my best intentions at the outset.

Emily initially thought that the issues I raised regarding feminist methodology were "bullshit." Why then did she continue to work on the MSS presentation and the revisions for this chapter? At first, she said she did so as an act of friendship. Subsequently, she explained, that through our ongoing dialogue she "finally came to understand the significance." She began to see the importance of a longer-term project designed to challenge how researchers study childhood sexual assault and assess the needs of survivors. Although she did not see how the project addressed the immediate needs of survivors, she recognized that "if nothing else, it will focus changes. People will start questioning themselves and that's not nothing."

DEFINING SURVIVORS' DISCOURSE

As a consequence of our personal commitment to shift the standpoint of discourse on treatment for adult survivors of childhood sexual abuse from a medical/psychiatric discourse to a survivors' discourse, we adopted a methodology that emphasized participation and empowerment. While Emily and I agreed to disagree on the centrality of feminist theories and practice for our activist project, we both found three key elements central to the work: the value of participation and empowerment of survivors in generating treatment alternatives; the significance of speaking out to contest societal processes of denial; and the necessity of friendship and support networks for sustaining us as we pursue our public activist agenda. These themes are also central to feminist theories about survivors' discourse itself. In this section, I explore the feminist theoretical challenges to expert discourse and demonstrate the value of feminist theory and practice for activism for and with adult survivors.

"Medical/psychiatric" or "therapeutic" discourses are forms of "expert needs discourses" described by Nancy Fraser (1989:173). Expert discourses are a means by which certain "needs" are translated "into objects of potential state intervention." They tend to be restricted to "specialized publics" and "as a result of these expert redefinitions, the people whose needs are in question are repositioned. They become individual 'cases' rather than members of social groups or participants in political movements. In addition, they are rendered passive, positioned as potential recipients of predefined services rather than as agents involved in interpreting their needs and shaping their life conditions" (174). Fraser contrasts "expert discourses" with "oppositional discourses" that derive from the "situated knowledges" (Haraway 1988:584) of those who do not share the privileged position of the professional group.[6] Haraway argues that "situated knowledges" generated from the point of view of "subjugates" will provide "more adequate, sustained, objective, transforming accounts of the world" (1988:584). In order to generate a discourse that can oppose the medical/therapeutic discourse on the treatment of adult survivors, we began from our standpoint as survivors and, in dialogue, actively analyzed our experiences with the goal of self-conscious reflection on the healing and telling processes.

Proponents of the mutual aid groups of the seventies and eighties also challenged "professional discourse" and "the expert" model for healing (Katz and Bender 1976). The so-called "self-help" movement utilized the benefits of "cogenerative dialogue" (Elden and Levin 1991:134) as a tool for indigenous knowledge creation as well as for personal recovery.[7] The "self-help" movement was influenced by the critiques of power developed by the social movements of the sixties and early seventies. The women's movement, in particular, utilized group-based consciousness-raising approaches to break down isolation, shift the site of knowledge creation, and help build a community of resistance (Peattie and Rein 1983). We drew upon consciousness-raising as a model for our dialogue. The process of empowerment occurs as we shift the site of knowledge creation from the "expert" to ourselves as actors with a perspective informed by our experiences and shaped by our dialogue and reflexivity (see Alcoff and Gray 1993; Fonow and Cook 1991; Haraway 1988).

One of the most significant resources for adult survivors that incorporates self-help and mutual aid perspectives is *The Courage to Heal: A Guide for Women Survivors of Child Sexual Abuse* (1988), a book written by Ellen Bass and Laura Davis with extensive material from women who are adult survivors themselves. Bass and Davis argue against the "expert" perspective often found in guides for mental health professionals.[8] The approach they advocate includes an emphasis on "breaking silence" and sharing experiences with others who are working to heal from the abuse (see Barringer 1992).[9]

Survivors experience empowerment when they speak out, especially when the expert mediator role is eliminated (Alcoff and Gray 1993). In their article on survivors' discourse, Linda Alcoff and Laura Gray argue that "we need to transform arrangements of speaking to create spaces where survivors are authorized to be both witnesses and experts, both reporters of experience and theorists of experience. Such transformations will alter existing subjectivities as well as structures of domination and relations of power" (1993:282). Beyond generating opportunities to reflect upon our experiences and standing witness to each other's processes, Emily and I critically reflected upon our oft-times differing understandings of the experience of childhood sexual abuse and speaking out. Our sense of empowerment grew throughout the course of our dialogue and was furthered when we affirmed each other's efforts to go public as theorists of our experience.

In our effort to generate and reflect upon our situated knowledge, we self-consciously explored the process and content of a dialogue between us as survivors, transcribing our discussions and reflecting upon them as a basis for subsequent conversations. We hope this reflexivity where we are "both observers (interpreters) and objects of observation (or interpretation)" (Morawski 1988:189) will add to the wider struggles to transform the discourse on adult survivors of childhood sexual abuse as well as contribute to our personal empowerment as authors of our lives.

LIMITS OF SURVIVORS' DISCOURSE

Despite the apparent value of the recovery discourse for survivors of numerous personal traumas, many critics detail the limits of such discourse, especially when manipulated by the mass media. These critiques must be addressed if we are to effectively contest the dominant discourse that shapes responses to adult survivors. For example, Norman Denzin maintains that in groups like Adult Children of Alcoholics, Adult Children of Sex Addicts, and Adults Recovering from Incest, as participants "attempt to take back their lives and to make sense of the experiences" they had growing up, they risk turning themselves into "commodities sold in the public market place." He is particularly concerned with the growing number of celebrities who are going public with their childhood traumas and the media attention that surrounds their disclosures. Denzin asserts that "we've entered an era where nothing is any longer hidden. The dividing line between public and private lives has dissolved; anyone's personal troubles can now serve as a front-page story, couched as a banal morality tale with a happy ending" (1990:13).

Alcoff and Gray also acknowledge the potential for co-optation that occurs when survivors speak out about childhood abuse. Echoing Michel Foucault, they caution that the confessional mode of speech characteristic of survivor discourse "participates in the construction of domination." Yet, they note, Foucault also demonstrates in his work that "speech is an important site of struggle in which domination and resistance are played out" (1993:263). Discourse initiated from the point of view of survivors has "paradoxically appeared to have empowering effects even while it has in some cases unwittingly facilitated the recuperation of dominant discourses" (262–63). To diminish the co-optation of survivor discourse, they argue that in addition to eliminating the "expert mediator," we abolish the separation "between experience and analysis" (282). They explain:

> A nonbifurcating ontology of experience and theory requires us to relinquish the idea that in reporting our experiences we are merely reporting internal events without interpretation. To become the the-

> orists of our own experience requires us to become aware of how our subjectivity will be constituted by our discourses and aware of the danger that even in our own confessionals within autonomous spaces we can construct ourselves as reified victims or as responsible for our own victimization. (284)

A self-reflexive and dialogic process as outlined in this chapter provides a safe context through which to critically assess the ways in which dominant discourse may infuse our own understandings. No one is immune from internalized oppression. A central part of our healing from childhood sexual abuse includes confronting how we have been made to feel responsible for the abuse. However, discourse generated by those who have experienced childhood sexual abuse differs fundamentally from recovery discourse produced by medical experts or psychologists. The process by which such situated knowledge is produced contributes to the sense of empowerment experienced by survivors and others within the so-called "recovery community." To ignore the process renders invisible the community context through which "recovery" takes place. Recovery discourses grounded in survivors' self-reflective understandings provide a site of resistance that can challenge the medical/psychiatric discourse, which has limited treatment options and has fed the denial of the broader community. The process of self-reflective dialogue among survivors of childhood sexual abuse goes beyond commonsense understandings to produce "theoretical knowledge grounded in lived experience" (Treichler 1989:74) to authorize survivors' situated knowledges.

FEMINIST PRAXIS AND THE DIALOGIC PROCESS

The consciousness-raising approach that serves as a model for our dialogue was premised on group members' standpoint as "insiders" sharing common experiences. The dialogic approach we adopt defies the "insider" (or community member) and "outsider" (or researcher) dichotomy that characterizes much of the literature on participatory action research (see Freire 1970, 1973). In fact, we experienced ourselves as both insiders and outsiders to each other's processes at various moments throughout our dialogue. Despite the commonality of our status as survivors of childhood sexual abuse, we held contrasting perspectives on a variety of significant issues. In the course of our ongoing dialogue, we recognized the difficulty in developing a common vision. Despite agreement on the overall goals to confront the denial of childhood sexual abuse and the mistreatment of survivors by professionals and others, we disagreed on who should be the audience, what language is appropriate for advocacy and education, and which strategies are effective. Even when we jointly identified questions for further discussion, upon reexamination we often interpreted the meaning of these questions differently. For example, Emily expressed concern that the critique of expert discourse would discourage survivors from seeking the support they need from professionals, whereas I thought it was important to distinguish between what survivors know and experience from what "experts" define for them. However, such distinctions did not emerge immediately. We contested a variety of issues before we recognized the source of our mutual misunderstanding. As we faced our differences in perception and understanding we experienced both frustration and disappointment. However, when we were able to struggle through our frustration and clarify our positions to gain mutual understanding, we experienced a deepened level of communication in subsequent conversations. As a consequence of ongoing dialogue, we shifted our understanding and, to a certain extent and on certain occasions, adopted the other's point of view; and in other instances, we have agreed to disagree.

In reflecting upon the process we used to construct this chapter, Emily and I discussed the dilemma of "interpretative authority" (Borland 1991) and aired our different goals and frustrations. We believe that a dialogic process provides a context in which conflicts in interpretation are made evident and, more importantly, can be renegotiated in a more egalitarian fashion than is found in traditional social science methodology. We do not purport to speak for other survivors. We do not believe that there can be a unified survivors' discourse. We expect that survivors experience abuse and subsequent recovery from a variety of standpoints influenced by a myriad of individual, social, cultural, and economic factors. On the other hand, we hope that our exchange will encourage others to engage in dialogue about their experiences in an effort to broaden the voices represented in the discourse on sexual abuse. We also recognize the shifting nature of discourse; that is, as we tell our story the salience of certain aspects of the story differs for each of us "in relation to [our] shifting interpersonal and political contexts" (Martin and Mohanty 1986:210). Our struggles to survive the traumas of childhood sexual abuse lead us to aggressively resist efforts of others to define us or to develop a totalizing image of "the incest survivor." In fact, it is this commitment that moved both of us to speak out.

Ongoing dialogue is required among others in varying social locations in order to ensure a diversity of representation in survivors' discourse. We have yet to explore how race/ethnicity, religious background, class, region, sexuality, among other social and contextual factors, shape the experiences, perceptions, and treatment needs of survivors. Although the pain, anger, and shame may be similar, the factors surrounding the abuse and the appropriate contexts for healing may vary. We also need to learn more about the contexts in which survivors find it safe to share their experiences with others. Feminist participatory research with adult survivors and other women who have experienced violence against them is a strategy that offers the potential for generating survivor-centered discourses that will broaden our understanding of the complex forces contributing to violence against women. This chapter models the ways that personal narrative and dialogue form the grounds for feminist participatory research.

Despite the theorizing about an alternative approach to knowledge construction and a commitment to feminist participatory research, this chapter is more an extension of my concerns than of Emily's. Since the issues dealt with derived from my social location as a feminist sociologist as well as an incest survivor and since the project was conceived in more abstract dialogue with others in the field attempting to develop alternative methodologies that are feminist, participatory, and emancipatory, the product clearly privileges my voice. Emily contributed her vision on the issues I raised and challenged my assumptions during our conversations as well as in response to drafts of the chapter. Through the dialogue, new issues were identified and new questions surfaced. As a consequence of her participation in the project, Emily said she developed a clearer understanding of feminism and a greater appreciation for the issues of methodology.

While I shaped the structure of the chapter and the research questions, Emily has been a powerful presence throughout the process, challenging the presuppositions, questioning the validity of the project, helping to clarify terms. Much of my thinking about motivations for and the effects of going public is informed by Emily's sensitive and grounded analyses of her own experiences. Earlier drafts of the chapter included direct and uninterrupted excerpts of our dialogue and listed our names as coauthors. The nontraditional format caused difficulty for some readers, and with each revision I found myself shifting the style to the more traditional academic format. What had begun as an attempt to bridge the activist/academic divide has failed in this context to a great extent. Yet the context is more academic than activist and consequently the outcome was inevitable. However, the honest self-reflection on the process effectively demonstrates the challenge of generating egalitarian feminist participatory research strategies.

CONCLUSION: BRIDGE-BUILDING LESSONS

We begin our academic and political work with a point of view grounded in our social, historical, and psychological biographies and bring different interests and resources to each endeavor. Further complicating the process is the diversity of sites through which texts are produced and distributed. Academic feminist discourse is produced within institutions organized by relations of ruling (Smith 1990). We can seek to change these patterns of dominance from within or by developing alternative sites or, when necessary, by severing our connections to the dominant institutions. At times, I find myself straddling all three approaches. A key solution for me has been continued dialogue and community work with those outside the academy. Emily, on the other hand, does not see the immediate relevance of academic feminist discourse for her goals. She wants to create a text shaped by her autobiography that will appeal to a wider audience than the text in which this chapter appears. However, we learned a great deal from each other and we take these lessons with us as we pursue the different avenues we chose. While Emily and I will continue on these differing paths, we share a common concern. As long as we continue to respect the differences between us, honoring them while also working to understand better the connections as well as the contrasts, we will strengthen the grounds upon which to build a more egalitarian emancipatory approach as a foundation for the broader struggle.

Our dialogic and reflexive process reveals the inadequacy of the distinction between "outsider" and "insider." Rather than one "insider" or "outsider" perspective, we all start from different standpoints and this contributes to numerous dimensions on which we can relate to members of various communities. Our positionality shapes the way we enter the "field" as activists or researchers and how we relate to different participants within a particular group. Members themselves experience differing relationships to the various groups and individuals who comprise their community. Furthermore, outsiderness and insiderness are not fixed or static positions; rather, they are ever-shifting and permeable social locations. Emily and I were simultaneously insider and outsider to each other's process at various points throughout our dialogue. While we often experienced these shifts as problematic and frustrating, we also benefited from the efforts we made to negotiate the sometimes surprising disjunctures and disagreements.

Recognizing the shifting nature of outsider and insider positions, however, does not negate the significance of situated knowledge for generating more relevant knowledge. My experience as a survivor of childhood sexual abuse provides me with a particular vantage point from which to view the experiences of other survivors as well as the basis for honest and open dialogue between us. However, as this account reveals, sharing the experience does not guarantee mutual understanding on a wide variety of relevant issues. Through the dialogic process some of these disparities were identified and reconciled, others remained unresolved.

It also would be misleading to imply that only survivors of childhood sexual abuse can learn from and contribute to knowledge generated from a survivors' standpoint. Both Emily and I maintain that those who have not experienced oppression of one sort or another can learn to see the world from the perspective of those whose lives are directly shaped by various systems of oppression (see Harding 1991:287). In fact, this assertion undergirds our desire to go public. We also hold that personal narrative and the dialogic process provide the bases for this learning to occur.

Survivors in self-help and mutual aid groups can also benefit from a feminist theoretical framework. All too often those who feel stigmatized by the wider community remain silent and internalize these negative messages (see Naples 1991, 1994). When healing takes place, the individualist psychological frames of enhancing self-esteem, building ego strength, gaining acceptance, or achieving upward mobility supersede the political analysis offered by feminist theories. However, when stigmatized groups shift from individualistic explanations to social, structural, and political analyses, they find that personal as well as collective empowerment ensues. While Emily did view her position as a survivor through political lenses, she did not see the relationship between childhood sexual abuse and broader relations of ruling. However, such a broadened view is necessary if we are to design research strategies and political interventions that will effectively challenge oppressive approaches. By creating bridges between feminist theorizing and grounded experiences through participatory strategies, feminist researchers can generate more relevant knowledge that in turn can help deepen the political analysis needed for effective activist interventions. This mutually reinforcing relationship between feminist theorizing and activism continues the very process that gave rise to feminist theories as well as to the political agendas now associated with feminist activism. The battered women's movement is a vivid example of the power of this mutually reinforcing relationship for fighting violence against women and generating collective solutions (Dobash and Dobash 1992).

Many oppressed groups successfully defied negative constructions and in the process created powerful social movements. Going public has been a key component of their success. The civil rights, gay and lesbian, disability rights, and welfare rights movements all provided sites through which self-defined "members" could claim a positive identity and challenge the abuse and inequities that circumscribe their lives. The women's movement in particular demonstrated the value of participation in an anti-hierarchical context and the significance of speaking out for personal empowerment and social change. Feminist theorists furthered the political project by demonstrating how "experts" in medicine, academia, law, and religion, among other institutions, silenced or devalued women's voices and controlled their lives (see, for example, Ehrenreich and English 1978; Jones 1985; Lerner 1986, 1993; National Association of Chicano Studies 1990; Tuchman 1989). Challenging the controlling power of "expert discourse" is one of the many goals that unite feminist theoretical and activist concerns. My work with Emily further demonstrates the mutually reinforcing relationship between feminist theorizing and activism yet also highlights the ongoing challenge to maintaining egalitarian and participatory research strategies.

NOTES

An earlier version of this essay was presented in the session "Feminist Research Agendas: Conflicts and Dilemmas" at the annual meeting of the Midwest Sociological Society in Des Moines, Iowa, on April 13, 1991. I am grateful for the helpful comments of Heidi Gottfried, Karen Hewitt, Francesca Cancian, Linda Williams, and Cynthia Truelove and for ongoing conversations with Susan Stern.

1. Stern (1994) distinguishes between pluralist participatory research and participatory research conducted for the purposes of social change and liberation. To this end, she applies the term *emancipatory participatory research* to describe the latter approach. We believe that the term *feminist participatory research* communicates both the social change thrust of our work as well as the significance of shifting the standpoint to center women's lives and voices.
2. After this unfortunate experience, she lost her desire to continue her college education.
3. Bloom (1990) elaborates thirty-five different "aftereffects" she identified in her work with adult survivors (see also Courtois 1988).
4. We do not oppose the use of medical intervention such as medications and hospitalization when necessary but the exclusive reliance upon medical and psychiatric explanations and treatments for the "aftereffects" of childhood sexual abuse often serve to pathologize the individual survivor and neglect to provide the context for long-term recovery.

5. In an earlier draft of this chapter, I used the term *mental masturbation* where the phrase *mental gymnastics* now appears. In notes taken during a discussion of the essay, I wrote down the former phrase and attributed it to Emily. When Emily read the draft, she stated emphatically that she had not used that term. The new phrase accurately characterizes her reservation without misrepresenting the point she wanted to make. Since we each had different recollections of the specific terminology used and we did not tape this particular discussion, I have chosen to modify the language while retaining what we both agree was the gist of Emily's original critique. As this one incident highlights, the process of clarification and revision is ongoing and requires continued dialogue and self-reflection.

6. Situated knowledge is generated through the self-reflexive analysis of those within a particular social location (see Haraway 1988). These social locations may be based upon class, geography, race/ethnicity, or another social identity, such as lesbian, elderly, or disabled. Situated knowledge differs from commonsense understandings that often form the basis for "inherent" or "traditional" ideologies discussed by George Rudé. Inherent ideologies are "based on direct experience, oral tradition or folk-memory" (Fisher and Kling 1990:73). In contrast, social actors generate situated knowledge when they self-consciously engage in the process of social analysis in order to understand the social construction of their location within the particular "relations of ruling" (Smith 1987) that shape their experience.

7. The term *indigenous* is frequently used to differentiate those who are members of a particular group or community from those who do not share the same economic, cultural, or racial/ethnic background as the group or community residents. Historically, the term has been used to describe members of non-Western and nonindustrialized cultures traditionally studied by anthropologists and more recently has been applied to low income community residents in urban settings or rural community residents. We use the term as a way to specify the origin of knowledge about the adult survivor. We therefore differentiate the knowledge generated by those who are "indigenous" to the experience of childhood sexual abuse, namely, those who have experienced childhood sexual abuse themselves, from those who have not had the experience, although we also acknowledge the wide range of experiences that are encompassed by the category of childhood sexual abuse. The term *indigenous* helps us capture the social location of the actors who are in the process of knowledge creation and furthers our attempt to specify the standpoint of a survivors' discourse.

8. *The Courage to Heal* (Bass and Davis 1988) and *Secret Survivors* (Bloom 1990) have come under attack recently for encouraging what is now termed "false memory syndrome." The gist of the critique is that since the authors of these books provide a list of symptoms and suggest that anyone who identifies with a number of those listed might be a survivor of childhood sexual assault, many people may be misled into believing they are survivors when their symptoms are a result of other mental health issues. Those who support Bloom's and Bass and Davis's contributions to healing argue that the fervor

with which the psychiatric community and the media are pursuing the few cases of reported false memory syndrome attests to the continued denial of childhood sexual assault as an extensive problem in this society (Wasserman 1992).

9. Laura Davis outlines what she describes as "the basic skills to healing." These skills include "taking care of yourself, building a support system, reaching out for help, creating safety, coping with crisis, and acknowledging the healing you've already accomplished" (1990:167). She also emphasizes the importance of "breaking silence": "One of the most damaging aspects of abuse is the silence that so often surrounds it. Most children endure terrible atrocities without ever being able to tell anyone. Secrecy increases feelings of shame in the victim and allows the abuse to continue unchecked. For most abused children, isolation and silence are a way of life" (234).

REFERENCES

Alcoff, Linda, and Laura Gray. 1993. "Survivor Discourse: Transgression or Recuperation?" *Signs* 18 (2): 260–90.

Barringer, Carol E. 1992. "The Survivor's Voice: Breaking the Incest Taboo." *NWSA Journal* 4 (1): 4–22.

Bass, Ellen, and Laura Davis. 1988. *The Courage to Heal: A Guide for Women Survivors of Child Sexual Abuse.* New York: Harper and Row.

Bass, Ellen, and Louise Thornton. 1983. *I Never Told Anyone: Writings by Women Survivors of Child Sexual Abuse.* New York: Harper Colophon.

Bloom, E. Sue. 1990. *Secret Survivors: Uncovering Incest and Its Aftereffects in Women.* New York: John Wiley and Sons.

Borland, Katherine. 1991. "'That's Not What I Said': Interpretive Conflict in Oral Narrative Research." In *Women's Words: The Feminist Practice of Oral History,* ed. Sherna Berger Gluck and Daphne Patai. New York: Routledge. 63–75.

Courtois, Christine. 1988. *Healing the Incest Wound: Adult Survivors in Therapy.* New York: Norton.

Davis, Laura. 1990. *The Courage to Heal Workbook: For Women and Men Survivors of Child Sexual Abuse.* New York: Harper and Row.

Denzin, Norman K. 1990. "Presidential Address on *The Sociological Imagination* Revisited." *Sociological Quarterly* 31 (1): 1–22.

Dobash, R. Emerson, and Russell P. Dobash. 1992. *Women, Violence, and Social Change.* London: Routledge.

Ehrenreich, Barbara, and Deirdre English. 1978. *For Her Own Good: 150 Years of the Experts' Advice to Women.* Garden City, N.Y.: Anchor Press.

Elden, Max, and Morten Levin. 1991. "Cogenerative Learning: Bringing Participation into Action Research." In *Participatory Action Research,* ed. William Foote Whyte. Newbury Park, Calif.: Sage. 127–42.

Fisher, Robert, and Joseph M. Kling. 1990. "Leading the People: Two Approaches to the Role of Ideology in Community Organizing." In *Dilemmas of Activism: Class, Community, and the Politics of Local Mobilization,* ed. Joseph M. Kling and Prudence Posner. Philadelphia: Temple University Press. 73–90.

Fonow, Mary Margaret, and Judith A. Cook. 1991. "Back to the Future: A Look at the Second Wave of Feminist Epistemology and Methodology." In *Beyond Methodology: Feminist Scholarship as Lived Research,* ed. Mary Margaret Fonow and Judith A. Cook. Bloomington: Indiana University Press. 1–15.

Foucault, Michel. 1972. *The Archaeology of Knowledge.* Trans. A. M. Sheridan Smith. New York: Harper and Row.

———. 1975. *The Birth of a Clinic: An Archaeology of Medical Perception.* Trans. A. M. Sheridan Smith. New York: Vintage/Random House.

Fraser, Nancy. 1989. *Unruly Practices: Power, Discourse, and Gender in Contemporary Social Theory.* Minneapolis: University of Minnesota Press.

Freire, Paulo. 1973. *Education for Critical Consciousness.* New York: Seabury Press.

———. 1970. *Pedagogy of the Oppressed.* Trans. Myra Bergman Ramos. New York: Seabury Press.

Friedan, Betty. 1963. *Feminine Mystique.* New York: Norton.

Gergen, Mary M. 1988. "Toward a Feminist Metatheory and Methodology in the Social Sciences." In *Feminist Thought and the Structure of Knowledge,* ed. Mary McCanney Gergen. New York: New York University Press. 87–104.

Haraway, Donna. 1988. "Situated Knowledges: The Science Question in Feminism and the Privilege of Partial Perspective." *Feminist Studies* 14 (3): 575–99.

Harding, Sandra. 1991. *Whose Science? Whose Knowledge?: Thinking from Women's Lives.* Ithaca: Cornell University Press.

Hartsock, Nancy C. M. 1987. "Rethinking Modernism: Minority vs. Majority Theories." *Cultural Critique* 7 (Fall): 187–206.

Haywoode, Terry. 1992. "Working Class Feminism: Creating Community-Based Social Change." Paper presented at the annual meeting of the American Sociological Association. Pittsburgh.

Jones, Jacqueline. 1985. *Labor of Love, Labor of Sorrow: Black Women, Work, and the Family, from Slavery to the Present.* New York: Vintage Books.

Katz, Alfred H., and Eugene I. Bender, eds. 1976. *The Strength in Us: Self-Help Groups in the Modern World.* New York: New Viewpoints.

Lerner, Gerda. 1993. *The Creation of Feminist Consciousness: From the Middle Ages to Eighteen-seventy.* New York: Oxford University Press.

———. 1986. *The Creation of Patriarchy.* New York: Oxford University Press.

Light, Linda, and Nancy Kleiber. 1988. "Interactive Research in a Feminist Setting: The Vancouver Women's Health Collective." In *Anthropologists at Home in North America: Methods and Issues in the Study of One's Own Society,* ed. Donald A. Messerschmidt. New York: Cambridge University Press. 185–201.

Maguire, Patricia. 1987. *Doing Participatory Research: A Feminist Approach.* Amherst, Mass.: Center for International Education, School of Education, University of Massachusetts.

Martin, Biddy, and Chandra Talpade Mohanty. 1986. "Feminist Politics: What's Home Got to Do with It?" In *Feminist Studies/Critical Studies,* ed. Teresa de Lauretis. Bloomington: Indiana University Press. 191–212.

Morawski, J. G. 1988. "Impasse in Feminist Thought?" In *Feminist Thought and the Structure of Knowledge,* ed. Mary McCanney Gergen. New York: New York University Press. 182–94.

Naples, Nancy A. 1994. "Contradictions in Agrarian Ideology: Restructuring Gender, Race-ethnicity, and Class." *Rural Sociology* 59 (1): 110–35.

———. 1991. "Challenging the Stereotypes: Women on Welfare in College." Paper presented at the annual meeting of the Society for the Study of Social Problems. Cincinnati.

National Association of Chicano Studies. 1990. *Chicano Voices: Intersections of Class, Race, and Gender.* Colorado Springs: National Association of Chicano Studies.

Peattie, Lisa, and Martin Rein. 1983. *Women's Claims: A Study in Political Economy.* New York: Oxford University Press.

Rew, Lynn. 1989. "Childhood Sexual Exploitation: Long-Term Effects among a Group of Nursing Students." *Issues in Mental Health Nursing* 10:181–91.

Smith, Dorothy E. 1990. *The Conceptual Practices of Power: A Feminist Sociology of Knowledge.* Boston: Northeastern University Press.

———. 1987. *The Everyday World as Problematic: A Feminist Sociology.* Boston: Northeastern University Press.

Stern, Susan. 1994. "Social Science from Below: Grassroots Knowledge for Science and Emancipation." Ph.D. diss., City University of New York.

Treichler, Paula A. 1989. "From Discourse to Dictionary: How Sexist Meanings Are Authorized." In *Language, Gender, and Professional Writing,* ed. Francine Wattman Frank and Paula A. Treichler. New York: Modern Language Association. 51–79.

Tuchman, Gaye, with Nina E. Fortin. 1989. *Edging Women Out: Victorian Novelists, Publishers, and Social Change.* New Haven, Conn.: Yale University.

Wasserman, Cathy. 1992. "FMS: The Backlash against Survivors." *Sojourner: The Women's Forum* (Nov.): 18–19.

Whyte, William Foote, ed. 1991. *Participatory Action Research.* Newbury Park, Calif.: Sage.

Williams, Mary Beth. 1990. "Post-Traumatic Stress Disorder and Child Sexual Abuse: The Enduring Effects." Ph.D. diss., Fielding Institute.

PART 3

Participatory and Liberatory Advocacy

CHAPTER 9

FRANCESCA M. CANCIAN

Participatory Research and Alternative Strategies for Activist Sociology

Many scholars have argued that feminist social researchers should do activist research that benefits women and challenges inequality (Cancian 1992; Cook and Fonow 1986; Gluck and Patai 1991; Nebraska Sociological Feminist Collective 1988). In particular, feminists have been urged to use participatory research methods that emphasize political action and community control over research (Maguire 1987; Mies 1983).

However, activist research often conflicts with academic standards. "Activist" research as I define it aims at empowering the powerless, exposing the inequities of the status quo, and promoting social changes that equalize the distribution of resources. Activist research is "for" women and other disadvantaged people and often involves close social ties and cooperation with the disadvantaged. In contrast, academic research aims at increasing knowledge about questions that are theoretically or socially significant. Academic research is primarily "for" colleagues. It involves close ties with faculty and students and emotional detachment from the people being studied. Social researchers who do activist research and want a successful academic career thus have to bridge two conflicting social worlds.

In this essay, I will analyze participatory research and other types of activist research, emphasizing their effectiveness in challenging inequality and their compatibility with a successful academic career. I will assume here that researchers will be more effective in challenging inequality insofar as they emphasize major changes in equalizing power, as opposed to improving services for the disadvantaged within the existing power structure, and they incorporate collective action into their research instead of restricting themselves solely to academic analysis, i.e., they include "practice" as well as "theory." I will also evaluate academic success by conventional criteria, such as the prestige of the institution in which researchers are employed and the places in which they publish.

My analysis of participatory research is based on a survey of the literature, informal contacts with numerous participatory researchers, and my own experience with this method. Interviews with nine activist sociologists with successful careers, most of them feminists, are the basis for examining alternative strategies.

Two major issues emerged in my analysis. First, activist researchers with academic careers face many difficulties in balancing the social worlds of academia, policymakers, and the public, or "the community." (The term *the community* tends to romanticize disadvantaged people and to cover up their internal differences and conflicts; but I will use the term since I have no better alternative.) Participatory researchers typically have strong ties to the community, because of their emphasis on community participation and collective action, but their relations with academia tend to be strained. In contrast, successful academics usually have weaker ties in the community but better relations with academia.

The second major issue in my analysis is the impact of organizational support on the success of activist projects. Participatory researchers who lack the full support of academic departments need institutional support for their research from unions, research organizations, or other sources. Successful academics, on the other hand, typically need activist organizations to sustain their community ties and their commitment to activism.

I begin this chapter by presenting the basic features of participatory research projects and describing the stages of participatory research, focusing on a project with women from a battered women's shelter. In the second part of this chapter I examine alternative strategies of activist research used by the professors I interviewed. I conclude by comparing the costs and benefits of different strategies of combining activism with an academic career.

PARTICIPATORY RESEARCH: AN OVERVIEW

Participatory research is a radical type of activist social research in which the people being studied, or the intended beneficiaries of the research, have substantial control over and participation in the research. Combining scientific investigation with education and political action, participatory researchers challenge inequality within the research process, as well as in the wider society.

Participatory research was developed in the seventies and eighties, primarily by researchers of industrializing countries who challenged conventional economic development projects and sought to empower poor rural and urban communities (Freire 1970; Huizer and Mannheim 1979; Tandon 1981, 1988). In the United States, the Highlander Center in Tennessee supported grass-roots projects on workers' education, racial justice, and rural development and became a major center of participatory research (Gaventa and Horton 1981; Horton 1990; for reviews of the field and bibliographies, see Cancian and Armstead 1992; Maguire 1987; Park, Brydon-Miller, Hall, and Jackson 1993).

Feminist scholars and participatory researchers have had little effect on each other until recently, despite their similarities. Like participatory research, feminist approaches to research and teaching often emphasize nonhierarchical power relations, popular knowledge, consciousness-raising, and political action (Cook and Fonow 1986). Some proposals for a feminist methodology are virtually identical with participatory research (Gluck and Patai 1991; Mies 1983). But there are important differences. Most feminist projects do not aim for a high degree of community participation, nor do they encourage political action; in these areas feminists have a lot to learn from participatory research, as Patricia Maguire (1987:123–28) points out in her excellent critique of the field. Participatory researchers, on the other hand, need to overcome their androcentric bias, which is evident in ignoring feminist theory and research, excluding gender issues from participatory research projects, giving inadequate attention to women's participation, and using male-centered language (Maguire 1987:62). In recent years, with increasing contact between the two approaches, many participatory researchers have overcome this bias and many feminists are becoming more interested in participatory, activist research. If these trends continue, the two approaches will be distinguished only by feminists' greater concern with women and gender and participatory researchers' commitment to one type of activist research.

Participatory researchers focus on power and are oriented primarily to community groups, not policy experts or academicians. These concerns underlie the four major characteristics of participatory research: participation in the research by community members, consciousness-raising and education of the participants, inclusion of popular knowledge, and political action.

One of the hallmarks of participatory research is that the intended beneficiaries of the research—who typically are members of relatively powerless groups—participate in all phases of the research as much as possible (Freire 1970; Tandon 1981). Projects that study "the oppressed" encourage participation by the people being studied. Projects that investigate "the oppressors" encourage participation by the people that the researchers intend to benefit. The degree of participation may be very limited or participants may have substantial power in all aspects of the project.

Secondly, teaching research skills and raising consciousness about power on the individual and social level are part of most participatory research projects. For example, there may be group discussions that attempt to reduce participants' feelings of self-blame, unworthiness, and incompetence and try to relate personal problems to unequal distributions of power in the community and the society. Another distinguishing feature of participatory research is valuing the popular knowledge of community members. Personal experiences and feelings as well as artistic and spiritual expressions are valued as useful ways of knowing.

Finally, participatory research includes political action, especially actions that cultivate "critical consciousness" and are oriented toward structural change, not toward adjusting people to oppressive environments (Brown and Tandon 1983). Some scholars argue that "real" participatory research must include actions that radically reduce inequality and produce "social transformation." However, many projects include little or no collective action and are limited to changing the behavior of individual participants, raising consciousness, and strengthening or creating community networks (Park 1978).

An example of a successful participatory research project is a study of the working conditions of bus drivers in Leeds, England. As a result of greater pressure at work accompanying government deregulation, bus drivers were experiencing increasing stress, accidents, and conflicts at home (Forrester and Ward 1989). With the help of professors from the University of Leeds, a group of eight bus drivers decided to do some research that would investigate stress at work and motivate the drivers' union to take action. They designed and carried out a survey of drivers and their families, studied accident records, and measured physical signs of stress.

The results of the project were mixed, which is typical of participatory research. The report presenting their findings failed to produce the desired action by the union. However, workers' stress became part of the agenda for the union and the national government, and the report was used by workers in other countries to document the need for improved working conditions. The participants in the research gained research skills and knowledge about work stress, and the professors produced academic papers on work stress and participatory research (Forrester 1989). The professors had a dual accountability (as they put it) to both the bus workers and to the university; their projects produced results that were valuable to both groups.

The support of a long-term organization was a critical element in the success of this project. An adult education program for workers at Leeds University had been organized by the researchers and unions several years earlier. The education program focused on work-related issues and accomplished a great deal of consciousness-raising, education, and training for both the professors and the workers before the research project began. The program also gave the professors institutional support and academic legitimation for their participatory research (Forrester and Ward 1989; Forrester and Thorne 1993).

Ideally, participatory research produces progressive social change on three levels (Maguire 1987:241). For individual participants, it develops confidence and critical consciousness. For the local community, it strengthens activist organizations and improves living conditions, and for the wider society it helps to transform the power structure. In fact, this ideal is usually unreachable or the degree of success is unknown. I believe that a project should be judged a success if it leads to progressive change on one or two levels.

THE STAGES OF PARTICIPATORY RESEARCH AND RELATIONS WITH THE COMMUNITY

To give a clearer picture of the process of participatory research and relationships between researchers and community members, I describe the typical stages of a project, focusing on Patricia Maguire's work with women from a battered women's shelter in Gallup, New Mexico (Maguire 1987). Participatory research begins with becoming oriented to a community or an organization, unless the researcher already is an insider. Then it proceeds to dialogues with groups of people to clarify community problems and research questions and possibly to raise consciousness and culminates in collective research and political action (Maguire 1987; Freire 1970; Vio Grossi 1981).

Maguire arrived in Gallup committed to doing a feminist project that would use the participatory research approach that she had learned in graduate school. The battered women's shelter was the only agency or group in town with an activist orientation to women's issues, so she began her project by working as a volunteer at the shelter and getting to know individual women. Building on her work at the shelter, she then interviewed some women about problems in everyday life since leaving the shelter. Each woman was invited to join a support group; nine Navaho, two Anglo, and two Hispanic women joined.

The group met biweekly for nine months and began discussing the issues identified in the interviews, such as difficulties in raising children and financial problems. These discussions enabled group members to gather and validate their commonsense knowledge about their situation, identify specific problems, and develop their confidence and ability to speak out.

In leading these discussions, Maguire, like all participatory researchers, encountered the problem of balancing the relative power of the researcher and community participants. Frequently, there is a tension between the goals of promoting critical consciousness and validating participants' experience. Thus, if a researcher assumes that she fully understands the structural causes of local problems, while community members understand very little, then consciousness-raising becomes indoctrination and domination. A related issue is the difficulty of teaching participants how local problems relate to structural inequalities. Maguire criticizes her project for failing to significantly raise consciousness about the effects of classism and racism on personal problems. She comments that the women resisted talking about these issues and she was afraid of imposing her views on the women or intimidating them (1987:199, 233).

The next phase of a project—doing research—is critical. Without it, participatory research becomes identical with community organizing or facilitating a support group. In Maguire's project, the women did not do anything resembling traditional research, but their discussions produced significant new knowledge about battered women that was useful to the women themselves and to Maguire and the shelter. In addition, Maguire herself conducted interviews, analyzed group meetings, and used the project as a major part of her doctoral dissertation. Like Maguire, many scholars who use elements of participatory research do not involve community members in the more traditional, academic aspects of their research, as my interviews with activist sociologists will show.

The final step of a participatory research project, achieving social changes that reduce inequality, is the most difficult to achieve. In Maguire's project the group made recommendations for improvements to the staff at the shelter, successfully opposed a staff proposal to accept male volunteers to contact new clients, and did informal peer counseling with shelter residents. However, the group did not achieve Maguire's goal of institutionalizing the inclusion of clients on the governing board of the shelter. Maguire concludes that achieving sustained social change requires more time and resources and the cooperative efforts of a team of researchers instead of only the effort of a single individual.

In sum, participatory research can be very effective in empowering participants and bringing about social change if it is supported by an organization and if researchers stay with the project for a long time. Without these supports, participatory research achieves more limited goals: it teaches participants critical thinking and research skills and significantly increases their confidence and self-esteem; it also offers participants the rewards of intense social contact and personal change.

CONFLICTS BETWEEN PARTICIPATORY RESEARCH AND ACADEMIC SUCCESS

While participatory research can be very effective in meeting activist goals, it is difficult to integrate with a successful academic career. In particular, sharing power over the research with community members makes it very difficult to produce publications that meet academic standards, and incorporating social action into the research slows down and complicates research projects and may antagonize academic colleagues and administrators.

My own limited experience in doing participatory research illustrates these conflicts. In a project on tensions between work and family, I organized a group of secretaries at my university to discuss stresses at home and work and to consider ways of improving their work situation. I began with the goals of doing a collective, participatory project that would improve working conditions for the secretaries, raise consciousness, and also result in academic publications for me. The members of the group discussed their problems and eventually decided to survey all the secretaries in the school about pressures at work. The survey, which was initiated, designed, and administered by the secretaries, consisted of two questions and showed that there was widespread agreement with the group's analysis of work pressures: the main problem was pressure from professors to complete last-minute work in a hurry. The survey succeeded in getting useful information, legitimating and publicizing the group within the school, and helping members feel more competent and powerful so that they could go on to take more ambitious actions. But the survey clearly was too limited to be an academic study. I decided not to argue for a more ambitious survey because that would have increased my power in the group and decreased their participation in the survey.

Over the nine months of this project, I became more involved with the group and more detached from my original academic goals. The survey led to meetings with the secretaries' supervisor to address problems at work, and I heard rumors that some colleagues outside my department disapproved of my activism. I produced some talks but no academic publications from the project, even though I had learned a lot about work and family conflicts and usually published something from my research projects.

In retrospect, I believe that this lack of academic productivity stemmed in part from my anxiety about the reactions of local colleagues. A bigger factor was my confusion about my goals in the project and how they differed from the secretaries' goals. For the secretaries, participating in a support group and improving their working conditions were the main goals. I shared their goals, but also wanted to produce research that would interest my colleagues, benefit my career, and contribute to general knowledge. I avoided seeing the differences between my goals and the secretaries', both because of my personal involvement with the group and my acceptance of the ideal that the only legitimate purpose of participatory research is to benefit community groups. I now believe that this ideal does not fit people like myself who value their membership and standing in academia.

My new participatory research project on family and community caring in a Mexican-American neighborhood has multiple goals. One goal is to promote social change by personally supporting a grass-roots community organization and developing a group of professors and students to support this organization. Another, relatively separate goal is to collect ethnographic and interview data on caring to be used for academic publications. My interviews with activist sociologists illustrate other ways of coping with the conflicts between participatory research and an academic career.

ALTERNATIVE STRATEGIES FOR ACTIVIST SOCIOLOGY

Participatory research is so strongly oriented to the community that it is difficult to maintain an academic career. It is especially difficult to produce the frequent publications required by a research university on the basis of research that faithfully follows the tenets of participatory research. However, the experiences of the sociologists I interviewed show that some elements of participatory research can be integrated with academic success.

My interviews with nine professors of sociology identified a variety of approaches to social change-oriented research, which I will briefly describe. For systematic studies of different types of applied and activist research, readers should consult the literatures on applied research (Freeman, Dynes, Rossi, and Whyte 1983; Fritz and Clark 1989), action research (Lewin 1946; Tichy and Friedman 1983), and other approaches (Reason and Rowan 1981; Whyte 1991).

In the interviews, I asked respondents to describe their activist research projects and the conflicts they experienced between activism and academic success. Eight interviews were by telephone and one was face to face, and they lasted for twenty to forty minutes. The individuals were selected informally and overrepresent my feminist network, but they were selected to be fairly diverse in age, ethnicity, methodological style, and research area. The criteria for inclusion were that the individuals defined themselves as doing activist research, or social change-oriented research that challenged inequality, and were academically successful in the sense of having a position at a major research university or publishing extensively in mainline sociology journals or prestigious publishing houses. I am using their names, with their permission, because I believe it will make my analysis more interesting and useful to sociologists who know them. In 1992 when I interviewed them, Nancy Naples and Stacey Oliker were assistant professors; Pauline Bart, Edna Bonacich, Mark Chesler, Troy Duster, Heidi Gottfried, Mary Romero, and Gary Sandefur were tenured professors. I will briefly describe some of the recent research of these sociologists, starting with studies that are the most similar to participatory research and the most community oriented.

The researcher whose work is closest to participatory research is Mark Chesler from the University of Michigan. He studied fifty self-help groups of parents of children with cancer and has published several articles describing his personal and professional experiences (Chesler 1991; Hasenfeld and Chesler 1989). The project was aimed both at advancing scientific knowledge on volunteer agencies and support systems and giving immediate help to parents and local groups by providing information on how to recruit new parents, run effective meetings, and work with the medical establishment. Chesler is a parent of a child with cancer and is an officer of the national organization of the self-help groups, the Candellighters' Childhood Cancer Foundation. Thus his research raises important issues about being an insider versus being an outsider to the community with which one is working.

Chesler's project includes many elements of participatory research. The project has several action components; for example, Chesler gives workshops for group leaders and consults with them, using findings from his study (and collecting new data). In addition, many of the questions that he researches were proposed by the organization or particular self-help groups. His research differs from participatory research in that community members do not have control over or participate in doing the research.

Two other sociologists that I interviewed also work closely with community organizations or unions. Edna Bonacich, from the University of California at Riverside, is studying the international garment industry by interviewing corporation executives, surveying manufacturers, and working closely with the International Ladies' Garment Workers' Union. Her goals are to contribute to union strategy by analyzing the structure of the industry and showing how owners are overrewarded while workers are exploited. As part of her volunteer work with the union, she meets with the director of organizing to plan needed research and participates in the union's Justice Center, where workers and union leaders conduct adult education sessions and try to develop a mass movement among workers. Her project is an example of studying "the oppressors" and encouraging the participation of the people whom the researcher intends to benefit, not the people being studied. Heidi Gottfried from Purdue University has done a variety of projects on the labor movement from a feminist perspective. She has worked as a pro bono consultant for labor unions (Communication Workers of America, 9 to 5), for example, by doing a demographic analysis of clerical workers to help in organizing drives.

Three other researchers—Nancy Naples, Pauline Bart, and Mary Romero—are less connected to particular community organizations or unions, but do research that is intended to benefit specific groups. Nancy Naples, from the University of California at Irvine, is studying community responses to adult survivors of childhood sexual abuse in rural towns. Currently she is surveying the extent to which service providers are aware of sexual abuse or deny its existence. The research questions guiding the survey were identified "in dialogue" with a group of incest survivors and an organization of service providers, the Iowa Coalition against Sexual Assault. The multiple goals of the study include providing evidence to support the coalition's advocacy efforts on behalf of sexually abused women. In another project on low-income women in two rural towns, Naples developed her research agenda in consultation with an activist organization focused on rural inequality, Prairie Fire, and with several individual activists and community workers in the towns. In addition, the director of Prairie Fire is on the board of the organization that funded Naples's project.

Pauline Bart, from the University of Illinois at Chicago, is evaluating Illinois's sexual assault laws in a project that involves extensive contact with individual rape victims, including lengthy interviews and observations of court proceedings and often expanding into giving material and psychological support. Mary Romero, of the University of Oregon, states that all of her research has been a response to "being part of the [Mexican-American] community and being active in it." Her current project explores the educational and career experiences of Latino academics and identifies the nontraditional avenues they have taken when faced with structural barriers. The goals of the study are to provide models of success for Latino youth and identify policies that would increase the number of Latino students and faculty in higher education.

The work of Troy Duster, from the University of California at Berkeley, falls between these six respondents and the two remaining, who give less emphasis to community organizations and are most different from participatory researchers. As director of the Institute for the Study of Social Change at Berkeley, he is involved in many kinds of projects. The institute supports progressive social research, emphasizing the areas of poverty and racial/ethnic minorities, and supports graduate training of minority students. Faculty at the institute try to "straddle the thin line" between activists working for immediate change and academic researchers investigating inequality with the hope of encouraging long-range change, according to Duster. In one of the more activist projects, researchers are surveying the health care needs of children in poor families and also are consulting with state legislators on improving health care policies.

The research of the final two respondents—Stacey Oliker and Gary Sandefur—is oriented to long-term changes in public policy and does not involve close ties with community organizations or collective action. Stacey Oliker, from the University of Wisconsin at Milwaukee, is studying the welfare system, doing a traditional ethnography of the personal lives of low-income women on "workfare," and interviewing welfare workers and administrators. Her research challenges the prejudices of policymakers and she hopes that publications on the project will be widely read and will help to improve government provision of goods and services. She is currently keeping a moderately "low political profile" in order to maintain trust with the welfare administrators she is interviewing, but will intensify her work with the media and with local welfare rights organizations when her fieldwork is completed. Gary Sandefur, from the University of Wisconsin at Madison, studies racial inequality and poverty, using mainstream quantitative methods. He is currently helping to organize a conference and volume on inequality in income and living standards, "Poverty and Public Policy: What Do We Know? What Should We Do?" bringing together academics, policymakers, activists, and media representatives. He has been active in community organizations but sees this work as separate from his role as a scientific researcher.

In comparing these nine professors to each other, to participatory researchers, and to more traditional sociologists, three issues stand out: the researchers' connections to academia, policymakers, and the community; the special importance of connections to activist community organizations; and the conflicts of researchers with their academic departments.

Ties to Academia, Policymakers, and the Community

As one would expect from successful professors, all nine respondents had strong ties to academia, and these ties seem to explain many of their departures from the ideal model of participatory research. All the professors retain control over the research process, probably so that they can meet academic standards and produce frequent scholarly publications. Community members do not participate in designing or doing the research, although they do heavily influence the research agenda of several respondents. Most of these researchers also avoid a radical orientation to social change that would alienate their colleagues. However, several of their projects did include collective action directed at challenging power relations, such as Bonacich's work on union organizing.

Compared to most sociologists in academia, all nine professors are more connected to community organizations and policy groups. Most of them also write for nonacademic publications. Bonacich has helped write a pamphlet for workers describing the organization of the garment industry, and Sandefur's volume will be written in nontechnical language to make it accessible to the educated public. Many use the mass media extensively, appearing on local TV, writing letters to the editor, and being interviewed for the newspapers. With the exception of Romero, who focuses on change within higher education, all the respondents insist that social change-oriented researchers must communicate with people outside the university.

Activist Community Organizations and Dual Accountability

Given the relatively strong ties of sociologists to academia, it can be difficult to maintain connections to the community and to understand the needs and interests of different community groups. Becoming involved with an activist community organization was a strategy used by several respondents to achieve these goals.

Community organizations are especially important in articulating a research agenda that addresses the interests and concerns of disadvantaged groups. Professors and policymakers—like other elite groups—tend to construct research agendas that reflect their own interests and experiences and that reproduce inequality. This is a fundamental proposition of social theory and the sociology of knowledge (Collins 1990; Harding 1991; Mannheim 1936). Therefore, the interests of disadvantaged groups are best articulated by members of those groups and "their" organizations. Unions and community organizations obviously do an imperfect job of challenging existing inequalities and representing the interests of different, conflicting segments of a community, but on the average, they do a better job than elite organizations.

Instead of working with an activist community organization, an alternative way of achieving dual accountability to both community and academic groups is to participate in a university organization dedicated to both activism and research, such as Troy Duster's Institute for the Study of Change or the Leeds Adult Education Center. However, university organizations probably will experience more pressure to avoid radical statements or actions than many community organizations.

Troy Duster described the "healthy tension" between the Bay Area activists who want to use the Institute of Social Change as a base for movement activities and his obligation to act as as "neutral researcher" in charge of an official university research organization. Most of the time, the institute maintains good relations with both activists and academics. But during a few politically "hot" times, the distinctions got blurred, he commented. "Some of them felt we had crossed over the line and critical eyes were cast by colleagues."

Conflicts with Departments

For many of the sociologists I interviewed, the "healthy tension" between activism and academic research became a major conflict between themselves and their departments. I will not identify respondents by name in discussing this sensitive topic, except for the published account of Chesler (Hasenfeld and Chesler 1989).

Chesler's account describes several conflicts with research and academic units at Michigan. For example, in the seventies, Chesler helped create the Educational Change Team, a research and social action organization focused on racism in high schools that was part of the Institute for Social Research at Michigan. "With a staff of scientists and practitioners and a communal and representative decision-making structure, the team received substantial federal and foundation funding for research and action projects." But "leaders of the Institute for Social Research argued that these projects contained an inappropriate balance of social research and social action, and 'invited' the team to locate its action work outside of the institute" (Hasenfeld and Chesler 1989:503). Several years later, "colleagues in the Sociology Department decided not to promote me to full-professor status. The principal reasons involved . . . the appropriate balance of scholarship and action in my work, and the general relevance of my work for advancing the intellectual frontiers of sociology as a discipline" (504). Since then, the department has become more tolerant of diverse types of research and Chesler has completed some research "that more nearly conformed to existing sociological research priorities" and published two books and several articles in "more 'mainstream'" journals. "Eventually I was promoted, and the disrespect and stigma now seem much diminished" (505). These are recurring themes of conflict for activist sociologists: the exclusion of social action from respected academic research, the narrow definition of what is sociologically significant and what kinds of publications are valuable, and the threat of heavy sanctions if these standards are violated.

Academic standards for posing research questions and writing are difficult to integrate with social change-oriented research, according to most of my respondents. One respondent remarked that most "theoretically significant" questions "are so narrowly defined that your work can't have any impact" on social change. Several respondents were in departments that discouraged graduate students from social change-oriented research, and one respondent described her department's successful campaign to pressure a tenured activist colleague to shift his research toward more positivist, conventional projects. Only one respondent reported no conflict between doing social change-oriented research and departmental expectations.

Publications are another arena of conflict between career advancement and activist research. Seven respondents mentioned writing different articles for academic and change-oriented audiences. Publications in nonacademic outlets count as "being a good citizen" and are accepted only "as long as I keep the other (academic) stuff going," commented one professor. To maintain professional standing, "At times I do alienating writing for sociology journals," commented another. A woman who wrote a book on preventing rape because so many women asked her about this topic found that a leading academic journal would not review the book because it was not theoretical enough.

In most sociology departments, academic standards devalue essential elements of activist research: advocacy of particular social goals, social change projects, and active involvement with community groups. But these elements are compatible with other academic subcultures and are valued in other disciplines, such as social work and medicine. For example, medical school faculty advocate reducing infant mortality and become involved in community health care projects. In the long run, if activist research is to flourish in sociology, departments will have to change (Cancian 1992). In the short run, activist sociologists in traditional departments will have to develop strategies for adapting to academic demands.

Several respondents seemed to be using the strategy of having a second career oriented to social change on top of their academic publications and activities; they were very productive in both arenas. This "two-career" strategy was successful but very demanding on the researchers' time and energy. One childless woman observed that if she had children, she would not have the time to be an activist as well as a successful professor. Other respondents confined themselves to publishing either in mainline sociology journals or in social change-oriented publications.

The conflict that professors experienced with their departments varied from extreme, bitter, mutual attacks to harmony and integration. The stronger the researchers' connections to activist community groups or unions, the more conflict they tended to have. But several other factors also influenced the degree of conflict.

The strongest indicators of conflict with departments were the lack of mainstream publications and integration with the department. One of the people with the highest conflict rarely published in sociology journals or attended American Sociological Association meetings and was marginally involved in department affairs. Another high-conflict person was well-integrated into the profession on a national level, in terms of publications, meetings, and personal connections, but extremely alienated from the department, which disapproved of the activist topics of this person's research. Another respondent with a similar pattern of very high national integration and high department conflict commented: "I'm so alienated in my department that I don't care what they think of me." Two of the professors with high conflict were harshly treated by their departments, denied promotions or raises, and cut off from close contact with departmental graduate students.

The intellectual stance of the department on the value of applied or activist research also had an important impact. Three respondents were in departments or official subgroups within departments that specialized in urban problems, social services, or social change. These respondents received departmental support for doing research linked to progressive social change and had many graduate students who wanted to work with them. But even these researchers experienced tensions between academic and activist allegiances; one commented on the problem of "being seen as a local politico, not a serious academic."

Evaluating Participatory Research and Alternative Strategies

How effective are participatory research and the alternative strategies used by my respondents in accomplishing the twin goals of activist feminists in academia: challenging sexism and other forms of inequality and having a successful academic career? Let us first consider the goal of challenging inequality.

Participatory researchers and my respondents who are closest to this approach seem to be the most effective in challenging inequality, if we focus on the research *process* and not the research *product.* By sharing control over the research with community members, by consciousness-raising and education of participants, and by valuing participants' knowledge, the process of participatory research empowers community members. Participatory research projects also challenge inequality in the wider society by incorporating social action within the project and by focusing on changing power relations, as opposed to providing better services within the existing system. Except for Chesler, and Bonacich's and Gottfried's involvement in union organizing, my respondents did not discuss doing research that included acting to challenge the existing power structure. Their activism centered on the findings or products of their research rather than the research process.

If we focus on research *products* as traditionally defined—the impact of research findings on promoting progressive social change in the wider society—it becomes more difficult to evaluate the different research strategies. A very democratic process, like the one used by Patricia Maguire, can have very little effect on inequality in the community. A very traditional, nondemocratic research process can have a powerful social impact. For example, demographers and sociologists who use mainline quantitative methods like those used by Gary Sandefur have documented the increasing income gap between rich and poor Americans over the past decade and seem to have changed the willingness of elected officials and voters to consider distributing resources more equitably. We know very little about how to produce long-term social change, i.e., how different kinds of evidence, arguments, books, or collective actions will help to create a more or less equal society. Therefore, the long-term effectiveness of alternative strategies of activist research are very difficult to evaluate.

On the other hand, there are many reasons to believe that research done in cooperation with activist community organizations will be more likely to produce findings that benefit the relatively powerless and challenge the existing power structure. Activist organizations will articulate the interests of disadvantaged groups more effectively than elite groups of academics and policymakers, on average. Given the importance of working with activist organizations and the overall uncertainty about how to create a more equal society, I conclude that feminist researchers committed to challenging inequality should encourage many different types of social change-oriented research and should pay special attention to research strategies that involve cooperating with activist community organizations.

Turning to the effectiveness of alternative strategies in contributing to academic success, the rank ordering of different strategies is the reverse. Participatory researchers and the sociologists I interviewed with the strongest ties to community groups tend to be the least successful in academia and to have the most conflict with their departments. The major requirement for academic success in research universities—publishing regularly in academic journals—is incompatible with doing research that is controlled by community members and that includes radical social change. Academic success also depends on being socially and professionally integrated with colleagues at a departmental and national level, a requirement that can conflict with developing close ties to activist community organizations.

To adapt to these conflicts, the sociologists I interviewed developed several successful strategies that enabled them to be academically successful while doing effective activist research: participating in an organization that is accountable to both academia and activists, like the Berkeley Institute; using the "two-career" strategy and having one career oriented to academic colleagues and another oriented to activism; and working in a sociology department that values activist research. Researchers who cannot use these strategies will have to develop alternative compromises.

Combining activism with an academic career means "swimming against the stream," Mark Chesler observes. But it also brings opportunities to do nonalienating research that contributes to social justice and public welfare.

NOTE

Part of the discussion of participatory research in this essay is taken from an unpublished manuscript, "Participatory Research: An Introduction," coauthored with Cathleen Armstead. A different version of this chapter was published as "Conflicts between Activist Research and Academic Success" in *Participatory Research, Part II,* edited by Randy Stoecker and Edna Bonacich, special issue of *American Sociologist* 24, no. 1 (1993): 92–106. I am grateful to the professors who were interviewed for their participation and their comments on an earlier draft of this chapter.

REFERENCES

Brown, L. David, and Rajesh Tandon. 1983. "The Ideology and Political Economy of Inquiry: Action Research and Participatory Research." *Journal of Applied Behavioral Science and Technology: An International Perspective* 19 (3): 277–94.

Cancian, Francesca M. 1992. "Feminist Science: Methodologies that Challenge Inequality." *Gender and Society* 6 (4): 623–42.

———. 1989. "Participatory Research and Working Women at the University: Democratizing the Production of Knowledge." Paper presented at the annual meeting of the American Sociological Association. San Francisco.

Cancian, Francesca, and Cathleen Armstead. 1992. "Participatory Research." In *Encyclopedia of Sociology,* edited by Edgar Borgatta and Marie Borgatta. New York: Macmillan. 1427–32.

Chesler, Mark A. 1991. "Participatory Action Research with Self-Help Groups: An Alternative Paradigm for Inquiry and Action." *American Journal of Community Psychology* 19 (4): 757–68.

Collins, Patricia Hill. 1990. *Black Feminist Thought: Knowledge, Consciousness, and the Politics of Empowerment.* Boston: Unwin Hyman. Reprint. New York: Routledge, 1991.

Cook, Judith, and Mary M. Fonow. 1986. "Knowledge and Women's Interests: Feminist Methodology in the Field of Sociology." *Sociological Inquiry* 56 (1): 2–29.

Forrester, Keith. 1989. "An Uncomplicated Democratic Demand?: Local Research Activities with Trade Unions." In *Contemporary Ergonomics,* ed. E. D. Megaw. London: Taylor and Francis. 68–73.

Forrester, Keith, and Colin Thorne, eds. 1993. *Trade Unions and Social Research.* Aldershot, England: Avebury.

Forrester, Keith, and Kevin Ward. 1989. "The Potential and Limitations: Participatory Research in a University Context." Paper presented at the Participatory Research Conference. University of Calgary, Alberta.

Freeman, Howard, R. Dynes, P. Rossi, and W. Whyte, eds. 1983. *Applied Sociology.* San Francisco: Jossey-Bass.

Freire, Paulo. 1970. *Pedagogy of the Oppressed.* New York: Continuum.

Fritz, Jan, and Elizabeth Clark, eds. 1989. *The Development of Clinical and Applied Sociology.* Special issue of *Sociological Practice* 7.

Gaventa, John. 1988. "Participatory Research in North America." *Convergence* 21 (2): 19–29.

Gaventa, John, and Billy Horton. 1981. "A Citizen's Research Project in Appalachia, U.S.A." *Convergence* 14 (3): 30–40.

Gluck, Sherna Berger, and Daphne Patai, eds. 1991. *Women's Words: The Feminist Practice of Oral History.* New York: Routledge.

Harding, Sandra. 1991. *Whose Science? Whose Knowledge?: Thinking from Women's Lives.* Ithaca: Cornell University Press.

Hasenfeld, Yeheskel, and Mark A. Chesler. 1989. "Client Empowerment in the Human Services: Personal and Professional Agenda." *Journal of Applied Behavioral Science* 25 (4): 499–521.

Huizer, Gerrit, and Bruce Mannheim, eds. 1979. *The Politics of Anthropology: From Colonialism and Sexism toward a View from Below.* Paris: Mouton.

Lewin, Kurt. 1946. "Action Research and Minority Problems." *Journal of Social Issues* 4 (4): 34–46.

Maguire, Patricia. 1987. *Doing Participatory Research: A Feminist Approach.* Amherst, Mass.: Center for International Education, School of Education, University of Massachusetts.

Mannheim, Karl. 1936. *Ideology and Utopia.* New York: Harcourt, Brace, and World.

Mies, Maria. 1983. "Towards a Methodology for Feminist Research." In *Theories of Women's Studies,* ed. Gloria Bowles and Renate Duelli Klein. Boston: Routledge and Kegan Paul. 117–39.

Nebraska Sociological Feminist Collective. 1988. *A Feminist Ethic for Social Research.* Lewiston, N.Y.: Edwin Mellen Press.

Park, Peter. 1978. "Social Research and Radical Change." Paper presented at the Ninth World Congress of Sociology. Uppsala, Sweden.

Park, Peter, Mary Brydon-Miller, Budd Hall, and Ted Jackson, eds. 1993. *Voices of Change: Participatory Research in the United States and Canada.* Westport, Conn.: Bergin and Garvey.

Reason, Peter, and John Rowan, eds. 1981. *Human Inquiry: A Sourcebook of New Paradigm Research.* New York: John Wiley.

Tandon, Rajesh. 1988. "Social Transformation and Participatory Research." *Convergence* 21 (2): 5–18.

———. 1981. "Participatory Research in the Empowerment of People." *Convergence* 14 (3): 20–29.

Tichy, N., and S. Friedman. 1983. "Institutional Dynamics of Action Research." In *Producing Useful Information for Organizations,* ed. R. Kilman and C. Thomas. New York: Praeger. 395–415.

Vio Grossi, Francisco. 1981. "Socio-Political Implications of Participatory Research." *Convergence* 14 (3): 43–51.

Whyte, William Foote, ed. 1991. *Participatory Action Research.* Newbury Park, Calif.: Sage.

CHAPTER 10

ROBERTA SPALTER-ROTH
AND HEIDI HARTMANN

Small Happinesses: The Feminist Struggle to Integrate Social Research with Social Activism

The struggle to balance social science inquiry with social activism has been central in the lives of two generations of women. The first generation of researcher/activists was also the first group of women to be trained as social scientists in the new research universities of the late nineteenth-century United States. During this period, academic social science was in the process of becoming specialized and professionalized but was still oriented toward the illumination and solution of social problems (Fitzpatrick 1990). As part of the first wave of the feminist movement, these women were confident that the positivist method of social science inquiry and the voice of the social science expert could be employed in the service of progressive reform. A second generation of women, schooled in both the social sciences and the social movements of the 1960s and 1970s, became researcher/activists during the second wave of the feminist movement. Like the first generation, these women also use academic social science to raise public consciousness, advance public recognition of social problems, mobilize political support to change public agendas, and encourage structural reform. But unlike the first generation, who was committed to scientific objectivity as the basis of social reform, the second generation is more critical of the power relations embedded in the positivist method of the social sciences and is more ambivalent about its ability to bring about social reform.

In this chapter we first contrast the methodological views of these two generations of women. We then situate ourselves and our current research on work and welfare within what we have labeled "the dual vision of feminist policy research." This vision is an attempt to synthesize the views of the two generations—to create research that meets both the standards of positivist social science and feminist goals of doing research "for" rather than "on" women. Ideally, the research that results from this vision should provide reliable evidence while maintaining the agency of the research subject. It should combine the standpoint of both the expert and the activist, the insider and the outsider. Attempting to achieve this synthesis results in occasional moments of triumph, when we feel we have succeeded, fairly frequent questioning of ourselves and the chances for successfully attaining the political goals of the women's movement, and, most often, the daily small happinesses of doing our work.

THE FIRST GENERATION

Women such as Sophonisba Breckenridge, Edith Abbott, Katherine Bement Davis, and Frances Kellor, described in Mary Jo Deegan's *Jane Addams and the Men of the Chicago School, 1892–1918* (1988) and Ellen Fitzpatrick's *Endless Crusade: Women Social Scientists and Progressive Reform* (1990), undertook advanced study in sociology, political economy, and political science at the University of Chicago. The University of Chicago became a leader in forging links between the social science experts it trained and political and economic elites. The university did this in order to obtain the massive resources required to institutionalize disciplinary-based social sciences within the higher education system (Silva and Slaughter 1984). Despite the university's efforts to educate professional social science experts rather than radical reformers, some professors urged their students to "get out into the streets" and observe social realities, to organize social movements, and to use scholarship to advance both knowledge and reform (Fitzpatrick 1990).

Unlike their male colleagues who became academicians, the women trained at the University of Chicago were more likely to work for government and private organizations, where they developed surveys and statistical data in the service of social reform. Fitzpatrick portrays these women's efforts to advance the social sciences (with their special claims to expertise resting on adherence to scientific methods and values), while increasing the public's recognition of the structural nature of social problems and promoting the creation of a social welfare state. Fitzpatrick describes them: "Enamored of scientific fact, [they] mounted social investigations at every turn, convinced that knowledge itself was the key to intelligent reform. Research often served as an engine for reform—powering legislative change and political alliances, drawing in philanthropists, and justifying more sweeping intervention by the state" (1990:xiii). For example, Frances Kellor was so enamored of the scientific methods of the day that she used the hotly contested scientific apparatus of the eugenics movement in her study of women prisoners. She set up experimental laboratories equipped with an instrument called a kymograph to take cranial measurements of women prisoners. Although she engaged in some of the more repellent aspects of social science methodology, she was among the first to view women's imprisonment as a social problem rather than a result of moral weakness.

Some of these women were attached to Hull-House, the Chicago settlement house that served as the center for a massive network of women reformers. Deegan (1988) describes them as a "community of women researchers and reformers" who lived together, did survey research together, and formed organizations and movements for social change together. Deegan labels these women "critical pragmatists" because they developed a theory of science that linked the gathering of empirical data with social action in order to advocate for public policy within a framework of progressive social values.

During the heady days of the progressive movement, these women used the surveys they conducted and the statistics they compiled to build considerable careers, to develop organizations and coalitions, to educate the public, and to develop laws, bureaus, and commissions around a series of progressive causes, such as the alleviation of poverty, unemployment, child labor, and dangerous working conditions. The reputation of these researcher/activists waned with the ebbing of the progressive movement, the coming of World War I, and, in Deegan's view, the maturation of masculinist, academic social sciences that were increasingly divorced from social action. Stripped of a supportive movement for social change and faced with decreased political support for progressive measures, some, such as Kellor, became increasingly probusiness in their orientation.

With the waning of their influence, the stories of these women were lost to generations of scholars, including those of a second feminist generation who attended graduate schools during the 1960s and 1970s. The members of this new generation found themselves in academic departments largely bereft of women scholars, research on gender inequalities, and women's experiences. The prevailing explanations of social phenomena appeared largely directed to other scholars or to administrators and managers rather than to advocates of progressive change. The stories of the Progressive Era scholar/activists were rescued from social science oblivion by the members of the second wave of feminist scholar/activists, who were in search of their disciplinary foremothers.

THE SECOND GENERATION

In contrast to their foremothers, who believed that the scientific method distinguished their efforts from that of do-gooders and rabble-rousers (with whom they often worked), the members of the second wave are much less at ease linking the positivist methodology of the social sciences and the detached standpoint of the social science expert with the goals of the women's movement. Like the members of the first wave, the members of the second wave of feminist researchers also have been involved in doing research to influence the formation and implementation of social policy. They have produced a body of policy-relevant research on topics such as comparable worth, spouse abuse, rape, divorce, displaced homemakers, family and medical leave, women's poverty, women's health, and employment discrimination. They, too, have formed or participated in organizations, written scholarly and popular articles, testified before Congress and state legislators, and attempted to gain a hearing for those who are usually voiceless in the policy process. In spite of, and in some cases because of, their experiences as researchers and activists (see, for example, Steinberg and Haignere 1991), the members of the second wave, unlike the first generation, are more critical of the relationship between quantitative data and women's lived experiences, between the researcher and the subject of the research, and between the scientific expert and the political activist.

Unlike the first generation of researcher/activists, the members of the second generation conceive of science as a social construct, its inquiries and methods shaped by relations of power, specific historical contexts, dominant ideologies, and the standpoint of the scientist (Keller 1984; Harding 1986; Kitzinger 1987; Collins 1991). In her review of feminist research practices, Shulamit Reinharz (1992) suggests that the response of feminist researchers to survey and other statistically based forms of research is particularly characterized by "a profound ambivalence." The debate is frequently argued in terms of quantitative versus qualitative research methods, with proponents of the former claiming that appropriate quantitative evidence can be used to put issues on the map, counter sexist (and racist) research, which continues to be generated in the social sciences, and identify differences among women and change over time (Jayaratne 1983; Reinharz 1992). In contrast, those who distrust quantitative methods criticize the failure of the questions, concepts, and categories used to reflect women's experiences (Collins 1991; Stanley and Wise 1991; Westkott 1990; Oakley 1981). They criticize the preoccupation with "hard facts" that break the "living connections" between the data and flesh and blood reality (Mies 1991), and they criticize the hierarchical relations between interviewer and respondent that permeate survey research (Oakley 1981).

Equally distasteful to second-generation feminist researcher/activists is the standpoint of the neutral social science observer/expert, rooted in the positivist understanding of the relation between science and politics in which science is perceived as free of power and politics (Mies 1991). Rather than take the stance of the objective expert and engage in what Mies (1991) labels as "spectator knowledge," feminist researcher/activists feel bound to contribute to women's liberation by producing research that can be used by women themselves (Acker, Barry, and Esseveld 1991) and that "speaks out" against injustice rather than speaking for others (Klein 1983).

Both generations of researcher/activists can be described as passionate scholars, although the former distinguished between disinterested science and passionate politics (but did both), while the later generation criticizes the methodologies that emphasize their separation.

OUR STORY

The stories of these two generations are of particular interest to us as research director and director, respectively, of the Institute for Women's Policy Research (IWPR), a Washington, D.C., feminist think tank. IWPR was founded to meet the need for women-centered, policy-oriented research with a special concern for the complexity of policy needs of women as they vary by race, ethnicity, and class. Like the first generation of researcher/activists, we use statistical analyses of quantitative data, often written in the language of the neutral social scientist, in order to raise consciousness, redefine agendas, and promote progressive change in women's interests. Like both generations, we are schooled in both mainstream social science and oppositional social movements and are committed to linking research with social movements for women's liberation. Like our second-generation cohorts, we are more self-conscious about the role of the scientific method in privileging the word of the researcher rather than the researched and distancing the expert from the activist and more realistic about the limitations of feminist social science to bring about progressive reform that undermines the capitalist-patriarchal system.

The research we produce reflects an attempt to synthesize the scientific and the political, the neutral and the oppositional. We refer to this methodological synthesis as the "dual vision of feminist policy research" (see Spalter-Roth and Hartmann 1991). We want our research to give credibility to the claims made by groups attempting to use the policy process to improve women's lives. The dual vision results from our efforts to conduct policy research that simultaneously puts women's claims at the center and meets the standards of mainstream social science research. Our research reflects both dominant methodological and critical oppositional views because we employ mainstream social science techniques but filter these techniques through a feminist prism that critically examines how these techniques are likely to reproduce and legitimate relations of domination and inequality within genders, races, and classes.

Reinharz (1992) credits the dual vision of feminist policy research with providing a "feminist way of seeing," a critical feminist perspective, and a positive way of resolving the ambivalence of feminists toward the practices and arrangements of survey and other statistically based research. Although Reinharz (1992) cites our attempts to deal with feminist ambivalence through the dual vision as a solution, we view *developing* a dual vision as an ongoing struggle to be faced in each study we do. In what follows we analyze how we applied the dual vision in one IWPR research project, *Combining Work and Welfare: An Alternative Anti-Poverty Strategy* (Spalter-Roth, Hartmann, and Andrews 1992). We emphasize our efforts to provide statistically valid social science evidence while maintaining the agency of research subjects and our efforts to maintain our credibility with both mainstream experts and feminist activists in order to contribute to redefining the welfare policy agenda from a feminist perspective.

COMBINING WORK AND WELFARE: AN EXAMPLE OF THE DUAL VISION OF FEMINIST POLICY RESEARCH

Combining Work and Welfare grew out of our concern with the furor to get single mothers "off the welfare rolls and into the workplace." During the reactionary eighties, under the Reagan and Bush administrations, Aid to Families with Dependent Children (AFDC) was increasingly portrayed by policymakers and the media as a program that "allowed women to live without a husband or a job" (Amott 1990) and as a program that perpetuated the American underclass and reinforced its "dependence on government handouts" (U.S. Library of Congress 1987). The rhetoric of dependency was used to promote a political and ideological consensus in which conservatives and liberals aligned to pass the Family Support Act (FSA) of 1988, legislation that strives to transfer responsibility for the support of poor minority children from the state (via AFDC) to the market (by requiring "able-bodied" mothers to find paid employment or to participate in the JOBS program) and to biological fathers (via increased child support enforcement).[1] The FSA assumed that women who participated in the AFDC program did not work at paid employment and that work and welfare are mutually exclusive alternatives for poor women. In previous research (IWPR 1989), we found that a substantial portion of single mothers employed in low-wage work participated in means-tested government programs (such as AFDC and food stamps) as a supplement to their wages.

Based on our previous research, and in the face of the increasingly vitriolic attacks on AFDC participants, we sought to conduct and disseminate additional research that would destigmatize these women, recast their use of welfare and their participation in work as successful survival strategies, and reshape the policy debate. John Lanigan, then of the Ford Foundation's Urban Poverty Program, funded a new IWPR study. This new study proposed to examine the survival strategies, including employment activities, participation in government programs, income sources, and poverty rates of a nationally representative sample of women who participated in the AFDC program for at least two months during a two-year period. The principal research questions to be answered were How do women participating in AFDC put together their families' income package? What portion obtain enough money to move their families out of poverty? and What factors increase their ability to combine paid employment and participation in AFDC and to use these income packages to move their families out of poverty?

The study is based on data from a nationally representative, longitudinal sample of 585 single mothers, drawn from the 1986 and 1987 panels of the U.S. Bureau of the Census Survey of Income and Program Participation (SIPP), a data set that provides detailed information on family composition, employment, participation in government programs, and income.[2]

The findings that resulted from the first phase of this study challenge the consensus that welfare perpetuates dependence and that paid employment is the ticket out of poverty for single mothers and their children. We found that approximately four out of ten women who participated in the AFDC program worked for a substantial number of hours over a two-year period (approximately 1,000 hours per year—about half-time employment, the average amount worked by mothers with young children). They either combined paid employment and AFDC participation simultaneously or cycled between them. These women, referred to as income packagers, *increased* their family income and *decreased* their burden on the taxpayer by combining work and welfare (see figure 1). Despite their substantial work effort, their average family income remained below the poverty threshold (at about 95 percent of the poverty threshold for families of their size). Their average hourly wages only slightly exceeded the minimum wage, despite the fact that they had an average of six years of work experience.

Those recipients we labeled as "more welfare reliant," because their income package was composed of an average of twenty-three out of twenty-four months of AFDC benefits and almost no paid employment, were more likely to be disabled, had slightly more children (2.2 as

Figure 1: Income Packagers Receive Less Public Assistance but Have Higher Family Income than More Welfare-Reliant Recipients

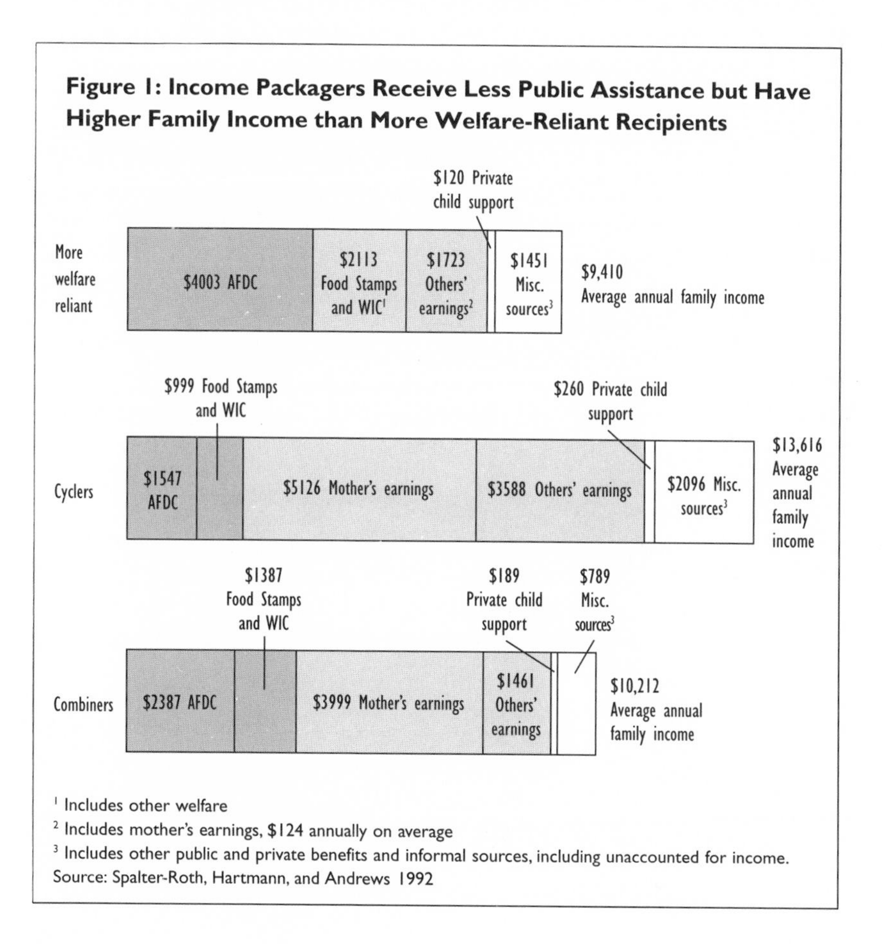

[1] Includes other welfare

[2] Includes mother's earnings, $124 annually on average

[3] Includes other public and private benefits and informal sources, including unaccounted for income.

Source: Spalter-Roth, Hartmann, and Andrews 1992

opposed to 1.8, on the average), and were less likely to be high school graduates. Despite stereotypes of a Black, never-married underclass, we found no significant differences between the "more reliant" and the "income packagers" in terms of their race or ethnicity and their previous marital history (see figure 2). Despite income supplements from other family members and miscellaneous sources, these women's families were the poorest.

We also found that high state-level unemployment rates have a negative effect on the probability of work/welfare packaging. For every one percentage point increase in state unemployment rates, the likelihood of including paid employment in the income packages declines by 9 percent. These findings indicate the importance of examining the economic context in which AFDC participants develop their survival strategies.

Based on these findings, we concluded that the current system of regulations does not enable AFDC participants who are doing paid work to move their families out of poverty. We recommended that the com-

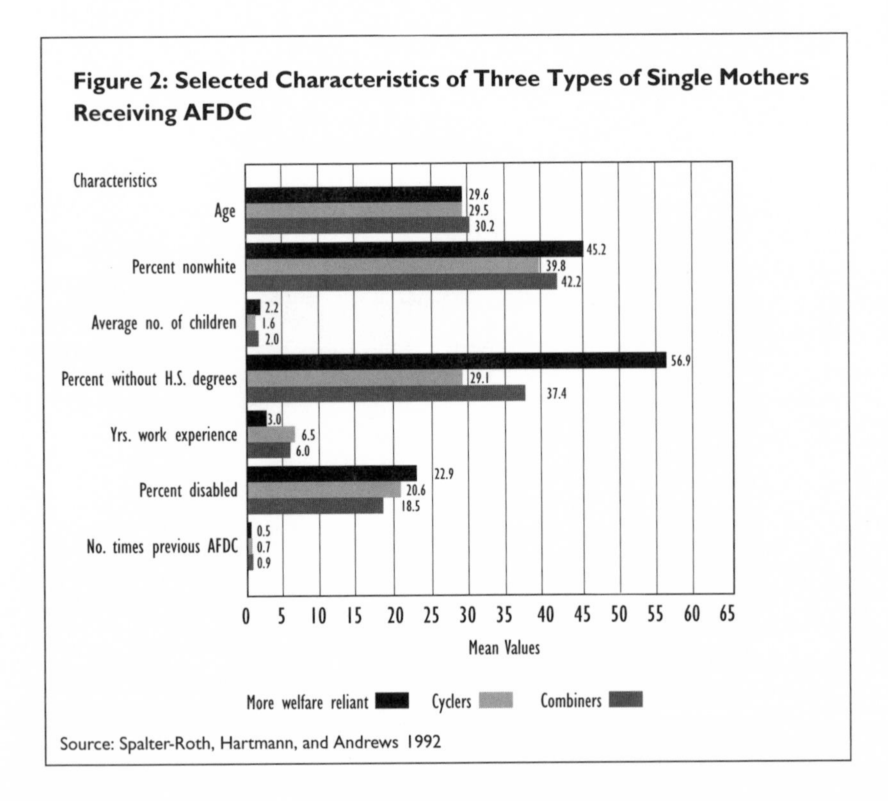

Figure 2: Selected Characteristics of Three Types of Single Mothers Receiving AFDC

Source: Spalter-Roth, Hartmann, and Andrews 1992

bining of work and welfare, along with income from other sources, be made legitimate because, at current levels, neither earnings nor means-tested benefits alone can provide a minimally sufficient income for single mothers and their families. We suggested additional policies that "make work pay," such as encouraging unionization, strengthening collective bargaining, increasing the minimum wage, and increasing available jobs through a full employment program. Finally, we concluded that not all single mothers can be expected to participate in paid employment. In particular AFDC participants with an above average number of children, little work experience and education, disabling conditions, limited access to other income sources, and living in areas with high unemployment rates are less likely to be able to do so. Higher benefit levels are a necessary poverty-reduction strategy for these women.

EVIDENCE AND AGENCY

Combining Work and Welfare, like the majority of IWPR studies, is based on the manipulation and analysis of nationally representative sample survey data usually collected by government bureaus. We use survey and statistically based research methods to provide the numbers that document the conditions of women as they vary by race, ethnicity, and class and to analyze whether public policies maintain, increase, or decrease these inequalities. Because we use secondary data analysis, we can be accused of engaging in the power relations found in the social arrangements of most mainstream research studies. We, not the respondents, choose the problem, design the study, analyze the data, and write up the results. We meet the subjects of our research in the most alienated and anonymous fashion, after they have been stripped of their names (to protect their anonymity), their own words, their own definitions of the situation, and after the connections between their responses to the survey questions and the "flesh and blood" reality of their daily lives have been severed.

Nevertheless, we believe the methodology we used in *Combining Work and Welfare* is appropriate for the goals of the dual vision. We used a large-scale data set to support claims about the representativeness of our findings.

We attempted to put these women at the center of our analysis. We portrayed them as active subjects engaged in survival strategies, albeit under structural and ideological conditions not of their choosing. To counterbalance the stripping process, we created "narrative diaries" from the data tape, allowing an individual woman's data record to tell her story. *Combining Work and Welfare* documents that women who participate in the AFDC program use welfare as a "cushion"—although an inadequate one—to support their families in the face of a low-wage, discriminatory job market. Rather than describing these women as passive victims, or as deviants enveloped in cultures of poverty or underclass behavior, we formulated measures of activities such as income packaging, combining work and welfare, and moving their families out of poverty.

Placing these women and their survival activities at the center of the analysis contrasts with the use by mainstream policy researchers of administrative counting units, such as the welfare "spell," and with the treatment of welfare recipients as subjects of experiments. In spell analysis the duration of the period of AFDC receipt is detached from the person receiving AFDC and the spell, not the person, becomes the unit of analysis. Spell analysis tends to focus on the numbers and length of spells, the reasons for entry and exit from spells, and the probability of spells lasting over time (see, for example, Bane and Ellwood 1994). Knowing how many spells occur in a given period, how long they are, and why they start or stop is useful for policy programming, planning, and budgeting purposes, but it is liable to displace women from the center of the analysis and to strip their behavior from its context and from its agency. Likewise, analysis of randomly assigned control group experiments, which compare the dollar amounts of AFDC receipt and earnings before and after a given treatment (usually participation in job training and other behavioral modification programs), can provide useful administrative data on program costs and benefits that can guide policy choices (see, for example, Gueron and Pauly 1991), but also generally treat AFDC recipients as objects of scrutiny rather than as subjects of their own lives.[3]

Like mainstream policy researchers, and like the first generation of feminist researcher/activists, our use of survey methods and statistical analysis in *Combining Work and Welfare* is an effort to provide reliable and generalizable evidence that can be used to inform public policy. In contrast to mainstream researchers, we are concerned with developing methodologies that reveal the agency of the women we study and the economic, ideological, and political context in which they make their lives. We believe this study reflects the critical standpoint of the dual vision of feminist policy research and combines the perspectives of first- and second-generation research/activists.

The use of secondary, anonymous data means, however, that we cannot directly ask the women whose lives we write about whether our perspective on their lives reflects their own. Nor can we directly organize them to bring about change in the conditions that negatively affect their lives. For our research to bring about progressive reform that liberates women we must not only seek to reform policy debate through research but must also work with social activists and policy advocates to ensure that the context in which the research is carried to the debate does benefit those who are its subjects.

EXPERT AND ACTIVIST

We want our research to be used by policymakers, by both mainstream and feminist researchers, by activists, and by women affected by policies. To fulfill this goal of producing *feminist* policy-relevant research, we attempt to synthesize the standpoint of the objective scientific expert with that of the participant in the women's movement.

In the case of *Combining Work and Welfare,* the purpose of the research was twofold. First, we wanted to counter policy and public discourse that stigmatized AFDC recipients as lazy, irresponsible, and solely dependent on taxpayer monies. Second, we wanted to suggest alternative policies to overcome the structures and patterns of inequality that they face, especially their dire poverty and their degraded treatment. Toward these ends, we distributed these findings widely through sale and complimentary distribution of the report, fact sheets (in English and in Spanish), press briefings, media interviews, meetings with advocacy groups, and public presentations.

In our efforts to provide credible evidence to demonstrate that current welfare policy stigmatizes the survival efforts of single mothers, we take the stance of the scientific expert. We do so because, for feminist researchers, the quest to gain credibility is difficult. Simply by having the term *women* in the institute's name, our work can be written off as biased, bleeding heart, and not worthy of consideration. Much like the first generation of researcher/activists, we use our reliance on the "scientific method" to gain credibility for our work by rhetorically reinforcing the distinction between science and ideology and by placing our research on the side of science. We introduce *Combining Work and Welfare* by distinguishing between our own use of random samples, "hard information," and "studies of actual behaviors" with the "fresh furor to get single mothers off the welfare rolls" inspired by "politics and ideology" (Spalter-Roth, Hartmann, and Andrews 1992:iii).

Part of our self-characterization as scientists is a performance and a rhetorical strategy to gain credibility for our analysis in the face of attack. By taking this standpoint, our research is more likely to be cited in the press as "hard fact" rather than rejected as the "whining of advocacy groups" (to use the words of a *Washington Post* reporter). As objective policy researchers, we are invited to present the research findings in the form of congressional testimony, and we are more likely than advocates to be invited to meetings convened by mainstream policy research organizations and other areas where policy is formulated. We hope this constant exposure helps to reframe the policy debate.

Yet when we are "inside" among policymakers and mainstream policy researchers, we speak out on behalf of women's interests in undermining systemic domination. Speaking out leads to our marginalization. Moreover, because of the questions addressed and the methods used, our research itself speaks out on behalf of women. At a recent meeting of the Advisory Committee to phase 2 of the *Combining Work and Welfare* project, a group composed of policy experts, program administrators, advocates, and researchers who accepted our invitation to provide guidance on the continuation of our study, a member from the Department of Health and Human Services described our research as inductive and as being concerned with the ability of welfare recipients to move out of poverty rather than off the welfare rolls. These characteristics were seen as making our research unusual—even unique—and, we inferred, less likely to be easily ingested and used by policymakers and program administrators. The advisor urged us not to change our methods or goals but to make our theoretical model, and its assumptions and expectations, more explicit.[4]

Our advisor's analysis of our research questions and policy goals was correct. These questions and goals are less likely to grow out of the mainstream research literature or administrative concerns than they are to grow out of our interactions with policy-oriented and grass-roots women's groups and from our own internationalization of the aspirations of the women's liberation movement. We often develop our research questions with women's advocacy groups and our interpretations of our findings through presentations to and discussions with them. If our findings mirror what advocates know to be true of women's lives, we consider them likely to be true or valid.

We have followed this validating procedure with *Combining Work and Welfare*, presenting and discussing our findings with many advocates. In spite of this activity, we are sometimes perceived as outsiders by these groups. Most recently we have been participating in a pro-welfare, women's economic survival coalition including the National Organization for Women (NOW), the NOW Legal Defense and Education Fund, and welfare rights groups. Among the purposes of this coalition is to move the policy agenda, under a new administration, from blaming poor women and their children for the results of welfare policy to implementing an agenda for their economic survival. As participants in this coalition, we were warned against disseminating research findings on the income packages put together by AFDC recipients because this information could be used by the media to reinforce powerful stereotypes of welfare cheats. As it turned out, this warning was accurate: an article written by a *Washington Post* reporter that went out over its wire service was published in the Madison, Wisconsin, *Capital Times* under the headline "Welfare Moms Work on Sly." Despite our chagrin over this misrepresentation of our findings, we think that the thousands of fact sheets and reports we have distributed have had a positive effect in stressing that many "welfare mothers" are already working to improve the financial lot of their children. In any case, we are reluctant to accede to the demands of advocacy groups to suppress study findings, despite their potential misuse. As we have reported elsewhere (Spalter-Roth and Hartmann 1991), tensions such as these—resulting in sleepless nights, day-long negotiations, and occasional name calling—typically occur between researchers and advocates, since researchers generally wish to expose findings while, in our experience, advocates wish to do so only when they feel sure that the findings will have positive political outcomes.

Despite the tensions and the marginality that result from our efforts to maintain our dual standpoint as credible research experts and as participants in an active women's reform movement, we hope that, in the long run, this dual standpoint increases rather than decreases our influence in the policy process. In the short-run our findings on work and welfare are less likely to affect the policy process than those of well-funded, well-connected mainstream research organizations such as the Manpower Research Development Corporation (MDRC). As Stacey Oliker (1994) suggests, MDRC was able to become the primary technical expert on the issue of "welfare reform" by gaining legitimacy for the use of an experimental design methodology that randomly assigned welfare recipients to treatment groups, by demonstrating that existing welfare experiments were marginally successful at moving recipients off the welfare rolls, and by bombarding the media and Congress with its findings. In contrast, our welfare policy proposals, even when modest in scope, tend to be critical of what exists. Further, we lack the resources to invest in large-scale publicity and dissemination campaigns.

But, as Oliker (1994) also notes, even groups such as MDRC, while much more likely to be treated as technical experts than is IWPR, did not set the welfare reform policy agenda implemented in the FSA. Rather, MDRC's research was used to legitimate an already existing political consensus that welfare was perpetuating the underclass and that public policy needed to "encourage self-sufficiency" and "help the needy to emancipate themselves" while providing cost savings to states (at least in the long run) by reducing the welfare rolls. MDRC's research demonstrated that state programs could move toward this goal. It is less likely that MDRC's research would have been perceived as useful by policymakers at the time of the FSA consensus if it had concluded, as IWPR's did, that moving recipients off the welfare rolls was less important than helping them to move out of poverty. In the longer run, IWPR's research, designed to reframe the debate, may be just as influential.

Although policy debates are often carried out in a discourse permeated by references to data (Weiss 1990), as if evidence always swayed minds and changed opinions, it is organized movements (be they right-wing, moderate, or progressive) that set the stage for policy change. An activist women's movement that carries the findings of our research and supports policy changes consistent with those findings can encourage policymakers to listen, especially when this movement contributes to electing members of Congress and presidents. By working in coalitions with advocates, our numbers and our scientific stance can legitimate feminist perspectives, if not during the initial policy formulation stage, then during the second or third go-round as policymakers face the likely failure of current policies based on blaming the victim. Our research helps to mobilize both the top and the bottom toward progressive policy change. Without a connection to the oppositional standpoints of activist women's groups involved in policy reform, our work either would be even more marginalized, as was the research of the first generation of researcher/activists when the progressive movement declined in influence, or, in search of an audience, would become more administratively oriented.

CONCLUSIONS

The first generation of researcher/activists believed that the scientific method, carried out through survey and other statistically based research methods, would illuminate social problems and provide the basis for enlightened state reform. From our standpoint as second-wave feminist critics, this view appears disingenuous about the power relations embedded both in the arrangements of social science research and in the public policy-making process. Can the more ambivalent notion of the dual vision of feminist policy research help to speak out against injustice and contribute to women's liberation? Under the pressure of deadlines and fund-raising, we do not spend a great deal of time consciously thinking about this issue. Rather, it is more a taken-for-granted assumption in our daily work lives. As old-time socialist-feminists, we believe that the capitalist patriarchal state, in general, defends the interests of those who control the means of production and reproduction. The result, in the case of welfare policy, is a system that stigmatizes single mothers, pressures them to take low-wage jobs, and treats them as social problems rather than as citizens and workers. But we also believe that strong countermovements and democratic coalitions among diverse groups of women (and men) can change state policy.

IWPR's research, such as *Combining Work and Welfare*, is not science for its own sake. Although we do not always have control over its use, we hope that it helps to heighten consciousness and to provide credible numbers that can help advocates to mobilize political support. Our research methodology, although it can perpetuate the distance between researchers and subjects, does place women at the center of the analysis, as subjects of their own lives rather than as subjects of experiments. Our dual standpoint as experts and advocates is a political strategy that calls for us to distance ourselves from "do-gooders" and "rabble rousers," as did first-generation research/activists, whenever this role seems strategically useful in the struggle for progressive change, and to work with advocates to formulate our research questions, validate our results, and disseminate our findings. The result can be uneasy relations with mainstream researchers, policymakers, funders, advocacy groups, and feminist activists. But, it can also result in exhilarating moments when we see the numbers that we have generated cited in newspaper articles or heard them spoken by members of Congress to support arguments for change. Between these occasional brief moments of triumph and the longer periods of questioning whether we are making a difference (when we feel marginalized by everyone—allies, opponents, and targets of influence alike), we persist day to day experiencing the small happinesses of doing work that we hope contributes to the liberation of women.

NOTES

1. The AFDC program, implemented as part of the Social Security Act of 1935, was designed, in part, by the Progressive Era researcher/activists. Modeled on state-level and private mother's aid and mother's pension programs, it aimed to prevent the transplanting of children from their households to orphanages because their widowed mothers were too poor to support them. This program operated using a regulatory model with intensive casework—including the investigation and monitoring of the moral fitness of the moth-

ers. AFDC is often given as an example of the social control aspects of the programs designed by Progressive Era reformers.

2. As with all Census Bureau surveys, the SIPP can be accused of having an androcentric bias because families are viewed as income-pooling units rather than the locus of struggle over the production and distribution of goods and services (Hartmann 1981) and definitions of employment do not include unpaid work. For an in-depth analysis of the androcentrism of U.S. Census Bureau surveys, see Anderson (1992).

3. While we believe it is possible to use these techniques in a woman-centered way, mainstream policy researchers generally do not. The questions they ask focus less on the structural conditions in which women try to put together their livelihoods and more on the outcomes of program interventions.

4. We were fascinated by the extent to which "theory-based," deductive models were clearly preferred—had higher status—in the committee discussion to experience-based, inductive models. Our study, which attempts to put what women actually do (combine work and welfare) at the center of the analysis was seen as experience-based or inductive. Especially in the field of economics, the latter approach is viewed as a "fishing" expedition. It is thought far superior to state one's expectations of how people will behave, based on theory, and then either confirm or fail to confirm one's expectations through empirical testing. With our usual ambivalence, we are currently considering whether we should restate our model so as to make our "expectations" clear. Stating one's theory-based expectation up front, common in much social science research, tends to place the objective, neutral researcher at the center of the analysis, rather than the experiences of subjects.

REFERENCES

Acker, Joan, Kate Barry, and Joke Esseveld. 1991. "Objectivity and Truth: Problems in Doing Feminist Research." In *Beyond Methodology: Feminist Scholarship as Lived Research,* ed. Mary Margaret Fonow and Judith A. Cook. Bloomington: Indiana University Press. 133–53.

Amott, Teresa L. 1990. "Black Women and AFDC: Making Entitlement Out of Necessity." In *Women, the State, and Welfare,* ed. Linda Gordon. Madison: University of Wisconsin Press. 280–98.

Anderson, Margo. 1992. "The History of Women and the History of Statistics." *Journal of Women's History* 4 (1): 12–36.

Bane, Mary Jo, and David Ellwood. 1994. *Welfare Relations: From Rhetoric to Reform.* Cambridge: Harvard University Press.

Collins, Patricia Hill. 1991. "Learning from the Outsider Within." In *Beyond Methodology: Feminist Scholarship as Lived Research,* ed. Mary Margaret Fonow and Judith A. Cook. Bloomington: Indiana University Press. 35–59.

Deegan, Mary Jo. 1988. *Jane Addams and the Men of the Chicago School, 1892–1918.* New Brunswick, N.J.: Transaction Books.

Fitzpatrick, Ellen. 1990. *Endless Crusade: Women Social Scientists and Progressive Reform.* New York: Oxford University Press.

Gueron, Judith, and Edward Pauly. 1991. *From Welfare to Work.* New York: Russell Sage Foundation.

Harding, Sandra. 1986. *The Science Question in Feminism.* Ithaca: Cornell University Press.

Hartmann, Heidi. 1981. "The Family as the Locus of Gender, Class, and Political Struggle: The Example of Housework." *Signs* 6 (3): 366–94.

Institute for Women's Policy Research. 1989. *Low-Wage Jobs and Workers: Trends and Options for Change.* Washington, D.C.: Institute for Women's Policy Research.

Jayaratne, Toby Epstein. 1983. "The Value of Quantitative Methodology for Feminist Research." In *Theories of Women's Studies,* ed. Gloria Bowles and Renate Duelli Klein. Boston: Routledge and Kegan Paul. 140–61.

Keller, Evelyn Fox. 1984. *Reflections on Gender and Science.* New Haven, Conn.: Yale University Press.

Kitzinger, Celia. 1987. *The Social Construction of Lesbianism.* Beverly Hills, Calif.: Sage.

Klein, Renate. 1983. "How to Do What We Want to Do: Thoughts about Feminist Methodology." In *Theories of Women's Studies,* ed. Gloria Bowles and Renate Duelli Klein. Boston: Routledge and Kegan Paul. 88–104.

Mies, Maria. 1991. "Women's Research or Feminist Research?: The Debate Surrounding Feminist Science and Methodology." In *Beyond Methodology: Feminist Scholarship as Lived Research,* ed. Mary Margaret Fonow and Judith A. Cook. Bloomington: Indiana University Press. 60–84.

Oakley, Anne. 1981. "Interviewing Women: A Contradiction in Terms." In *Doing Feminist Research,* ed. Helen Roberts. London: Routledge and Kegan Paul. 30–61.

Oliker, Stacey. 1994. "Does Workfare Work?: Evaluation Research and Workfare Policy." *Social Problems* 4 (2): 195–213.

Reinharz, Shulamit. 1992. *Feminist Methods in Social Research.* New York: Oxford University Press.

Silva, Edward, and Sheila Slaughter. 1984. *Serving Power: The Making of the Academic Social Science Expert.* Westport, Conn.: Greenwood Press.

Spalter-Roth, Roberta M., Heidi I. Hartmann, and Linda Andrews. 1992. *Combining Work and Welfare: An Alternative Anti-Poverty Strategy.* Washington, D.C.: Institute for Women's Policy Research.

———. 1991. "Science and Politics and the 'Dual Vision' of Feminist Policy Research: The Example of Family and Medical Leave." In *Parental Leave and Child Care: Setting a Research and Policy Agenda,* ed. Janet Shibley Hyde and Marilyn J. Essex. Philadelphia: Temple University Press. 41–65.

Stacey, Judith. 1988. "Can There Be a Feminist Ethnography?" *Women's Studies International Forum* 11 (1): 21–27.

Stanley, Liz, and Sue Wise. 1991. "Feminist Research, Feminist Consciousness, and Experience of Sexism." In *Beyond Methodology: Feminist Scholarship as Lived Research,* ed. Mary Margaret Fonow and Judith A. Cook. Bloomington: Indiana University Press. 265–83.

Steinberg, Ronnie, and Lois Haignere. 1991. "Separate but Equivalent: Equal

Pay for Work of Comparable Worth." In *Beyond Methodology: Feminist Scholarship as Lived Research,* ed. Mary Margaret Fonow and Judith A. Cook. Bloomington: Indiana University Press. 154–70.

U.S. Library of Congress. Congressional Research Service. 1987. "New Ideas on Welfare," *Albuquerque Journal,* Nov. 9, 1986, B2. In *Welfare Reform: National Consensus/National Debate Overviews [Newspaper Editorials and Public Opinion Polls].* CRS Report no. 87–556-L, Saundra Shirley-Reynolds and Roger Walke. Washington, D.C.: Congressional Research Service.

Weiss, Carol H. 1990. "The Uneasy Partnership Endures: Social Science and Government." In *Social Scientists, Policy, and the State,* ed. Stephan Brooks and Alain-G. Gagnon. New York: Praeger. 97–111.

Westkott, Marcia. 1990. "Feminist Criticism of the Social Sciences." In *Feminist Research Methods: Exemplary Readings in the Social Sciences,* ed. Joyce McCarl Nielsen. Boulder: Westview Press. 58–68.

CHAPTER 11

RONNIE J. STEINBERG

Advocacy Research for Feminist Policy Objectives: Experiences with Comparable Worth

Since 1978, I have worked as an advocacy researcher, primarily with unions and women's organizations in the United States and Canada, on the issue of comparable worth. Comparable worth, also referred to as pay equity, involves correcting for the underpayment of wages to those performing such historically female jobs as registered nurse, legal secretary, clerk, food service worker, and housekeeper because that work has been and continues to be performed primarily by women. Along with advocacy researchers such as Lois Haignere, Helen Remick, Lynda Ames, and Patricia Armstrong, I performed a variety of research and analytical activities in political contexts that bring scholarship to bear on social issues explicitly for the purpose of achieving change in structural arrangements in power relations—in my case, primarily on behalf of women.[1]

I have not only played the narrowly technical roles of information-gatherer, researcher, and teacher but I also have participated in developing and carrying out political and legal strategies for achieving pay equity objectives, including writing final legal arguments presented before an administrative tribunal. I have used my scientific credentials and "expert" status, along with conventional social science research methodologies, as a power resource to further this policy goal (Larson 1984). Throughout this work, I have juggled the explicit contradiction between the openly political and biased character of advocacy for specific policy objectives and the supposed political neutrality and bias-free assumptions of scientific inquiry. Advocacy researchers, thus, live within these and other tensions. And the complications of advocacy research are compounded because I work explicitly as a *feminist* social scientist on an explicitly *feminist* reform.

The role of the feminist advocacy researcher is a meaningful but problematic one. For those of us politicized in the sixties and drawn to feminism in the seventies, the selection of sociology as a critical discipline in which to conduct our intellectual work satisfies our need to identify issues and conduct research that contributes to social change. Yet, once we move onto the terrain of politics, working directly on policy initiatives, the stakes become high and the contradictions intensify. On the one hand, advocacy research within the comparable worth movement has the potential to dramatically affect the lives of those employees, especially those who perform historically female work. Some of that potential has been realized. According to an Institute for Women's Policy Research study, twenty states implemented some pay equity initiative in the eighties. Overall these states spent more than $527,000,000 (in 1990 dollars) on pay equity wage adjustments (Hartmann, Aaronson, and Sorenson 1993). At the individual job level, these initiatives can yield 10–20 percent wage adjustments, involving salary increases of over $3,000. For librarians and registered nurses, the adjustments can run as high as $5,000 to $8,000. In every state that implemented some form of pay equity, the gap in wages between male and female workers declined (Hartmann, Aaronson, and Sorenson 1993). On the other hand, the attempt to use research as a resource in accomplishing one's political goals involves serious technical, political, and ethical challenges (Steinberg 1986). Not one pay equity initiative approached, in its actual wage adjustments, the correction in wages that would have occurred had compensation systems been fully cleansed of gender bias based on current technical knowledge (Acker 1989; Evans and Nelson 1989; Steinberg 1991; Haignere 1991; Blum 1991).

My experiences over the sixteen years of my involvement with pay equity have not been uniform. The use and significance of advocacy research changed at different stages of this reform's trajectory. Moreover, the impact and control of the advocacy researcher over the research product changed at different stages. In what follows, I highlight the issues of use and control of research to examine the tensions inherent in the advocacy researcher role to determine how these tensions emerged and whether they can even be resolved. I also examine the unresolvable contradictions between science and advocacy and reflect upon the relationship between principles of feminist methodology and this type of advocacy research.

• • •

The Center for Women in Government (CWG) was a year old when I arrived from the Wellesley College Center for Research on Women to continue my research on equal employment policies for women (Steinberg-Ratner 1980). The structure of CWG embodied some of the tensions inherent in advocacy research. At that time, CWG had an activist executive director and board chair, both of whom had recently left staff positions organizing for the American Federation of State, County, and Municipal Employees (AFSCME), the largest public employee union. Yet, CWG was located in a university, at the State University of New York at Albany (SUNYA), within the School of Public Administration, and I was the only researcher on staff. I was subordinate to people who didn't really value research for its own sake, as you would expect in a university, but for its use in achieving social change. SUNYA provided no direct funding, but did provide intellectual credibility, space, and minimal infrastructure. However, through their own political connections, Executive Director Nancy Perlman and Board Chair Linda Tarr Whelan secured a state legislative appropriation in the SUNYA budget directly to CWG. This small appropriation was supplemented with grants and contracts. Since we were primarily a soft-money institution, we began by working on more palatable issues to ensure our survival. By the time we attempted to gain funding for comparable worth research, we had completed over a dozen projects.

Indeed, we began to work on pay equity without any funding and largely on "our own" time. Along with Phyllis Palmer of George Washington University and Teresa Odendahl, then of the Business and Professional Women's Foundation, I organized the first research conference on pay equity. Nancy Perlman and I participated with others in founding the National Committee on Pay Equity (for which Nancy Perlman served as the first president of the board and I served as chair of the Research Task Force). We shaped, with congressional staff, the first federal hearings on the reform and appeared among those who testified. We gave many unpaid talks on pay equity to whomever would invite us, ranging from the Social Action Committee of New York City 9 to 5 to the Phil Donahue show.

We knew that we had made some progress when the opposition appeared out of the woodwork, often turning what had previously been one-sided speaking engagements into debates. Proponents spent a lot of time defining and redefining the reform in defensive reaction to vocal opposition from the business roundtable, chambers of commerce, and personnel management associations. We debated whether we could compare "apples and oranges," that is, dissimilar jobs; we debated the nature of the market (Marshall and Paulin 1984); we debated the cost of adjusting wages for undervalued jobs. We even debated whether or not there *was* sex discrimination in the labor market (Steinberg 1986, 1987). We thought we had that one under control when the National Research Council report concluded that a substantial portion of the wage gap was due to discrimination that was a byproduct of occupational segregation (Treiman and Hartmann 1981). But, shortly after, under funding from the U.S. Commission for Civil Rights—a major opponent of the reform—the economist June O'Neill argued that most of the wage gap could be explained away by differential hours of work, by age, and by marital status (used inappropriately as a proxy for choice). Proponents then had to compile and make accessible to the general public social science research that emphasized the role of employer decision-making in the allocation of workers to positions and in the compensation of positions relative to one another. At that time, the opposition's reliance on individualistic free choice arguments resonated much more effectively with American ideology about the labor market.

Social scientists were drawn into the comparable worth debate early on, and political debates rested heavily on the shoulders of competing technical analyses. The sides drawn were not simply feminist versus antifeminist, but, with a few exceptions, were also divided by discipline. Sociologists and social psychologists often prepared the case for comparable worth, with economists and industrial psychologists providing the intellectual arguments against.

• • •

In these early years, Lois Haignere, who joined the CWG staff in 1981, and I worked with activists in New York State and across the country, first participating in building a case for the reform and then trying to measure wage discrimination. Proponents' efforts gained enormously in 1981 by the court decision in *Gunther* (which indicated that the court would accept certain explicit inequities between dissimilar jobs as constituting wage discrimination under Title VII), by the final report of the National Research Council, *Women, Work, and Wages* (Treiman and Hartmann 1981) (which cautiously concluded that employment discrimination could be corrected through a policy of comparable worth), and by a successful strike over pay equity by public employees in San Jose, California (Steinberg 1984b). By 1981, comparable worth had moved from an abstract pie-in-the-sky political demand to a doable reform priority that trendsetter states like Minnesota and Oregon had actually begun to consider and implement (see Steinberg 1990, 1991 for a fuller discussion).

Research was an integral part of these efforts. Especially important was breaking down somewhat complicated arguments into ones that were comprehensible to the average public employee and to the electorate in general. It further involved strategically presenting ideas in a way that undercut the opposition's ability to discredit us. Two success stories from my personal experience are relevant here: In early 1982, I was asked by members of the West Virginia chapter of the National Organization for Women to be their keynote speaker at the forum held on the evening before their annual Women's Day Lobby, because members viewed pay equity as their primary legislative priority for the coming year. They invited leaders of the two political parties to speak briefly on these issues as well. I introduced pay equity briefly but devoted most of my time to identifying myths about the reform and answering the predictable charges of the critics. The leaders of the political parties were asked to respond to my talk. Knowing the arguments previously leveled against the reform, I was able to address them with not easily discredited factual information. The politicians' remarks were visibly vacuous. The next day the legislature unanimously passed a bill to establish a task force to examine the problem of pay equity in that state. While the vote had more to do with the substantial gender gap in the midyear elections and with political tactics to deflect meaningful action for the issue, the event and my speech added icing to the cake.

A similar encounter with Morris Abram, a member of the U.S. Commission on Civil Rights, reveals how such dialogues often try to discredit and defeat reform. In my testimony before the commission, I described the New York State Comparable Pay Study, from which I concluded that wage discrimination could be measured and that compensation systems could be cleansed of race and gender bias if a political commitment existed (Steinberg 1984a). Abram tried to discredit my position, first by pointing out that my political values undercut my credibility as a scientist, imputing that scientists don't have values. And second, he reduced comparable worth to a process of communistlike wage setting that scientists would control, almost mocking the idea of scientific control. Our exchanges went as follows:

> Vice Chairman Abram: Do you feel that the concept [of comparable worth] should be broadened, as a matter of public policy, to embrace an evaluation in which people, regardless of their race, color, or creed or in jobs that are lower paid but are higher rated, should have their pay raised as a matter of public policy?
>
> Dr. Steinberg: Are you asking me to speak as an expert or as a citizen?
>
> Vice Chairman Abram: Well, as an expert.
>
> Dr. Steinberg: I don't think that as an expert I can answer that question.

Vice Chairman Abram: All right. As a citizen, then.

Dr. Steinberg: As a citizen, yes. I do believe as a matter of personal principle that individuals who are in low-paid positions, regardless of race or sex, national origin, or the like, should be paid fairly in the labor market. . . .

Vice Chairman Abram: Have you thought very deeply or long about what it would mean to have wage scales established in this country, even absent discrimination in the conventional sense, by the not learned people who practice psychometrics, sociometrics, and econometrics?

Dr. Steinberg: I don't think the idea that social scientists bring empirical findings back to policy-makers means that social scientists are setting an inflexible wage policy. I don't think that follows. . . .

Vice Chairman Abram: I gather, then, that you feel, if I am expressing your feelings correctly—tell me; if not, tell me also—that what is involved, as a citizen looking for justice and equity; is the reorganization of the way in which wages are established in this country.

Dr. Steinberg: No. No, I disagree with that.

Vice Chairman Abram: You do?

Dr. Steinberg: Yes.

Vice Chairman Abram: Okay.

Dr. Steinberg: And I disagree with that because in the New York State context and in most public sector work organizations—Federal, State, county, and municipal—some form of classification system with more or less formal allocation of positions into job titles already operates. These systems are already used as the basis for allocating jobs across a wage structure.

When we are undertaking a comparable pay study, we start at the point at which work organizations already operate and use their own methodologies to seek adjustment in the procedures that they already use. We are not reorganizing the way wages are structured in the society. We are using the very technologies already in use and adjusting them to eliminate discrimination. (U.S. Commission on Civil Rights 1984:62–63)

Because he controlled the direction of the questioning, I chose not to challenge the premises of his questions (except about the reorganization of wage setting, where he was factually inaccurate), but to disagree with the conclusions that followed from his premises. In a limited sense, this strategy worked. The commission's report on the hearings does not attack bureaucratic wage-setting procedures on scientific grounds. Instead, the commission offered classic free market economic rhetoric and concluded that the wage gap was not a product of labor market discrimination. These were not efforts at understanding but at winning, for both sides.[2]

Research at the early stages of the reform also involved grappling with the goal of comparable worth, especially with the issue of nondiscriminatory compensation systems. Although it took almost ten more years before the development of gender-neutral comparisons systems, in the early eighties, we found it necessary to develop standards on the *absence* of discrimination in compensation practices. During presentations, for example, personnel managers, often from private sector firms, would ask what they could do informally to determine if there was wage discrimination in their compensation practices. Building on the work of Helen Remick (1980, 1981, 1984) and of Donald Treiman and Heidi Hartmann (Treiman 1979; Treiman and Hartmann 1981), I developed a set of systematic standards for assessing job evaluation systems around maximizing consistency and inclusiveness of work performed in each of three steps of the job evaluation process: in the ways jobs are described, in the evaluation procedures, and in salary setting. Lois Haignere and I used these standards as the basis for our assessment in Massachusetts and spoke about them often at forums (Steinberg 1984a, 1990; Steinberg and Haignere 1987). As we put forth these standards, we somewhat arrogantly thought that they might eventually be treated by practitioners *as if* they carried the strength of law. Ironically, we did manage to have some impact. Finally, in 1991, they were incorporated into specific guidelines on gender neutrality issued by the Ontario Pay Equity Tribunal in a major decision.

Throughout the early efforts to establish pay equity guidelines, it was exciting to participate in the process of legitimating and establishing the parameters of the reform—to take on the business roundtable and even high-level Reagan appointees; to persuade audiences that the reform was not an absurd proposal of radical feminists out to destroy the economic system of the country. At many moments we thought it would be a miracle to achieve any reform even faintly resembling the objectives associated with comparable worth. In this context, we were exceptionally positive about any initiative that occurred. With hindsight, we realized that several of these early initiatives had actually established precedents that limited the scope of subsequent initiatives. Once one jurisdiction had taken the most conservative and narrow approach to adjusting wages, calling it pay equity and getting away with it politically, other jurisdictions had little incentive to correct fully for all of the wage discrimination identified by proponents. By the early nineties, my assessments of pay equity accomplishments were much less positive (compare, for example, Steinberg and Haignere 1984 to Steinberg 1991).

• • •

By the early eighties, comparable worth initiatives had taken off around the country, stimulated in part by Judge Tanner's decision in *AFSCME v. Washington* as well as by the fear of the gender gap that surfaced in the 1982 midterm elections. The implementation of pay equity had begun.

This profound change in the trajectory of the reform had a significant impact on our role as researchers. Proponents no longer had exclusive control over the definition of pay equity. Nor did they have a monopoly on the research conducted in its name. Rather, at the state level, politicians who moved forward with the reform and administrators who implemented legislation and collectively bargained agreements redefined the reform, and not simply through the process of political compromise. The process was more like "containment," in which pay equity was implemented in terms of the lowest wage adjustments politically feasible, with traditional compensation practices maintained virtually intact and with other political agendas attached to the initiative, some of which were in fundamental contradiction to pay equity (Steinberg 1991). Research on wage discrimination was now both subject to serious constraints and could be used to subvert the reform it was intended to help.

Jurisdictions might decide on the total appropriation for pay equity adjustments long before receiving any study results on the extent of wage discrimination. In at least two states and one city of which I am aware, policymakers told researchers (in this case, working for compensation consulting firms) to present findings that fell within the amount of funds appropriated. In other words, they were to design studies with predetermined results that "worked" for politicians. Most consultants complied.

An advocacy researcher almost inevitably faces such situations if the reform on which she works is taken seriously politically. Once there is money to be made in conducting research, the field of available researchers broadens well beyond the handful of pioneering advocacy researchers. Advocacy researchers like CWG, whose primary commitment is to the reform, are often marginalized at this point, dismissed as purists, and replaced by profit-making companies waiting to conduct research fulfilling the needs of those willing to pay their rates. Many of these consulting firms conducted pay equity studies using the job evaluation systems that had been cited by advocacy researchers as the very one saturated with gender bias. It should come as no surprise that these studies found little or no wage discrimination. Our often unpaid role as advocacy researchers under these circumstances was to point out the deficiencies of these studies and hope that pro–pay equity activists would employ our study to force the jurisdiction to undertake another study, or, at best, to avoid implementing the one that had been conducted.

CWG also bid on but received few contracts to conduct pay equity studies, primarily because we were viewed as politically "uncontrollable," and because we did not have a track record in the field of compensation.[3] Often, a more palatable management consulting firm would get the contract instead. Palatability referred to a demonstrated sensitivity to the political and fiscal constraints surrounding the reform. My colleagues and I at CWG used systematic social science techniques as the basis for arriving at justifiable estimates of wage discrimination, regardless of fiscal and political difficulties. As social scientists committed to what Joan Acker (1989) has called "true comparable worth," we carried a double stigma that almost ensured our early elimination from the pool of consultants considered, often as a political compromise, in which our removal was contingent on the elimination of one of the traditional management consulting firms. Ironically, this purism eventually turned to our advantage, when our "blessing" on a number of Canadian initiatives was sought.

Nonetheless, when we did participate in an initiative, we invariably came to loggerheads with policymakers over recommendations that they found troublesome because of their political implications. For example, Lois Haignere and I received a contract from the Special Committee on Comparable Worth of the Massachusetts legislature. As part of our findings, we noted that wage scales varied considerably as a function of sex-segregated union bargaining units. The special committee feared the response of the male-dominated unions to this finding and to the recommendation that further investigation and possible correction was needed to achieve pay equity. Although they asked us to drop this recommendation, we refused. The committee took over a year to release our report and we were contractually prohibited from sharing our conclusions with activist proponents. When the report was released, the committee, not surprisingly, rejected our recommendation, citing the possibility that our recommendation might "compromise the right of employees to bargain over wages" (Special Committee on Comparable Worth 1986:4). Yet, management in most public jurisdictions does not consider it a "compromise" to restrict labor's bargaining rights to percentage wage increases, treating the issue of the level of base pay as a management prerogative beyond the scope of collective bargaining.

This story recounts a situation in which proponents with high credibility conducted research that was selectively implemented and used to legitimate other policy agendas not necessarily consistent with pay equity. Information gathered by the state was then withheld from citizens and those representing its employees, both the report we prepared and the details of the wage agreements with the unions. The state's actions could not be assessed. Our efforts as advocacy-researchers were undercut by the power of the special committee, the Department of Personnel, and the Office of Employee Relations. It may sound naive to have assumed otherwise but our sense of the staff and political leadership of the special committee led us to assume their genuine commitment to this reform.

• • •

One of the reasons the members of the special committee could control unilaterally their pay equity initiative was weak external political support. At that time, only a few individuals representing organizations of little consequence to the relevant politicians made any noise. This weak political base constrained the outcome of the New York State Comparable Pay Study as well and limited our advocacy. Part of the problem lay in the changing role of CWG from advocate to researcher.

In the early eighties, CWG was the major political force pressing for pay equity in New York State public employment, along with union women leaders and several high-level state administrators. In 1982, the Civil Service Employees Association (CSEA), the largest of the three unions representing public employees in New York State and the Office of Employee Relations agreed, as part of its contract negotiations, to undertake a comparable pay study. It allocated $500,000. CWG positioned itself as the "natural" choice to conduct the study. The state delayed but finally, after eighteen months, signed a contract with CWG.

Both labor and management had reservations about CWG. Management was primarily uncomfortable giving a feminist advocacy organization that much control over a study of such consequence, even if this feminist center was university-based. Labor's problems hinged on issues of control and was also fueled by union leadership hostility toward the CWG director and the former chair of its board, who had earlier attempted to organize employees away from CSEA. CWG had to mobilize its women's networks within each group to counteract this resistance. Although CWG received its contract, management offered another contract to a mainstream consulting firm as protection against the possible results of our study.

In retrospect, the state and the unions didn't have to worry about CWG's stance as an advocate. Giving CWG the research contract effectively tied its hands from playing an advocacy role. In other words, CWG's critical political role up to that point as an advocate for comparable worth had to be put on the back burner in order for it to carry out defensible social science research on wage discrimination in state government employment.

The study remains the largest comparable pay study yet undertaken and the first undertaken using defensible social science techniques by explicit proponents of the reform (Steinberg, Haignere, Possin, Chertos, and Treiman 1985). Initially, as director of this study, I was given considerable discretion, by New York State and CSEA and within CWG, to design the study consistent with the standards of pay equity and gender neutrality that we had earlier delineated. The analysis involved a 112-item questionnaire designed essentially from scratch and distributed to over 37,000 employees in over 2,900 different job titles. The questionnaire asked a large sample of employees what they did on their job. The 73 percent response rate reflected our almost obsessive concern with collecting a data base that would prove invulnerable to political attempts to discredit the study. The final step used the data collected to construct a statistical model of the state's implicit wage policy. This model was adjusted to remove the effect of gender and race in wages as the basis for estimating wage discrimination.

The initial independence was short-lived. Soon after the study began, the state created a staff position within the Office of Employee Relations to monitor our activities (at least initially) full-time. A second staff position was established to monitor the concurrent management compensation study. Every detail of every decision we made was documented in required monthly reports and in regular face-to-face meetings. Within six months of the study's initiation, the contract monitor had constituted an advisory committee, the key players of which came from the Department of Personnel, the Office of Employee Relations, the Governor's Office, and the Division of the Budget. By contrast, the CSEA (now our only possible source of protection apart from a few well-placed women in the administration) assigned review of the study to an overworked director of research and to one of his overworked staff researchers. The union monitors requested nothing from us. We sent them the monthly reports as a matter of courtesy and often involved them in design decisions that could not be justified solely on technical grounds and that management would have preferred to make unilaterally.

Design features of the study were often crafted in the political process, because they involved serious political and fiscal issues and because they could not be justified solely on technical grounds or on past research practice. We "lost" on many decisions. If CWG still played primarily an advocacy role, it would have fought a stronger and more openly political battle for its preferred options. Or, if CWG or feminist advocates within government or the unions had built a strong external political base, these groups could have fought for the design options we thought were both intellectually plausible and politically desirable. Without that base, as researchers, we could only make more or less convincing intellectual arguments to management and labor. More often than not, the union supported management preferences. This situation did not affect the technical quality of the research, but it did affect what we were "permitted" to study. It is one important reason why the designers of the study arrived at unusually low estimates of wage discrimination.

Most of the political action surrounding the pay equity study occurred *within* the management Advisory Council to the Technical Monitor. The constant fights climaxed almost one year into the study, when shortly before we were scheduled to distribute the questionnaire (carefully planned for a time of the year selected to maximize returns), the Division of the Budget stopped payment to CWG as a way of terminating the study. It questioned the methodological rigor and hired two male industrial psychologists as consultants with no experience or expertise in either compensation or pay equity to review all our work to that point. For the next few months, we waited for their review, which required a 110-page rebuttal by CWG's comparable worth team. In the end, we made one or two insignificant changes in our design. The obstruction was removed through political channels and we continued on the project, distributing our questionnaire in early December, probably one of the two worst times during the year to distribute a survey.

This review could have terminated the study if our research design had been vulnerable to the consultants' criticisms. But it was not. Precisely for these reasons, we followed, to the letter, mainstream social science quantitative techniques, conducting a preliminary field assessment and a pilot test of our questionnaire, validating each question included, conducting tests of reliability and validity of our instrument, and using rigorous sample selection procedures, just to offer a few examples. We even introduced a procedure called jackknifing to determine confidence levels around our estimates because of the unusual need to sample within our unit of analysis.

Yet, this conservative approach alone would not in itself have yielded the relatively low estimates of wage discrimination presented in the final report. Through some nasty political maneuvering, the state was able to get CWG to agree contractually to a limited analysis of wage discrimination. Specifically, the wage model used as the basis for estimating wage discrimination did not correct for a major source of gender and race bias in its compensation policy. All we could do in the final report was note this "oversight" in the wage model and point out (on two pages of a 360-page report) its implication for lowering the estimates of wage discrimination.

The study found that jobs with 100 percent female incumbents paid, on average, two full salary grades less than jobs with 100 percent male incumbents, net of other job characteristics. Similarly, it found that a job with 100 percent minority incumbents (of which there were few) lost about one-half a salary grade for no other reason than racial composition of the job. These estimates are based on wage models in which characteristics differentially associated with female-dominated and minority-dominated jobs are set at no value or even at negative values.

In retrospect, this outcome would have been different if there had been a strong *external* proponent base, independent of management and labor. Several women leaders, especially within management, worked tirelessly against these contractual limitations but, as insiders, they simply didn't command enough power. Where was labor? Our estimates proved sufficient to enable labor leaders to declare victory with their female members, without having to justify to their more powerful male members a set of wage adjustments that appeared to threaten male wage advantages and their assumed cost of living increases.

But the story does not end here. Several months before the release of the study report, and even before the model had been estimated, labor and management, as part of its regular collective bargaining agreement, negotiated the formation of an implementation task force solely controlled by management. The task force hired a staff of seventeen to use CWG's study and the concurrent management study as recommendations from which the task force would develop and implement a compensation policy model consistent with pay equity. The task force was located within the Department of Personnel, headed at that time by Karen Burstein, who had just resigned as CWG's president of the board and who was without a doubt the most vocal insider pay equity proponent.

In developing this model, the task force used *only* the data collected by CWG. As policymakers, members of the task force could set the parameters of the wage model at any value they wanted since they were using statistical models to *make* state policy, not to capture it. By playing with the parameters, the task force constructed a compensation model that yielded even lower pay equity wage adjustments than those estimated by CWG. By using CWG's data, the state could claim it was following CWG's approach to pay equity, which it was not. Only the broadest parameters of the model were shared with labor and many of the crucial details were withheld, even when the unions requested the information. Thus, unlike CWG's study, which was subject to detailed scrutiny at every phase, the task force shared its model with no one (see Steinberg, forthcoming, for a fuller discussion of why those who advocated for pay equity participated fully in shaping this outcome).

CWG's hands were tied in responding. It did, after all, agree to issue a report with conservative estimates and would have to reject its own report. Also, as a soft-money institution that relied heavily on state funding, it appears that CWG also had to be cautious in what it said about New York State government. The state strategy appeared to count on this and largely worked. It somewhat shifted the considerable anger that male and female employees felt from the state to CWG.

It also set a precedent for further conservatizing the direction of reform initiatives elsewhere. Perhaps because we used this careful methodology, the New York State study established a major pay equity precedent and confused the use of social science techniques with the separate issue of procedures for cleansing gender and race bias in the wage structure. It opened the way to arguments that the New York State "policy-capturing" approach should become the standard approach to estimating wage discrimination, resulting in a permanent redefinition and dilution of the reform. Indeed, in Canada, I have reviewed at least two systems, one constructed by a labor union and the other by management with labor's agreement, that followed this format. In both cases, employees have brought cases against both management and labor before the Pay Equity Tribunal, arguing correctly, in my opinion, that this approach does not achieve pay equity.

I left CWG one month prior to the completion of the comparable pay report, directing the finishing touches from Philadelphia and my new position as assistant professor of sociology at Temple University. By that time, and certainly by the time New York State announced the formation of the implementation task force, I was deeply dissatisfied and even, at times, depressed, over the fate of comparable worth research and with my role, however modest, in contributing to the containment of the reform. The New York State study had been designed so carefully that every facet of it was defensible in a court of law. That degree of care was necessary at that time, when the context was one of great skepticism over the measurement of wage discrimination "scientifically," especially by a group of feminist proponents. We did "prove" that a rigorous and sophisticated study of wage discrimination could be completed, but we were not able politically to complete a pay equity study that eliminated all of the sources of gender bias.

Moreover, because we used sophisticated quantitative methods, the details were inaccessible to the very employees who were supposed to benefit from the results of the study. Because of inaccessibility, the results could also be manipulated by New York State without the employees knowing that they were receiving substantially low wage adjustments. With hindsight and further experience as an advocacy researcher, I see that both of these shortcomings derive from the lack of a political base supporting the reform external to the state and independent of those conducting research.

• • •

Between 1985 and 1990, I conducted very few projects as an advocacy researcher. I was much more careful to involve myself only in projects that I believed would contribute positively to the realization of pay equity. Even here, I was not always accurate in my judgment. I worked, for example, as a technical adviser with a female-owned consulting firm on a study for the city of Philadelphia. The project was "protected" by the very effective Commission on the Status of Women, which established a feminist-controlled advisory committee. Even so, the study was never implemented. The research was methodologically vulnerable and the consultants had failed to gain union support. The combination of bad research and bad consultant-union relations left the commission director and advisory committee without any leverage. I withdrew from the project at the point I felt that my association added credibility to research that would undercut "true comparable worth."

By contrast, my most successful and least frustrating experiences involved work with women's organizations or with unions strongly committed to pay equity because their membership was overwhelmingly female. Here the combination of strong external political support for pay equity and credible and legally defensible technical work created the conditions for more fully realizing the objectives of "true comparable worth." Three projects are noteworthy successes.

In 1985, I advised Pam Ryan of the National Education Association

(NEA) to develop a job evaluation system inclusive of educational support personnel in public schools. This system would enable the union to develop independent estimates of wage discrimination for its female-dominated and minority-dominated classes and take those estimates to the bargaining table as the basis for achieving pay equity, and where necessary, use those estimates to gain the support of school board officials and other elected representatives responsible for financing wage adjustments. She had such a customized system developed, and the union's Human and Civil Rights Division now assists state affiliates in undertaking pay equity initiatives. Between 1985 and 1990, more than twenty local affiliates in thirteen states used the system (Ryan forthcoming).

In 1986, following the NEA study, I designed an equitable compensation system for use by the California School Employees Association (CSEA), which represents over 800 local bargaining units. In this project, I merged six existing and minimally acceptable job evaluation studies. I also compiled a notebook of job descriptions to be used by local bargaining committees and computed a set of standardized job evaluation points for each job title in the notebook. Local union bargaining committees receive the notebook and use it to find the best match between their job titles and the generic job titles. Although the job evaluation systems I selected to include in the equitable compensation system were not gender neutral, every other aspect of the project was consistent with standards of pay equity as understood by proponents. Wage adjustments for educational support personnel using this system averaged 20 percent.

In 1987 I served as a technical consultant to Federation of University Employees Local 24 at Yale University for a pay equity assessment they conducted. We decided to use that study for educational and media purposes alone and to use a different strategy for devising a pay equity proposal that would be put on the bargaining table. I asked the members of the Collective Bargaining Committee to examine the wage structure for the jobs they represented, to decide subjectively what they as a group thought an equitable wage structure should look like, and then to see what wage adjustments were necessary to achieve that realigned wage structure. They conducted this exercise without recourse to any system of job evaluation and placed their proposed reorganized wage structure on the bargaining table. Yale University accepted the union's proposed reorganization to increase wages on average by 28 percent, to be implemented over a four-year period.

None of the preceding examples represents the use of a job evaluation system fully cleansed of gender and race biases. Yet, each improves on traditional job evaluations conducted by management consulting firms in significant ways and thus, the wages paid to female-dominated jobs are closer to a nondiscriminatory wage. In addition, the technical pay equity work is kept separate from the political jockeying that pervades studies controlled by joint labor-management committees or legislative task forces. Finally, this approach has the significant advantage of extensive involvement by employees in the research and information-gathering phase, educating them in the process and investing them in seeing that the results are implemented.

I thought that, by the late eighties, I had come to the limit of what I could contribute to the technical development of pay equity. The irony of "retiring" just at the point of maximum intellectual independence was not lost on me, as few researchers who work in the political arena have the luxury of an independent source of income. Yet, until 1989, there were few projects that I believed would make a significant difference in the trajectory of the reform.

• • •

In 1988, the Canadian province of Ontario passed a pay equity act with potentially far-reaching consequences for the measurement of gender bias and the determination of gender neutrality. I once again became involved, and between 1989 and 1994 engaged in a variety of projects primarily under the auspices of one union, the Ontario Nurses' Association (ONA). I served as an expert witness on two cases and provided technical assistance to the legal counsel on a third.

I had not anticipated the formidable difficulties in the role of expert witness. Some of the tensions associated with using positivist methods in political contexts to bring about feminist social change resurfaced. These experiences also made clear the imbalance of power between labor and management and between the "gendered state" and feminists. Even after winning two of the tribunal cases (the third has yet to be decided) and even after having proponent definitions of gender bias and gender neutrality written into precedent-setting tribunal decisions, the end results seriously compromised pay equity adjustments. Two stories illustrate these tensions.

Among the more innovative and far-reaching of the provisions of the Ontario Pay Equity Act is the one that states that discrimination is embedded in compensation practices and the one that requires the use of gender-neutral job comparison systems to identify and correct this systemic discrimination. However, the law does not provide any specific guidelines for what constitutes gender neutrality in a job comparison system beyond joint recognition by labor and management. It also identifies the Pay Equity Tribunal as the arbiter of standards of gender neutrality (Steinberg and Walter 1992). ONA, representing 54,000 registered nurses, 98 percent of whom are female, immediately reached an impasse with employers over the issue of gender neutrality requiring resolution by the tribunal.

I was one of three expert witnesses (and the expert on job evaluation) in the second of these gender neutrality cases, *Women's College Hospital,* involving ONA against three hospitals. I was on the stand for eighteen days over a five-month period: one day to qualify as an expert, five days in direct examination, eleven days in cross-examination, and one day in redirect examination. During my nineteen months on the case, I wrote a lengthy report on gender bias in job evaluation in general and in the system under examination by the tribunal for use in evaluating the work of registered nurses in these hospitals. ONA's lawyers prepared me for testimony and cross-examination.[4] I worked with the team of lawyers representing the union to assist in structuring their strategy, including the selection of witnesses and evidence, the preparation of evidence used by other witnesses, and the development of issues for cross-examination. I also wrote drafts of sections of the written final argument.

These activities suggest a broader role than is usually played by expert witnesses. It occurred, I believe, because the case law was in the very early stages of development and because so much of the substance of this case hinged on contentious substantive issues about the scope of comparable worth, the meaning of gender bias, the content and value of female-dominated work, and the standards of gender neutrality. It also occurred because the position of ONA on gender neutrality was built largely on my and Lois Haignere's intellectual work. In these cases, the differences in definitions of gender neutrality involved millions of dollars in pay adjustments.

The case highlighted the tension between the positivist premises of "expertise" and the essentially unprovable character of certain features of the argument that women's work is systematically undervalued (Larson 1984). The argument that women's work is systematically undervalued is premised on accepting both that some job content in historically female work is not captured in traditional job evaluations (which can be demonstrated) and that there is *value* or *complexity* of work performed in female-dominated jobs (which cannot be demonstrated empirically in the same way).

Of course, the other side has similar difficulties in demonstrating lack of complexity and value. But, it has the market and market-based wage rates as an "objective" criterion of value. It can argue that the existing wage is an adequate measure of the complexity of the job and of its value to the organization. The premises underlying the market model are more hidden than the premises about compensation practices associated with comparable worth. This gives the other side a significant power advantage.

It is easy for feminist social scientists to understand the subjectivity of the wage and its gendered character (Kessler-Harris 1990). It is also easy to discuss these issues with other feminists who share this perspective. Yet, place that feminist in an adversarial context like a courtroom as a pay equity expert and she finds that she must overcome a prevailing view that believes in this heuristic device called the market. In this context, she must expose the subjective character of the wage and its inappropriateness as a measure of value in work. She must point out the empirical inaccuracies of the market model. And she has no external criterion like the wage. To a pay equity proponent, the wages for female-dominated work include discrimination, which artificially lowers pay for the work performed. In other words, at this juncture in the development of case law, the expert must convey an alternative worldview and illustrate how it exposes the gender bias of traditional evaluation systems and how that bias treats as invisible much of a registered nurse's work. These objectives go beyond what positivistic social science can yield.

Further, while I relied heavily on case study methodology of the actual job evaluation system at issue, the opponent expert relied on "scientific" experimental studies of bias in job evaluation that had been published in refereed journals. Once again, he looked more like a scientist than I. True, his work had internal validity, but the studies were not generalizable to the case of the registered nurses in the three hospitals under examination. In this case, we had to take on two complex issues: the empirical accuracy of the neoclassical market and the validity of experimental versus quasi-experimental designs.

In an adversarial context, these differences can prove a nightmare for the unconventional "expert" in cross-examination. In cross-examination, the opposing lawyer attempted to discredit the standards of gender neutrality I developed by discrediting me as a scientist. She not only used the standard tactics of lawyers, who uncover inconsistencies in written work and mistakes in citations in the expert's published articles, but she also ridiculed my references to face validity, my references to the use of stereotyping, and my reliance on "commonsense understanding." She wanted, for example, to know what I meant when I said that job evaluation systems "reproduce" the wage hierarchy or that they embed "cultural understandings" about women's roles that are outdated. These are arguments that may work in the classroom, or even in refereed articles within journals sympathetic to the social construction paradigm, but imagine scrutiny of the social constructionist framework by positivists for six hours a day for eleven days. Like the chair of the U.S. Commission on Civil Rights, the opposing counsel's intent was not to understand but to discredit and dismiss. My arguments and those made by the legal team were only effective to the degree to which they resonated with the worldviews of the members of the tribunal. The tribunal took eleven months to issue its decision. Fortunately, two of the three members of the tribunal shared enough of the feminist worldview to rule in our favor.

This decision and the prior one, *Haldimand-Norfolk* (May 29, 1991), were major victories for pay equity advocates. Articles, reports, and testimonies by Lynda Ames, Pat Armstrong, Lois Haignere, and me were cited in the text of the decision as justification for the guidelines issued. Under the right political conditions, the standards could be used as the basis for designing new job evaluation systems and mandating their implementation.

In both cases, the tribunal required each side to put on the table a job comparison system that met its guidelines for gender neutrality in the evaluation of the work of the registered nurse and corrected for the specific problems with the two traditional job evaluation systems under scrutiny. It specified a sixty-day limit for each side to put a specific proposal on the bargaining table. Lawrence Walter and I worked feverishly on the development of that system.

Management of the municipality of Haldimand-Norfolk in effect refused to comply with the decision and ONA brought them back to the tribunal, which led to a second decision in which the dispute resolution unit, Review Services, within the Pay Equity Commission was given jurisdiction to resolve this case. The decision also specified that Review Services retain me as ONA's pay equity expert and allow me the opportunity to finalize and pilot test the system directly in the municipality. Then Review Services had to either use or modify the Gender Neutral Job Comparison System (GNCS) for use in making its final determinations of wage discrimination in the work of registered nurses, public health nurses, and RN case managers.

The development and final modification of the GNCS was one of the most intellectually and politically challenging research projects of my career. Now I was no longer the critic but the architect of an alternative system that, if utilized, would itself be subject to intense scrutiny. While a few others had attempted to design gender-neutral systems, this was the first specifically required by a government body and designed by a visible pay equity proponent. It was necessary to take great care in the procedures for data collection and analysis because it was likely that the municipality would contest ONA's GNCS.

The system had to include *all* work performed in the municipality, whether the work was associated with female-dominated or male-dominated jobs. The tribunal required that a comparison system positively identify and value "characteristics of work, particularly women's work, which [are] historically undervalued or invisible." Valuable work is defined as follows: "If the skill, effort, responsibility, and working conditions are required in the normal performance of work, they must be of value to the organization whether or not those requirements have been consciously recognized or previously valued by the employer" (*Haldimand-Norfolk,* No. 6:116, 118).

In modifying the GNCS questionnaire and job evaluation framework according to tribunal guidelines, it was important to gather information on the content of male-dominated jobs because traditional evaluation systems were not inclusive of their *work content* either, in that systems of job evaluation rely very heavily on location in the organizational hierarchy. Getting this information was not easy. While the tribunal decision provided formal access, gaining cooperation was another matter. For three years prior to my arrival and during the duration of the tribunal proceedings, job incumbents encountered inaccurate information on pay equity and its consequences from management and the local newspapers. The week before I arrived to conduct my research, there was an anti–pay equity article in the papers almost every day, including one describing this U.S. social scientist who was being "brought in" to resolve this issue. The male employees I interviewed believed that they were underpaid. Some had been told that pay equity adjustments would lead to layoffs of male workers in their offices. Others had been the subject of a separate management consultant report issued several weeks before my arrival indicating that their units were padded with excess workers and recommending a reorganization that would result in layoffs. To add insult to injury, the questionnaire was eighty-two pages long and took most employees a full working day to fill out. The employees were also being asked to return for an interview about how to make the questionnaire more inclusive of their work. Leann Sherbaty of Review Services and I managed to gather the information we needed, using the few male allies among the group to our advantage (e.g., one was married to one of the registered nurses who brought the case). We even turned around a few of the men.

The GNCS questionnaire was substantially revised, the evaluation frame was extensively modified, and both were finally submitted to Review Services. As of this writing, Review Services is deliberating on the project. This represents an important precedent in the use of a proponent-developed evaluation system by a neutral government body to resolve a highly contentious pay equity dispute. Because the politics of implementation was largely kept separate from the technical work, the GNCS represents a first attempt at measuring wage discrimination as proponents understand it.

In the other case, *Women's College Hospital,* the resolution took a more political direction. While the details are beyond the scope of this essay, it is noteworthy, if only to understand the context in which this research work occurs, that ONA put a version of the GNCS on the bargaining table as it had in *Haldimand-Norfolk* to fulfill its requirement under the tribunal decision. Both sides agreed to use ONA's questionnaire as the basis for gathering information, but management refused to use the evaluation system to determine job worth. Instead, each side brought to the bargaining table a male job it believed was equivalent to the registered nurse position. Labor picked a middle-level management job and management picked a male professional position, senior dialysis technician. The difference in pay between the registered nurse and the senior dialysis technician was $12,000. Although ONA wanted a precedent established in finding nursing work equivalent to managerial work, it accepted management's male comparator. But it didn't get the $12,000 adjustment. Instead, it was able to bargain a $1.13 per hour adjustment for the registered nurses, which comes to about one-fifth of the pay difference. Since the case took three years to resolve, the nurses also received $4,100 in back pay, far short of the $36,000 in lost wages figured on the basis of the jointly agreed upon male comparator. Even when management and labor agree on a dollar figure for the extent of wage discrimination, labor is not powerful enough to bargain for full adjustment of wages for female-dominated jobs. In this case, wage adjustments were not based on the GNCS. However, to ONA's credit, the compromise kept the GNCS intact—i.e., it was not modified to dampen its gender neutrality (see Steinberg and Jacobs 1994 for a fuller account of this case, especially the role of the provincial government in contributing to the containment of the adjustments).

• • •

Throughout this chapter, as I have recounted my experiences as an advocacy researcher, I have attempted to point to conditions that make feminist advocacy research more effective. Two factors in combination maximize the benefits that can be gained from research as a power resource. First, effective advocacy research requires knowledgeable external political advocates willing and able to exert pressure when necessary. Second, it requires advocacy researchers committed to conducting defensible studies of publishable quality and who can leave a project at the point at which it is contained or undercut. My experiences with Local 34 at Yale University and with ONA illustrate successful efforts at using research to gain pay equity. The Philadelphia initiative indicates that advocacy alone is insufficient. New York State and Massachusetts indicate that advocacy researchers alone also prove insufficient to achieve "true comparable worth" (see Glazer and Glazer 1989 for the identification of similar factors as preconditions for ethical resistance or whistle-blowing).[5]

It is also critical for the advocacy researcher not to be financially beholden to the reform or to any group, even an advocacy group. The fact that by 1988, not one of the advocacy researchers that I mention in this chapter relied for their salaries on pay equity work is not trivial. It is hard to do feminist advocacy research in a political context without making serious compromises in your research to support the position of those paying your salary. But financial independence is a luxury few have been able to achieve. And those who have it do their advocacy research on top of another full-time work obligation.

Nor is it easy to build a base of external political support for comparable worth. More often than not management, often working hand in glove with labor, successfully kept feminist advocates at the margins of an initiative once a jurisdiction had agreed to undertake a study (see, for example, Acker 1989 on Oregon). So, paradoxically, the very conditions that would make it possible to use social science research effectively in an advocacy context rarely if ever exist at critical junctures of the reform's trajectory.

There is a catch-22 for the advocacy researcher: credible pay equity studies must use techniques that are difficult for employees to understand. Yet, for the results of such a study to capture all of the determinants of wage discrimination and be implemented, it is *essential* that employees, at least employees in female-dominated and minority-dominated jobs, understand the study enough to provide a base of support for it. For both of these conditions to occur, advocates must translate this information and provide it to employees directly, sometimes even bypassing union leaders, who may be withholding information from members for their own reasons. Yet, this requires the very redistribution of power from overwhelmingly male policymakers, administrators, and labor leaders to predominately female pay equity proponents, a redistribution of power that would itself be a reflection of the achievement of pay equity and other, related feminist reforms.

I have discussed other ways in which advocacy research can backfire, in some cases, badly. As director of the New York State Comparable Pay Study, I moved from the margins of the policy-making process to the position of inside technical expert. Even in those instances in which I was ostensibly given great latitude over the design of the research, policymakers were able to use such threats as cutting off the monies to complete the study and several other power plays to contain the reform. In New York State, for example, the management could hide behind the *facts* of the study while abandoning the *substance* of the findings. In my work as a technical monitor, I give a project some credibility but have no leverage to insist on the use of my recommendations, beyond disengagement. While some advocacy researchers might find the potential to influence a sufficient incentive to participate—after all, some impact is better than none—my position is one of greater purism.

Moreover, I have identified tensions and contradictions associated with advocacy research, some of them unresolvable. These tensions flow from the larger tension between advocacy and science. Political contexts operate according to very different norms than university contexts. Maintaining the integrity of the research process is not easy, but it is crucial to effectiveness. Indeed, in both the New York State study and as an expert witness, I found it necessary to put to one side the role of proponent and emphasize the role of scientist. I see no way around this choice.

Tensions also emerge from the contradictions between feminist social science and science in working for pay equity. As a feminist, I am critical of institutionalized science and regard detachment and balance as a gendered posture that denies the inevitable biases and values of the researcher. I am offended by the position of indifference to research subjects, who are faceless, disembodied, and genderless (Harding 1986; Jayaratne and Stewart 1991). I also reject positivistic conceptions of objectivity or of the reality of the social world "as a system of distinct, observable variables, independent of the knower" (Maguire 1987:13). Rather, I view objectivity as intersubjectivity, a view that implicates the knower in the construction of reality.

Despite these serious criticisms of positivism, I conduct research that relies very heavily on validity and reliability to bolster its credibility, and I assume the role of social science expert on wage discrimination and comparable worth. I generalize my findings about gender bias in traditional job evaluation systems and offer "theories to account for regularities in observable social behavior" (Maguire 1987:14). I even operate within the contradiction of using my reputation for integrity and my recognition as an expert as a power resource to influence the political process (see Larson 1984).[6] In addition, most of my research is inaccessible to the employees who stand to benefit from its findings. Although I have worked on participatory research projects with employees, my research does not attempt to develop special relations with the people who hold female-dominated jobs. These characteristics of the advocacy research I conduct violate important methodological standards of feminist research, especially its more purist formulations (Smith 1979, 1987, 1989). While I do not deny my feminism or my biases, I also strive, when necessary, to assume a more scientific stance (Reinharz 1992:240). Unless the dominant worldview were to change radically, I do not think that these contradictions between advocacy research for pay equity and feminist methodology are resolvable.

Nonetheless, I view the advocacy research in which I am engaged as largely consistent with feminist methodology in its more inclusive formulations. As Harding suggests it is not the use of particular data-gathering techniques that makes feminist research part ways with positivist science but rather three other characteristics. First, feminist research topics are generated from the perspective of women's experiences. Second, the research is conducted *for* women. Third, the researcher does not stand above that which is researched. Thus, feminist research differs from mainstream science in its theoretical framework, its purpose, and in the relationship of the researcher to the subject. Shulamit Reinharz (1992) develops a grounded definition that is remarkably similar to the one put forth by Harding. She rejects the idea that there is a research method unique to feminist research and argues instead that it is a "perspective" that "involves an ongoing criticism of nonfeminist scholarship," that is "guided by feminist theory," and that "aims to create social change" (1990:240).

My work on pay equity encompasses these characteristics. And it is precisely *because* of the alternative methodology involved in being a feminist advocate conducting research in explicitly political and change-oriented settings for less powerful groups that the *methods* I use in my research be rigorous, subject to replication, and defensible. Thus, while feminist advocacy researchers are critical of science and feel all too strongly the limitations of its claims to objectivity and universal truth at a practical level, we use these methods because they legitimate our expertise and because they legitimate the findings we introduce into the policy arena. Given the ease with which any social science study can be pulled apart by those of other ideological persuasions in adversarial contexts, I believe that it is often preferable to rely on conventional social science research methods.

Advocacy research differs from academic research in several important respects. It differs in the *purposes* of the research. Advocacy research is carried out with an explicit social change agenda. Academic research is conducted primarily to contribute to a body of knowledge within the researcher's field of specialty.

Advocacy research differs in the *context* in which it is carried out. Because of the adversarial nature of the policy-making process around issues such as pay equity and because of the potentially costly financial consequences of the reform, research produced by a proponent is subject to immediate scrutiny by other experts who are hired by opponents precisely to find fault with the study.

Advocacy research differs from academic research in the degree to which the principal investigator has *control of the research design.* Unlike academic social science (or even academic feminist research), in which research assumptions are shaped by the principal investigator and the norms of the subspecialty in which she works, advocacy researchers often fight to maintain control of the study process and product. And they frequently lose.

And working in a political context raises the issue of who controls the *results.* Certainly the events in New York State make it clear that policymakers use research to protect their actions and implement policies that are not necessarily consistent with pay equity. Where norms of academic research strongly favor maximum disclosure, the norms in political contexts favor withholding information to maximize one's power over opponents.

There are several other differences between advocacy and academic social science: the sources of funding, time constraints, and the potential consequences of the results. One of the ways that management controls the research product is by controlling the funds. Academic funding sources may identify research priorities and assess the quality of the research design and the capability of the principal investigator to fulfill the work in the proposal, but this bears little relationship to the type of control experienced in political contexts and to the use of funds to secure that control.

Time deadlines also seriously constrain the quality of results in advocacy settings. Academic social scientists may take years to complete their research projects. They may not be promoted and others may be first to publish research on related issues, but other consequences are slight. By contrast, advocacy researchers operate in a world of short attention spans, budget cycles, contract deadlines, legislative sessions, and elections. If you miss a deadline, you may lose the opportunity to get monies appropriated for pay equity adjustments. The politician providing key support for the initiative may be voted out of office, as happened at a critical moment in Washington State (Remick 1980). Or, a key supporter may be reelected and regard support for pay equity as no longer necessary to build an electoral constituency. You could lose political momentum. In Oregon, for example, even modest delays in an initial study contributed to losing millions of dollars in appropriations for pay equity adjustments and to dismantling a legislative task force, on which several strong and technically knowledgeable proponents sat (Acker 1989). On the other hand, as Lois Haignere has noted, "when meeting the deadline becomes the ultimate goal, the reform suffers." Unrealistic deadlines become one way to replicate the status quo, and another way to provide "the appearance that pay equity has been achieved, when it has not" (1991:168).

Finally, there is always the risk of findings that would contradict the policies for which one is advocating. This seemed highly implausible in our studies. A large body of academic research had already pointed out the considerable effect of segregation on the depression of wages by gender and race, although only recently has it begun to examine the mechanisms through which segregation translates into lower wages. Though we expected to find variations in the extent of wage discrimination in different work organizations, we did not expect to find a workplace in which female-dominated jobs were paid at an equal rate to equivalent male-dominated jobs. And thus far, we haven't.

This chapter offers one look into the world of advocacy research as I have experienced it working on one especially difficult policy issue. Examining the tensions, dilemmas, and contradictions of advocacy research is important not only for its own sake but also because many feminist sociologists express ambivalence about careers comprised solely of academic research and teaching. Many have expressed great curiosity and, on occasion, even envy at the work that I do and its direct impact on the wages of women and minorities engaged in primarily low-paid, historically female work. This desire for direct participation, as researchers, in change efforts is not unique to feminist sociologists, but feminist sociologists are more likely to feel these frustrations because it is difficult to do feminist research, with its explicit emphasis on social change, as a pure ivory-tower activity. At the same time, I sense in these conversations a romanticism and a lack of understanding of the challenges, frustrations, and unresolvable double-binds associated with conducting research in a political context for social change.

To be sure, the work carries great personal significance, carries great potential for dramatic impact on the lives of women and minority employees, stretches one's creative faculties, forces one to be quick on one's feet, and offers many technical, political, and ethical challenges. Yet, the struggle to use research as a resource in accomplishing one's political goals represents a serious uphill battle, given the differential power resources in the political arena. One can write about power differentials and their impact in the abstract. Unless one does advocacy research, one can't imagine, I believe, what it feels like to sit in an audience and hear one of the commissioners on the U.S. Commission on Civil Rights glibly admit to an audience that the commission report knowingly distorted the definition of pay equity because the members believed that they could get away with it. "When you've got the ball," he said, "you can throw it any way you want."

I welcome my feminist colleagues to engage in more advocacy research, but I hope that as they enter the political arena, they arrive better prepared than I was for the ways research can be used, controlled, undercut, and backfire and for the loss of time or ability to plan their workday, let alone their free time. Then again, I want to reassure them that sometimes they can even contribute somewhat to making the lives of some employed women and minorities just a little bit better.

NOTES

1. Almost all of the initiatives in which I participated in the United States involved examining and correcting for potential wage discrimination on the bases of gender *and* race.

2. Although that is often true among academics as well, in this context, the stakes and consequences go far beyond recognition of one's personal intellectual contributions and the personal rewards accorded to those whose paradigms are in favor.

3. Ironically, those consultants who did have a track record in compensation were the ones who had been implementing gender-biased job evaluation systems. From the vantage point of proponents, the longer the track record, the more likely was the consultant *not* to understand pay equity and the poorer the quality of the study. For a number of these consultants, gender bias in job evaluation amounted to using the words *male* and *female* in the process of evaluating jobs.

4. The system of cross-examination of experts is different in Canada than in the United States. In Canada, an expert is not allowed to discuss any aspect of the case, including how to handle cross-examination, after she is asked the last question in direct examination and until she is finished testifying. My understanding of U.S. procedure is that the expert and counsel can discuss how to handle cross-examination while it is taking place.

5. It appears, as well, that a disproportionate percentage of ethical resisters are drawn from the ranks of professionals, reflecting some of the tensions between scientific and bureaucratic or political norms.

6. Larson provides an insightful discussion of the further contradictions between the political character of professionalism, its roots in nineteenth-century liberal political philosophies, and the value-free and detached posture that "experts" put forth. This posture obscures the contradictions between science and politics and legitimates the expert's qualifications, allowing her a special voice in consideration of public policy issues because of her monopoly on specialized knowledge.

REFERENCES

Acker, Joan. 1989. *Doing Comparable Worth: Gender, Class, and Pay Equity.* Philadelphia: Temple University Press.

Blum, Linda. 1991. *Between Feminism and Labor: The Significance of the Comparable Worth Movement.* Berkeley: University of California Press.

Bridges, William P., and Robert L. Nelson. 1989. "Markets in Hierarchies: Organizational and Market Influences on Gender Inequality in a State Pay System." *American Journal of Sociology* 95 (3): 616–58.

Evans, Sara M., and Barbara Nelson. 1989. *Wage Justice: Comparable Worth and the Paradox of Technocratic Reform.* Chicago: University of Chicago Press.

Glazer, Myron Peretz, and Penina Migdal Glazer. 1989. *The Whistle-Blowers: Exposing Corruption in Government and Industry.* New York: Basic Books.

Haignere, Lois. "Pay Equity Implementation: Experimentation, Negotiation, Mediation, Litigation, and Aggravation." In *Just Wages: A Feminist Assessment of Pay Equity,* ed. Judy Fudge and Patricia McDermott. Toronto: University of Toronto Press. 160–71.

Haldimand-Norfolk (No. 6) (1991) 2 P.E.R. 105.

Harding, Sandra. 1987. "Introduction: Is There a Feminist Method." In *Feminism and Methodology: Social Science Issues,* ed. Sandra Harding. Bloomington: Indiana University Press. 1–14.

———. 1986. *The Science Question in Feminism.* Ithaca: Cornell University Press.

Hartmann, Heidi, Stephanie Aaronson, and Elaine Sorenson. 1993. *Pay Equity Remedies in State Government: Assessing Their Economic Effects.* Washington, D.C.: Institute for Women's Policy Research.

Jayaratne, Toby Epstein, and Abigail Stewart. 1991. "Quantitative and Qualitative Methods in the Social Sciences: Current Feminist Issues and Practical Strategies." In *Beyond Methodology: Feminist Scholarship as Lived Research,* ed. Mary Margaret Fonow and Judith A. Cook. Bloomington: Indiana University Press. 85–106.

Kessler-Harris, Alice. 1990. *A Woman's Wage: Historical Meanings and Social Consequences.* Lexington: University of Kentucky Press.

Larson, Magali Sarfatti. 1984. "The Production of Expertise and the Constitution of Expert Power." In *The Authority of Experts,* ed. Thomas L. Haskell. Bloomington: Indiana University Press. 28–80.

Maguire, Patricia. 1987. *Doing Participatory Research: A Feminist Approach.* Amherst: Center for International Education, School of Education, University of Massachusetts.

Marshall, Ray, and Beth Paulin. 1984. "The Employment and Earnings of Women: The Comparable Worth Debate." In *Comparable Worth: Issue for the 80's* by the U.S. Commission on Civil Rights. Washington, D.C.: U.S. Government Printing Office. 1:201–20.

Reinharz, Shulamit. 1992. *Feminist Methods in Social Research.* New York: Oxford University Press.

Remick, Helen. 1984. "Major Issues in A Priori Applications." In *Comparable Worth and Wage Discrimination,* ed. Helen Remick. Philadelphia: Temple University Press. 99–117.

———. 1981. "The Comparable Worth Controversy." *Public Personnel Management* 10 (4): 371–83.

———. 1980. "Beyond Equal Pay for Equal Work: Comparable Worth in the State of Washington." In *Equal Employment Policy for Women; Strategies for Implementation in the United States, Canada, and Western Europe,* ed. Ronnie Steinberg-Ratner. Philadelphia: Temple University Press. 405–19.

Ryan, Pam. Forthcoming. "Fair Pay—We're Worth It!: The NEA Pay Equity Program for Educational Support Personnel." In *The Politics and Practice of Pay Equity,* ed. Ronnie Steinberg. Philadelphia: Temple University Press.

Special Committee on Comparable Worth, Massachusetts State Legislature. 1986. Second Report of the Special Committee on Comparable Worth. June.

Smith, Dorothy. 1989. "Sociological Theory: Methods of Writing Patriarchy." In *Feminism and Sociological Theory,* ed. Ruth Wallace. Newbury Park, Calif.: Sage. 34–64.

———. 1987. *The Everyday World as Problematic: A Feminist Sociology.* Boston: Northeastern University Press.

———. 1979. "A Sociology for Women." In *The Prism of Sex: Essays in the Sociology of Knowledge,* ed. Julia A. Sherman and Evelyn Torton Beck. Madison: University of Wisconsin Press. 135–87.

Steinberg, Ronnie. 1991. "Job Evaluation and Managerial Control: The Politics of Technique and the Techniques of Politics." In *Just Wages: A Feminist Assessment of Pay Equity,* ed. Judy Fudge and Patricia McDermott. Toronto: University of Toronto Press. 193–218.

———. 1990. "The Social Construction of Skill: Gender, Power, and Comparable Worth." *Work and Occupations* 17 (4): 449–82.

———. 1987. "Radical Challenges in a Liberal World." *Gender and Society* 1 (4): 466–75.

———. 1986. "The Comparable Worth Debate." *New Politics* 1 (1): 108–26.

———. 1984a. "Identifying Wage Discrimination and Implementing Pay Equity Adjustments." In *Comparable Worth: Issue for the 80's* by the U.S. Commission on Civil Rights. Washington, D.C.: U.S. Government Printing Office. 1:99–118.

———. 1984b. "'A Want of Harmony': Perspectives on Wage Discrimination and Comparable Worth." In *Comparable Worth and Wage Discrimination,* ed. Helen Remick. Philadelphia: Temple University Press. 3–27.

———. Forthcoming. "'We Did It Our Way': Pay Equity in New York State." In *The Politics and Practice of Pay Equity,* ed. Ronnie Steinberg. Philadelphia: Temple University Press.

Steinberg, Ronnie, and Lois Haignere. 1987. "Equitable Compensation: Methodological Criteria for Comparable Worth." In *Ingredients for Women's Employment Policy,* ed. Christine Bose and Glenna Spitze. Albany: State University of New York Press. 152–82.

———. 1985. *Review of Massachusetts Statewide Classification and Compensation System for Achieving Comparable Worth.* Albany: Center for Women in Government.

———. 1984. "Separate but Equivalent: Equal Pay for Work of Comparable Worth." In *Gender at Work: Perspectives on Occupational Segregation and Comparable Worth,* ed. Congressional Caucus for Women's Issues. Washington, D.C.: Women's Research and Education Institute of the Congressional Caucus for Women's Issues. 13–26.

Steinberg, Ronnie, and Jerry Jacobs. 1994. "Pay Equity in Nonprofit Organizations: Making Women's Work Visible." In *Women and Power in the Nonprofit Sector,* ed. Teresa Odendahl and Michael O'Neill. San Francisco: Jossey-Bass. 79–120.

Steinberg, Ronnie, and Lawrence Walter. 1992. "Making Women's Work Visible: The Case of Nursing; First Steps in the Design of a Gender Neutral Comparison System." *Proceedings,* Third Institute for Women's Policy Research Conference. Eds. Roberta Spalter-Roth, Debbie Clearwaters, Melinda Gish, and Susan A. Markham. Washington, D.C.: Institute for Women's Policy Research. 309–16.

Steinberg, Ronnie, Lois Haignere, Carol Possin, Cynthia Chertos, and Donald Treiman. 1985. *The New York State Comparable Pay Study: Final Report.* Albany: Center for Women in Government.

Steinberg-Ratner, Ronnie. 1980. *Equal Employment Policy for Women: Strategies for Implementation in the United States, Canada, and Western Europe.* Philadelphia: Temple University Press.

Treiman, Donald. 1984. "Effect of Choice of Factors and Factor Weights in Job Evaluation." In *Comparable Worth and Wage Discrimination,* ed. Helen Remick. Philadelphia: Temple University Press. 79–89.

———. 1979. *Job Evaluation: An Analytic Review.* Washington, D.C.: National Research Council.

Treiman, Donald, and Heidi Hartmann. 1981. *Women, Work, and Wages: Equal Pay for Jobs of Equal Value.* Washington, D.C.: National Academy Press.

U.S. Commission on Civil Rights. 1984. *Comparable Worth: Issue for the 80's.* Vol. 2, *Proceedings.* Washington, D.C.: U.S. Government Printing Office.

Women's College Hospital (4 August 1992) 0008-89; 0011-89; 0029-89; 0034-89; 0036-89 (P.E.H.T.).

CHAPTER 12

NANCY C. M. HARTSOCK

Theoretical Bases for Coalition Building: An Assessment of Postmodernism

This essay explores some of the theoretical bases and supports for coalition. In general, I suggest that political theory can be useful for politics and policy by helping to reveal possible new coalitions and alliances. This function is particularly important for groups who have been dominated and marginalized and consequently whose culture and vision of the world are systematically made invisible as we are forced to examine our experience through the eyes of dominant groups. The axes of domination are several and different groups are privileged along some and disadvantaged along others. Thus, in any effort at coalition building or alliance formation, close attention must be given to the specific situations of each group as defined by axes of gender, race, class, and sexuality.

Because of these features of social life, feminist theory must locate itself in terms of both victimhood and complicity. Attention to the specifics of each group's situation must recognize that the subordination of different groups is often obtained and maintained by different mechanisms. As a result of these differences, one must expect the feminisms of different groups to emphasize the political issues that are most salient in that particular social location: white feminists' efforts to bring the concerns of the private sphere into public life, Black feminists' emphasis on economic issues, Latina feminists' attention to issues of language and the family all illustrate the ways in which certain issues become unavoidable for some groups while they remain less salient for others.

This argument leads to an emphasis on difference and heterogeneity, a stress on the multiple possibilities for understanding the world, and the importance of multiple points of view. These emphases are shared with many postmodernist theories, and thus it would seem that these theories might be important resources for those who are thinking about theoretical bases for coalitions. Postmodernist/post-structuralist theories' stress on dissonance, incommensurability, depthlessness, or the need to move to the margin has led some feminist theorists to find them attractive. I am, however, among those who are less sanguine about these theories. The work of postmodernist theorists such as Richard Rorty and Michel Foucault represent less an alternative to the overconfident theories of the Enlightenment than a parasitic continuation of its preoccupations. Postmodernist theories represent the situated knowledges (Haraway 1988) of a particular social group—European-American, masculine, and racially as well as economically privileged (Hartsock 1989–90). Postmodernist theories should be understood as a situated knowledge that reveals itself as "the felt absence of the will or the ability to change things as they are . . . the voice of epistemological despair" (Sangari 1987:161).[1]

But alternative understandings are possible, and feminist theory faces tasks that require moving to a new terrain, one not defined by the Enlightenment and the theoretical reaction against it; feminist theory must be understood not only as analysis but also as an instrument of struggle against dominant groups and a tool for the empowerment of the dominated. The task facing all theorists committed to social change is that of working to construct some theoretical bases for political solidarity; theoretical bases that are no substitute for collective action and coalition building but a necessary adjunct to them.

Postmodernism is a very complex topic and the label covers a wide variety of ideological positions, from Richard Rorty's liberal version to Fredric Jameson's relocation of postmodernism onto a Marxist terrain. As such a complex phenomenon it is, then, difficult to characterize the political position it represents. Far from being a resource for the development of new and more inclusive social movements, postmodernist theories represent and express the voices of the powerful.[2] It is, however, the destabilized voice of the powerful being forced to come to terms with the voices of the disenfranchised. This may seem an odd claim since the abandonment of the imperial certainties of the Enlightenment would seem to put postmodernism on the side of liberation struggles. There are other models of incommensurability and difference, especially those that come out of the experiences of marginalized and oppressed groups, which open possibilities for both resistance and transformation.

Postmodernist/post-structuralist theories, as they have been received in the United States, present several problems as models for change. First, they represent unsatisfactory and parasitic alternatives profoundly constituted by the Enlightenment. Second, in these theories both the Enlightenment and postmodernism have been redefined in liberal and pluralist terms.[3] Third, postmodernism should be recognized as a discourse of the powerful attempting to come to terms with the voices of others.[4] The result is that this body of theory can be of little help in the project of constructing active coalitions for change.

POSTMODERNISM AND THE ENLIGHTENMENT TRADITION

Postmodernist theories are reacting against a particular body of thought; most frequently this body of thought is termed "the Enlightenment." The specifically modernist and Western tradition of political thought had several distinctive epistemological features. First, the "god-trick" was pervasive: the tradition depended on the assumption that one could see everything from nowhere, that disembodied reason could produce accurate and "objective" accounts of the world.[5] Second, and related, the Enlightenment was marked by a faith in the neutrality of reasoned judgment, in scientific objectivity, in the progressive logic of reason in general and science in particular. Third, Enlightenment theories claimed to assume human universality and homogeneity, based on the common capacity to reason. Differences were held to be fundamentally epiphenomenal. Thus, one could speak of human nature, truth, and other imperial universalities. Fourth, all this had the effect of allowing for transcendence through the omnipotence of reason. Through reason, the philosopher could escape the limits of the body, time, and space to contemplate the eternal problems related to humans as knowers. Finally, Enlightenment political thought was characterized by a denial of the importance of power to knowledge and concomitantly a denial of the centrality of systematic domination in human societies. The subject/individual and power were held to be distinct.[6]

These fundamentally optimistic philosophies both grew out of and expressed the social relations of the expanding market/capitalist societies of Europe (Mouffe 1988).[7] At the same time, many of the philosophers who were central to Western political thought also contributed to the development of ideologies that supported colonialism, the slave trade, the expansion of Western patriarchal relations, and so forth. Thus, despite a stated adherence to universal principles, I argue that the epistemological and political thought of the Enlightenment depended on the dualistic construction of a different world, a world onto which was projected an image of everything that ruling class, male

Europeans wanted to believe they were not. Edward Said named the fundamental dynamic of the process clearly when he stated that the creation of the Orient (and one might add, the creation of various other racial, gender, and even class categories) was an outgrowth of the will to power. "Orientalism," he states, "is a Western style for dominating, restructuring and having authority over the orient" (1978:3).

It must be remembered that this Eurocentric, masculinist, and capitalist world was constructed not only in theory but more importantly in fact through such practices as the Atlantic slave trade, the development of plantation agriculture in the North American colonies, the introduction of markets and private property in Africa, the colonization of large parts of Asia, Latin America, and Africa, and the introduction of European forms of patriarchal and masculinist power. These constituted the means by which the duality and the domination of Europe, and later North America—the "rich North Atlantic democracies" as Richard Rorty has termed them—were institutionalized in fact as well as in thought. Duality, inequality, and domination were established in the name of universality and progress; ironically, power relations were institutionalized in and through a mode of thinking that denied any connections between knowledge and power or between the construction of subjectivity and power. The philosophical and historical creation of devalued Others was the necessary precondition, then, for the creation of the transcendent, rational subject who could persuade himself that he exists outside time and space and power relations, the subject who is the speaker in Enlightenment philosophy.

The social relations that both express and form the material base for the theoretical construction of this Enlightenment subjectivity have been rejected on a world scale over the last several decades.[8] Decolonization struggles, movements of young people, women's movements, racial liberation movements—all represent the diverse and disorderly Others beginning to take political power, to demand participation in the "public realm," and to chip away at the social and political power of the unmarked, autonomous "individual." As a result of these social and political changes, some European and American intellectuals are beginning to reject many of the totalizing and universalizing theories of the Enlightenment.

First, let me take up my own view that postmodernist theories remain imprisoned on the terrain of Enlightenment thought and fail to provide the ground for alternative and more emancipatory accounts of subjectivity and practice. Moreover, despite their own desires to avoid universal claims and despite their stated opposition to these claims, some imperial and universalist assumptions creep back into their work. For those of us who have been marginalized and subjugated in various ways and who need to understand the world systematically in order to change it, postmodernist theories at their best fail to provide helpful alternatives to the Enlightenment.

THE FAILURES OF POSTMODERNISM

Rather than simply argue against a generalized postmodernism, I will discuss the ways the issues of concern appear in the work of two quite different theorists, Richard Rorty and Michel Foucault.[9] Because they emerge from quite different intellectual traditions and have divergent political views, together they can stand for a substantial range of postmodernist thought. Both Rorty and Foucault reject each of the several Enlightenment assumptions I listed at the beginning of this essay, although in different ways. Yet despite profound differences in their stated projects, and indeed in their work, both ultimately inhabit the terrain defined by the Enlightenment. At best their postmodernist theories criticize Enlightenment assumptions without putting anything in their place. And at worst they recapitulate the effects of Enlightenment theories that deny the dominated the right to participate in defining the terms of interaction.

Both Rorty and Foucault claim to have rejected the "god-trick," the view of everything from nowhere. Rorty has done so in the name of rejecting "Epistemology." It must be noted that his choice of terminology implies that the epistemology of the West constitutes the only possible theory of knowledge. Without *that* theory, we must give up claims to knowledge. Because of their different styles and intellectual ancestors, it may be surprising to argue that Foucault makes a very similar move. But Foucault's arguments that truth must be seen as simply legitimized errors, that what we have called reason is born from chance, and that the essence of things must be understood to have been fabricated "in piecemeal fashion from alien forms" (1977:142–43) represent a similar rejection of Enlightenment assumptions: he, like Rorty, concludes that if one cannot see everything from nowhere, one cannot really see anything at all. Thus, both argue for taking parodic and satiric positions, for taking the position that one is not in a position to take a position, and their analyses indicate that they take the position that if one cannot engage in the god-trick, there is no such thing as knowledge.[10]

Foucault's attack is far more systematic and thorough than Rorty's. Not only does he reject the gaze from nowhere but he is also clear that the attack must include the subject who claimed to engage in disembodied knowledge gathering. Thus, unlike Rorty, Foucault argues that the question of the subject must be attended to by "creating a history of the different modes by which, in our culture, human beings are made subject" (1983:208), or, as I would put it, are made objects or "objectified subjects."

Second, both Rorty and Foucault reject the neutrality of disembodied reason. Rorty argues simply for abandoning claims to rationality, objectivity, and certain knowledge. One should give up the process of constructing theoretical schemes and instead be reactive and peripheral. Foucault too attacks the notion of reason, of the solemnity of history, and argues for a reverence for irreverence. One must reject, he states, the "great stories of continuity" (1977:140, 163). Thus, once reason has been exposed as biased rather than neutral, the very possibility of knowledge must be abandoned. Once again, the assumptions underlying this form of argument point to the implicit conclusion that if the objective knowledge (falsely) claimed by Enlightenment thought is not available, then one must abandon the search for any knowledge at all.

Third, both Rorty and Foucault argue in their different ways that we must give up on human universals. Rorty argues that instead we should accept the notion of incommensurable discourses and abandon the search for commensurability. Foucault's argument takes a different form to reach similar conclusions: one must unmask the demagogy cloaked by universals such as truth, laws of essences (Foucault 1977:158). One must be suspicious not only of claims to universal truths but even of claims to reject these truths. Indeed, at least one commentator has argued that Foucault "doesn't take a stand on whether or not there is a human nature. Rather, he changes the subject" (Rabinow 1984:4).

Fourth, both Foucault and Rorty reject the search for transcendence and omnipotence. But they put forward alternatives that lead in the direction of passivity and immobility. Rorty tells us we must abandon the search for truth in favor of joining in edifying conversation. Because the great certainties available to omnipotent and eternal reason no longer obtain, one must settle for conversations rather than search for knowledge. Nor do there appear to be urgent issues of social change or justice that need to be addressed by means other than a conversation.

Foucault's political commitments appear to be quite different, yet his counsels lead in very similar directions. He has argued that we should at least unmask and criticize political violence (Rabinow 1984:5).[11] But at the same time his rejection of the hope of transcendence leads him to conclude that the only possibilities open to us involve the tracing of the ways humans have been subjugated. Marshall Berman has eloquently summed up the conclusion to which Foucault presses us: "Do we use our minds to unmask oppression—as Foucault appears to be trying to do? Forget it, because all forms of inquiry into the human condition 'merely refer individuals from one disciplinary authority to another,' and hence only add to the triumphant 'discourse of power.'" "There is no point in trying to resist the oppressions and injustices of modern life, since even our dreams of freedom only add more links to our chains; however, once we grasp the total futility of it all, at least we can relax" (1982:34).

THE FAILURES OF POSTMODERNISM 2

Rather than simply dismiss postmodernism as not useful to feminist theory, I want to situate its theories both historically and politically. Postmodernism should be seen as a representation of a discourse of the powerful at the point where they are confronted and destabilized by dominated groups. This discourse is an expression of the voices of those who are the heirs to the legacy of the Enlightenment in the context of the late twentieth century. That is, I want to add to Jameson's historical location of the cultural phenomenon of postmodernism the idea that its intellectual expression also has a historical and social location, that it is the theoretical and intellectual expression of the historical and political displacement experienced by the powerful—i.e., European-American, white, masculine, class-privileged, universal, and previously unmarked individuals.[12]

As the intellectual reflex of a particular group at a particular historical conjuncture, it reflects and expresses the purposes of some actors or agents but not other purposes and other agents. Or rather, when other actors and agents make similar moves, the meaning and significance of their actions differ in important ways. In particular, the options offered by postmodernist theories represent useful strategies to the extent that one is part of the dominant group. Those of us with various forms of privilege need to be reminded that the world is a more varied place than is usually evident from dominant positions. In addition, those of us with various forms of privilege need to question the imperial certainties of the past and highlight lack of certainty and inability to name the world in any conclusive way. But to the extent that we have been excluded and marginalized and are involved in efforts to create and claim new subjectivities and alliances the discourse of postmodernist theory will not help.

My move to name this as a discourse of the powerful was originally stimulated by a suspicious conjunction: At the moment in history when so many groups of marginalized Others were involved in redefining themselves, doubt arose about the nature of the "subject," about the possibilities for theories that could describe the world. And I found myself asking, "Why is it, exactly at the moment when so many of us who have been silenced begin to demand the right to name ourselves, to act as subjects rather than objects of history, that just then the concept of subjecthood becomes 'problematic'? Just when we are forming our own theories about the world, uncertainty emerges about whether the world can be theorized?" (Hartsock 1987).

And related, there is the question of the subject who claimed this objective knowledge. Without the possibility of objective knowledge, the view from nowhere, this subject is endangered. One must ask who are/were the subjects who have been so roughly reminded that there are alternatives to their vision of the world? Who are the heirs to the overconfidence of the Enlightenment? And what sort of subject is it whose existence is now threatened? Not members of oppressed groups, the objects of history in the process of attempting to become the collective subjects of history. One gets the sense in reading a number of postmodernist theoretical claims that this is the voice of the universal man realizing that there are others out there. I am reminded of Jameson's writing on the demographies of postmodernism: "The West thus has the impression that without much warning and unexpectedly it now confronts a range of genuine individual and collective subjects who were not there before . . . new people, other people . . . even though their bodies and their lives filled the cities and certainly did not materialize yesterday" (1988:356–57).

THE FAILURES OF POSTMODERNISM 3

The third major failing of postmodernist theories is located in its particular reception in the United States, in the ways European ideas have been adopted and adapted. Kathi Weeks argues that in the adaptation of European ideas in the United States, the vitally important presence of Marxism was dropped out. The result is a misinterpretation of the post-structuralist project in such a way that the political commitments and purposes of the authors have been recast as a kind of liberal individualism (Weeks 1992:chap. 4). Weeks argues that Neitzsche's and Foucault's specific and limited critiques of universalizing theory have been fashioned into a general indictment of modernism altogether (1992:104). She argues that Foucault's critique was transformed in the United States into a paradigm debate between modernists and postmodernists and she uses Thomas Kuhn's classic book on the philosophy of science, *The Structure of Scientific Revolutions*, to discuss the ways a set of questions, assumptions, methods, values, and criteria of validity are put together (115). She stresses that one paradigm cannot be falsified by another because they do not share the same criteria of validity (117).

She argues that once Foucault's condemnation of naturalized models of the subject is expanded into a radical rejection of modernism altogether it can be conflated with other critiques of subjects, agents, and individuals, such as Rorty's liberal critique. And she argues further that this is part of a process of constructing a paradigm that opposes postmodernist theories to a straw figure of Enlightenment liberalism (130). Marxist theory then becomes invisible, or the Western Marxist tradition is conflated with orthodox, scientific, or Stalinist Marxism (133). The end result, she holds, is that a heterogeneous tradition of thought is reduced to "its most vulnerable member (that is, Enlightenment liberalism) which is then dismissed as inadequate" (136). Thus constructed is another version of liberalism, not Enlightenment liberalism, but a liberal, individualist, and peculiarly U.S. interpretation of post-structuralist/postmodernist theories.

IMPLICATIONS FOR FEMINIST THEORY

What does this body of thought mean for feminist theory? How are these points incorporated/transformed or not transformed by feminist theory?[13] I believe there are several malign results. And here I am not reassured by what I have heard from graduate students in feminist theory classes. There seem to be several taken-for-granted positions that are common knowledge.

First, there is the emphasis on constantly shifting subject positions: nothing lasts long enough to be named, or if named should be immediately problematized, interrogated, or destabilized. In the process, agency and transformative activity disappear. Second, there is an emphasis on difference and heterogeneity, with difference always coded as Other. The result is that we end up with "interesting stories about endlessly particular and elaborated lives. But this misses the structured texture of politics" (di Stefano 1991:199). Or, as Linda Gordon has put it, simply stressing the existence of difference obliterates the way that groups are "created in their relationships with each other" (1991:106). I would add that these relationships are not only created by/with each other but that their creation cannot be understood apart from the relations of power that constitute both the relationship and the groups.

It is important to pay attention to the continuing salience of the central axes of domination that run along lines of race, gender, and class (that forbidden word in U.S. politics—often coded as race, but very real as it emerged in the Zoe Baird hearings).[14]

Third, one finds in feminist theory a dismissal of identity politics as simplistic and limiting: "We are all too multiply situated for that" is a common response. Yet, identity politics (or, in my terms here, attention to subjectivity) has been an important resource for political change. The construction of new identities has allowed for the formation of new groups—the demographies of the postmodern world. Despite the difficulties and problems of identity politics, most prominently demonstrated at this writing by the situation in Bosnia-Hersegovina, the construction of group identities remains a potentially politically important resource.

Fourth, in feminist theory, questions have emerged about the possibility of knowledge of the world. There is a sense that we can never get beyond the texts; or indeed, that there *is* nothing beyond the texts. One ends up with simply one situated reading versus another. In my experience, even the term *we* can become suspect because in the midst of shifting subject positions the points of connection between different locations can be seen as theoretically problematic.

The end result is that politics and political change can be reduced to analyses of discourses and a series of individual readings can replace a more collective agenda. This is what Donna Haraway (1988) has referred to as "self-induced multiple personality disorder," and I would add that it is often coupled with a politics of liberal pluralism. All this represents an extension of the claims feminist postmodernist theorists make, but I want to stress the directions of theorizing that can lead to a disabling of political action and a thoroughgoing relativism.

CONTRIBUTIONS OF MARXIST THEORY

This critique should not be taken as an indication that I am a supporter of the Enlightenment as defined by postmodernist theorists. We do need historically specific and contingent accounts of our social relations. We do need to recognize the relevance of change over time, and we need to recognize that groups of people working together can contribute to change. We do need an understanding of objectivity that differs from that of Enlightenment faith in the neutrality of reason.

Parts of the Marxist tradition represent an important resource for developing such an account—for insisting on the impossibility of neutrality and the necessity of engagement, for recognizing that the social relations in which we live structure (though do not determine) the ways we understand the world; and for providing tools that can allow us to trace the ways our concepts and categories both structure and express the ways we interact with the world. As Haraway so eloquently puts it, "'Our' problem is how to have *simultaneously* an account of radical historical contingency of all knowledge claims and knowing subjects, a critical practice of recognizing our own 'semiotic technologies' for making meanings, *and* a no-nonsense commitment to faithful accounts of a 'real' world . . . friendly to earthwide projects of finite freedom" (1990:187).

What does this mean in terms of feminist tasks for the future if we are to develop theoretical and political bases for coalition? We need to recognize/insist on important axes of domination and we must retain categories such as oppression, exploitation, and white supremacy rather than talk only about a sanitized "difference." As bell hooks has put it, "words like *Other* and *difference* are taking the place of commonly known words deemed uncool or too simplistic, words like *oppression, exploitation,* and *domination*" (1990:51–52).

Related to this is that we need to think more about identity politics. Identity is not something formed unproblematically by existing in a particular social location and therefore seeing the world in a particular way. My effort to develop the idea of a feminist standpoint, in contrast to "women's viewpoint," was an effort to move in this direction. Chela Sandoval's (1990) notion of the importance of strategic identity for women of color represents an important advance, as is her development of the notion of oppositional consciousness.[15]

Sandoval argues that U.S. Third World feminism can function as a model for oppositional political activity in the United States. She proposes that we view the world as a kind of "topography" that defines the points around which "individuals and groups seeking to transform oppressive powers *constitute themselves* as resistant and oppositional subjects" (1991:4; emphasis added). She holds that once the "subject positions" of the dominated are "self-consciously recognized by their inhabitants" they can be "transformed into more effective sites of resistance" (4). She discusses a "differential consciousness," which she states operates like the clutch of an automobile, allowing the driver to engage gears in a "system for the transmission of power" (14). Here, her views parallel those of Gramsci, who suggests that we rethink the nature of identity: "Our capacity to think and act on the world is dependent on other people who are themselves also both subjects and objects of history" (1971:346). In addition, one must reform the concept of the individual to see it as a "series of active relationships, a process in which individuality, though perhaps the most important, is not the only element to be taken into account." Individuality, then, is to be understood as the "ensemble of these relations. . . . To create one's personality means to acquire consciousness of them and to modify one's own personality means to modify the ensemble of these relations" (352). Moreover, Gramsci holds that each individual is the synthesis of these relations and also of the history of these relations, a "precis of the past" (353). Thus, Gramsci argues that human nature is simply a complex of social relations. I am shifting his argument slightly to argue that identity is a complex of social relations, a social construction, by means of which individuals constitute themselves.

DEVELOPING ALTERNATIVE VISIONS

In the spirit of recognizing the important achievement of constructing consciousness and identity I propose to read a number of statements of the view from below. While the phenomenological specifics differ, there are a number of connections to be drawn and similarities to be seen in the epistemologies contained as possibilities in the experience of dominated groups, groups who represent new forms of historical agency. In particular, white feminists can learn a great deal about the possibilities of solidarity from U.S. feminists of color and postcolonial subjects. At the same time, white feminists have some experiences that can provide and facilitate shared understandings.

To understand these perspectives and the knowledges they support, generate, and express, we must understand at least the outlines of the situations of oppression from which they emerge. Or put more clearly, the existential problems to which the worldviews of the oppressed must respond. Most fundamentally, the dominated live in a world structured by others for their purposes—purposes that at the very least are not our own and that are in various degrees inimical to our development and even existence. Domination takes a variety of forms, both globally and locally. There is, for example, an implicit "assumption of 'the West' as the primary referent in theory and practice." At the very least, as Carlos Fuentes puts it from the perspective of Mexico, "The North American world blinds us with its energy; we cannot see ourselves [because] we must see YOU" (1988:85).

As a result of this definition, dominated groups experience a series of inversions, distortions, and erasures that can become epistemologically constitutive. Or, in Sandoval's terms, can become the critical points around which individuals constitute themselves. "The presupposition is that, owing to its structural situation in the social order and to the specific forms of oppression" inherent in that situation, each group lives the world in a way that allows it to see, or rather "makes it unavoidable to see and to know, features of the world that remain obscure, invisible, or merely occasional and secondary for other groups" (Jameson 1991).

Let us look more specifically at one of the most powerful experiences, that of inversion. One of the most frequently mentioned features of the consciousness of the dominated as they become conscious of both relations of domination and possibilities for change is a recognition of the "insanity" or "unreality" of the "normal." Thus, Michelle Cliff writes of light-skinned middle-class Jamaicans, "We were colorists and we aspired to oppressor status. . . . We were convinced of white supremacy. If we failed, . . . our dark part had taken over: an inherited imbalance in which the doom of the creole was sealed." She steps back to look at what she has written and states that this "may sound fabulous, or even mythic. It is. It is insane" (1988:78). Or consider a U.S. Black woman who told her interviewer, "I have grown to womanhood in a world where the saner you are, the madder you are made to appear" (Gwaltney as quoted in Collins 1989:748).

Eduardo Galeano, writing of the situation in Latin America, notes that "'Freedom' in my country is the name of a jail for political prisoners and 'democracy' forms part of the title of various regimes of terror; the word 'love' defines the relationship of a man with his automobile, and 'revolution' is understood to describe what a new detergent can do in your kitchen" (1988b:124–25). He adds, "Why not recognize a certain creativity in the development of a technology of terror? Latin America is making inspired universal contributions to the development of methods of torture . . . and the sowing of fear" (114–15).[16]

This sort of understanding of the inversions created for the oppressed leads to a re-understanding of the dominant group. As this understanding changes, it is striking how similar the descriptions are. Thus, one can begin to ask questions and formulate descriptions that are vastly different. Thus, we find questions raised among feminist, Third World, and postcolonial writers. "Besides possessing more money and arms is it that the 'First World' is qualitatively better in any way than our 'underdeveloped' countries? That the Anglos themselves aren't also an 'ethnic group', one of the most violent and anti-social tribes on this planet?" ("Documented/Undocumented" 1988:132). And there is also the observation by a student of Black radicalism that "there was the sense that something of a more profound obsession with property was askew in a civilization which could organize and celebrate—on a scale beyond previous human experience—the brutal degradations of life and the most acute violations of human destiny." He adds that the suspicion mounts that "a civilization maddened by its own perverse assumptions and contradictions is loose in the world" (Robinson 1984:442–43). Descriptions such as this remind me of my own characterization of "abstract masculinity" by its fascination with death (Hartsock 1983).

The result of this kind of experience for knowledge and epistemology is expressed in Gabriel García Márquez's Nobel Prize address. He presents the rich statement that "our crucial problem has been a lack of conventional means to render our lives believable. This my friends, is the crux of our solitude. . . . The interpretation of our reality through patterns not our own serves only to make us ever more unknown, ever less free, ever more solitary" (as quoted in Galeano 1988a:262).[17] The result is that the dominated and marginalized are forced to recognize (unlike whites and males and Europeans) that they inhabit multiple worlds. W. E. B. Du Bois has described this situation from an African-American perspective: "It is a peculiar sensation, this double consciousness, this sense of always looking at one's self through the eyes of others, of measuring one's soul by the tape of a world that looks on in amused contempt and pity" (as quoted in Ladner 1971:273–74).

The significance of this experience for developing theory has been described in a number of ways. I have argued in my feminist standpoint essay that for (white) women in Western industrial society, the experience of life under patriarchy allows for the possibility of developing an understanding both of the falseness and partiality of the dominant view and a more complex vision of social relations. Others have made similar arguments about the nature of the knowledge available to the subjugated. Thus, Kumkum Sangari, discussing García Márquez's marvelous realism, writes that for "Third World" people, the difficulty of arriving at fact through the "historical and political distortions that so powerfully shape and mediate it" leads them to assert a different level of factuality, "a plane on which the notion of knowledge as provisional and of truth as historically circumscribed is not only necessary for understanding but can in turn be made to work from positions of engagement within the local and contemporary" (1987:161). She argues that marvelous realism operates because "if the real is historically structured to make invisible the foreign locus of power, if the real may thus be other than what is generally visible, . . . then marvelous realism tackles the problem of truth at a level that reinvents a more comprehensive mode of referentiality" (163).

Gloria Anzaldua, writing out of the experience of a Latina living on the Mexico-Texas border, describes a similar phenomenon in terms reminiscent of Sangari's discussion. She points not only to the experience of living in two realities and thus being forced to exist in the interface but also to "la facultad," the capacity to see in surface phenomena the meanings of deeper realities, to see the "deep structure below the surface." And she argues that "those who are pounced on the most have it the strongest—the females, the homosexuals of all races, the dark skinned, the outcast, the persecuted, the marginalized, the foreign." It is a survival tactic unknowingly cultivated by those caught between the worlds, but, she adds, "it is latent in all of us" (1987:37–39).

The knowledges available to these multiple subjectivities have different qualities than that of the disembodied and singular subject of the Enlightenment. Moreover, despite the specificity of each view from below, several fundamental aspects are shared. Among these are the qualities of multiplicity, of being locatable in time and space and particular cultures, of being embodied in specific ways, and, finally, of operating as social and collective points of view, indeed, operating as standpoints. While I cannot discuss these qualities in detail, I can lay out a few of their general outlines.

These are knowledges located in a particular time and space—in Donna Haraway's terms, situated knowledges. They are therefore partial, the knowledges of specific cultures and peoples. As an aspect of being situated, these knowledges represent a response to an expression of specific embodiment. The bodies of the dominated have been made to function as the marks of our oppression.

One can describe the shape of these knowledges by attending to the features of the social location occupied by dominated groups. Because of these features, these knowledges express a multiple and contradictory reality; they are not fixed but change and recognize that they change with the changing shape of the historical conjuncture and the balance of forces. They are both critical of and vulnerable to the dominant culture, both separated off and opposed to it and yet contained within it. Gloria Anzaldua's poem expresses these characteristics:

> To live in the Borderlands means
> you are at home, a stranger wherever you are
> the border disputes have been settled
> the volley of shots have shattered the truce
> you are wounded, lost in action
> fighting back, a survivor.
>
> (1987:14)

All these mark achievement through struggle, a series of ongoing attempts to keep from being made invisible, to keep from being destroyed by the dominant culture. There is no way these situated knowledges can be characterized as "natural."

Even more than this, however, the development of situated knowledges can constitute alternatives: they open possibilities that may or may not be realized. To the extent that these knowledges become self-conscious about their assumptions, they make available new epistemological and political options. The struggles they represent and express, if made self-conscious, can go beyond efforts at survival to recognize the centrality of systematic power relations. They can become knowledges that are both accountable and engaged. As the knowledges of the dominated, they are "savvy to modes of denial," which include repression, forgetting, and disappearing.[18] Thus, while they recognize themselves as never fixed or fully achieved, they can claim to present a truer, or more adequate, account of reality. As knowledges that recognize themselves as the knowledges of the dominated and marginalized, these self-consciously situated knowledges must focus on changing contemporary power relationships and thus point beyond the present.

In conclusion, I believe that feminist theory can be useful in the effort to come together while recognizing our differences. Theoretical analysis can point to the shared structural features of accounts of the world whose specific phenomenological contents differ profoundly. Recognizing our experiences in the lives of others can strengthen our resolve to do the difficult political work of coalition building.

NOTES

1. Sangari makes a similar case when she argues that the tenuousness of knowledge in the West is a symptom and critique of the contemporary social and economic situation in the West.

2. I distinguish between postmodernist theories and postmodernism as a cultural condition, finding Jameson's argument about postmodernism as the cultural logic of late capitalism very interesting and fruitful. We do face an ever-increasing commodification of social life: the question is how to understand and cope with it. The ways this is understood and acted upon differs profoundly with social location. Katie King suggested to me that telecommuting was an interesting example of this. On the one hand, for professionals, it offers a way to combine work and family and contribute to the improvement of the environment by not driving to work; on the other hand, for those less skilled it becomes another form of piecework.

3. I owe this insight to Weeks (1992).

4. This is not a statement about the theorists of postmodernism but rather a statement about the discourse itself and its lineages, attachments, and points of definition.

5. I owe the phrase *god-trick* to Haraway (1988).

6. This is the case made about "Enlightenment epistemology." Clearly there were other worldviews extant, but we have received "Enlightenment epistemology" as the dominant one and the one that postmodernists argue against.

7. See my critique of the ways assumptions express the epistemology of the commodity (1984:chap. 5).

8. I use the term *subjectivity* rather than *identity* to mark what I see as the achievement of developing a political worldview. Thus one can speak of European-American men of the ruling class but to speak of subjectivity is to speak of the epistemology and account of the world that grew from this identity.

9. I have analyzed their work in more detail in "Postmodernism and Political Change" (n.d.).

10. Donna Haraway (1988) has argued that relativism itself is another form of the god-trick.

11. Foucault argues that one should not fight for justice since that is a notion too tied to power.

12. Jameson first made this argument in an article of the same title (1984). It is considerably expanded in *Postmodernism: The Cultural Logic of Late Capitalism.*

13. I see feminist postmodernism as embodying the same contradiction Zillah Eisenstein (1981) identified in liberal feminism—the attempt to meld two mutually exclusive worldviews.

14. Heidi Gottfried called to my attention the statement by Susan Bordo that "too relentless a focus on historical heterogeneity . . . can obscure the trans-historical hierarchical patterns of white, male privilege that have informed the creation of the Western intellectual tradition" (1990:149). In addition, there is Christine di Stefano's question, "Are some differences more basic than others?" (1990:78). Clearly my concerns are not unique.

15. She makes an excellent point in her essay on the development of the category of "women of color" out of the consciousness-raising sessions at the 1981 NWSA meetings. Much of what follows comes from Sandoval (1991).

16. See also Galeano's (1988b:117) remarks about the importance of the consumption of fantasy rather than commodities.

17. García Márquez's work makes important points about incommensurable realities. He argues that ordinary people who have read *One Hundred Years of Solitude* have found no surprise, because "I'm telling them nothing that hasn't happened in their own lives" (as cited in Sangari 1987:164).

18. These are Donna Haraway's terms.

REFERENCES

Anzaldua, Gloria, 1987. *Borderlands.* San Francisco: Spinsters, Aunt Lute.

Berman, Marshall. 1982. *All That Is Solid Melts into Air.* New York: Simon and Schuster.

Bordo, Susan. 1990. "Feminism, Postmodernism, and Gender Skepticism." In *Feminism/Postmodernism,* ed. Linda J. Nicholson. New York: Routledge. 133–56.

Cliff, Michelle. 1988. "If I Could Write This in Fire, I Would Write This in Fire." In *Graywolf Annual Five: Multicultural Literacy*, ed. Rick Simonson and Scott Walker. Saint Paul: Gray Wolf Press. 57–82.

Collins, Patricia Hill. 1989. "The Social Construction of Black Feminist Thought." *Signs* 14 (4): 745–73.

di Stefano, Christine. 1991. *Configurations of Masculinity*. Ithaca: Cornell University Press.

———. 1990. "Dilemmas of Difference." In *Feminism/Postmodernism*, ed. Linda Nicholson. New York: Routledge. 63–82.

"Documented/Undocumented." 1988. In *Graywolf Annual Five: Multicultural Literacy*, ed. Rick Simonson and Scott Walker. Saint Paul: Gray Wolf Press.

Eisenstein, Zillah. 1981. *The Radical Future of Liberal Feminism*. Boston: Northeastern University Press.

Foucault, Michel. 1983. "The Subject and Power." In *Beyond Structuralism and Hermeneutics*, ed. Hubert Dreyfus and Paul Rabinow. Chicago: University of Chicago Press. 208–26.

———. 1977. *Language, Counter-Memory, Practice: Selected Essays and Interviews*. Ed. Donald Bouchard. Ithaca: Cornell University Press.

Fuentes, Carlos. 1988. "How I Started to Write." In *Graywolf Annual Five: Multicultural Literacy*, ed. Rick Simonson and Scott Walker. St. Paul: Gray Wolf Press. 83–112.

Galeano, Eduardo. 1988a. *Century of the Wind*. New York: Pantheon.

———. 1988b. "In Defense of the Word: Leaving Buenos Aires, June, 1976." In *The Graywolf Annual Five*, ed. Rick Simonson and Scott Walker. St. Paul: Graywolf Press. 113–26.

Gordon, Linda. 1991. "On 'Difference.'" *Genders* 10 (Spring): 91–111.

Gramsci, Antonio. 1971. *Prison Notebooks*. Ed. and trans. Quintin Hoare and Geoffrey Nowell Smith. New York: International Publishers.

Haraway, Donna. 1990. *Simians, Cyborgs, and Women*. New York: Routledge.

———. 1988. "Situated Knowledges: The Science Question in Feminism and the Privilege of Partial Perspective." *Feminist Studies* 14 (3): 575–99.

Hartsock, Nancy C. M. 1989–90. "Postmodernism and Political Change: Issues for Feminist Theory." *Cultural Critique* 14 (Winter): 15–33.

———. 1987. "Rethinking Modernism: Minority vs. Majority Theories." *Cultural Critique* 7 (Fall): 187–206.

———. 1984. *Money, Sex, and Power: Toward a Feminist Historical Materialism*. Boston: Northeastern University Press.

———. 1983. "The Feminist Standpoint: Developing the Ground for a Specifically Feminist Historical Materialism." In *Discovering Reality*, ed. Sandra Harding and Merrill Hintikka. Dordrecht: David Reidel.

———. N.d. "Postmodernism and Political Change." Ms.

hooks, bell. 1990. *Yearning: Race, Gender, and Cultural Politics*. Boston: South End Press.

Jameson, Fredric. 1991. *Postmodernism: The Cultural Logic of Late Capitalism*. Durham: Duke University Press.

———. 1984. "Postmodernism: The Cultural Logic of Late Capitalism." *New Left Review* 146:54–92.

Ladner, Joyce. 1971. *Tomorrow's Tomorrow.* New York: Anchor Books.

Mouffe, Chantal. 1988. "Radical Democracy: Modern or Postmodern." In *Universal Abandon,* ed. Andrew Ross. Trans. Paul Holdenraber. Minneapolis: University of Minnesota Press. 31–45.

Rabinow, Paul, ed. 1984. *The Foucault Reader.* New York: Pantheon.

Robinson, Cedric. 1984. *Black Marxism.* London: Zed Press.

Said, Edward. 1978. *Orientalism.* New York: Vintage.

Sandoval, Chela. 1991. "U.S. Third World Feminism: The Theory and Method of Oppositional Consciousness in the Postmodern World." *Genders* 10 (Spring): 1–24.

———. 1990. "Feminism and Racism: A Report on the 1981 National Women's Studies Association Conference." In *Making Face, Making Soul/Haciendo Caras,* ed. Gloria Anzaldua. San Francisco: Aunt Lute Foundation. 55–71.

Sangari, Kumkum. 1987. "The Politics of the Possible." *Cultural Critique* 7 (Fall): 157–86.

Weeks, Kathi. 1992. "The Standpoint of Theory: Modernism, Postmodernism, and Feminism." Ph.D. diss., University of Washington.

Contributors

JOAN ACKER has written extensively on feminism and sociological theory and on gender and organizations. Her recent work includes *Doing Comparable Worth: Gender, Class, and Pay Equity* and articles such as "Hierarchies, Jobs, Bodies: A Theory of Gendered Organizations" and "Gendering Organizational Theory."

KATE BARRY coordinates women's programs and teaches women's studies at Lane Community College in Eugene, Oregon. She has written on feminist ethics and the feminist philosophy of science.

FRANCESCA M. CANCIAN's research has focused on family, gender, and feminist methods. Recent publications include the books *Love in America: Gender and Self-development* and *Making War/Making Peace,* co-edited with J. William Gibson, and articles such as "The Feminization of Love" and "Feminist Science."

LINDA CARTY is an antiracist activist who teaches sociology. The focus of her scholarly work is the ideological and material significance of Third World women's labor in international capitalism. She is the editor of *And Still We Rise: Feminist Political Mobilizing in Contemporary Canada.*

EMILY CLARK is a life-long resident of Iowa, where she is raising three sons and managing a family-owned business. She is interested in writing a book that chronicles how she confronted and healed from incest in order to share her story with other survivors and health care professionals.

JOKE ESSEVELD has completed several research projects on women and employment in Sweden. The research culminated in a book co-authored with Karen Davies, *Playing Hop-Scotch in the Swedish Labor Market: A Study of Unemployed Factory Women.*

SHERRY GORELICK has pursued the analysis of social contradictions in such diverse nooks and crannies as "Undermining Hierarchy: Problems of School in Capitalist America," "Jewish Success and the Great American Celebration: The Cold War vs. the World War in Social Science," *City College and the Jewish Poor,* and "Boom and Bust in Higher Education: Economic and Social Causes of the Current Crisis." Her published work in feminist methodology began with "The Changer and the Changed: Methodological Reflections on Studying Jewish Feminists." She is currently working on a book on Jewish feminists and the Israeli-Palestinian conflict. She teaches sociology and women's studies at Rutgers University.

HEIDI GOTTFRIED teaches sociology and women's studies at Purdue University. Two telephone operators in Detroit, Michigan, inspired her to initiate research *on* and *for* women workers. Almost a decade later, she continues to write and reflect on women and work issues. Her most recent publications include "In the Margins: Flexibility as a Mode of Regulation in the Temporary Service Industry," "The Impact of Skill on Union Membership: Rethinking Gender Differences," "Constructing Difference: The Making of Gendered Subcultures in a Japanese Automobile Transplant" with Laurie Graham, and "Learning the Score: Gender and Resistance in the Temporary Help Service Industry."

HEIDI HARTMANN is an economist and director of the Institute for Women's Policy Research and has written extensively on feminist theory and policy issues. Publications include the National Research Council reports *Women, Work, and Wages: Equal Pay for Jobs of Equal Value,* co-edited with Donald Trieman, and *Women's Work, Men's Work: Sex Segregation on the Job,* co-edited with Barbara Reskin; articles such as "The Unhappy Marriage of Marxism and Feminism" and "Capitalism, Patriarchy, and Job Segregation by Sex"; and numerous essays and reports produced at IWPR with Roberta Spalter-Roth and others. She has recently been awarded a MacArthur Fellowship.

NANCY C. M. HARTSOCK is the author of *Money, Sex, and Power* and has written extensively on feminist theory. She is working on a collection of her essays, "The Feminist Standpoint Revisited and Other Essays," and a critique of postmodernist theories.

PIERRETTE HONDAGNEU-SOTELO's research has focused on immigration, domestic work, and activist stances in sociology, and her articles have appeared in *American Sociologist, Clinical Sociology Review, Gender and Society, Social Problems,* and *Qualitative Sociology.* She has also written *Gendered Transitions: Mexican Experiences of Immigration* on the intersection of gender and Mexican undocumented immigration.

NANCY A. NAPLES is a faculty member in sociology and women's studies at the University of California at Irvine. She has written on low income women's community-based activism, social policies designed to counter poverty in the United States, and the construction of inequality in a rural context. Her articles have appeared in *Gender and Society, Rural Sociology,* and *Social Problems.* She is currently writing the book "Grassroots Warriors in the War on Poverty: Activist Mothers, Community Workers, and the State." Her activism includes work with PrairieFire Rural Action and California Women's Law Center.

LEILA J. RUPP teaches women's history and lesbian/gay history at Ohio State University. She is the author of *Mobilizing Women for War: German and American Propaganda, 1939–1945* and the coauthor, with Verta Taylor, of *Survival in the Doldrums: The American Women's Rights Movement, 1945 to the 1960s.* She is currently writing a book on the history of the international women's movement and, with Verta Taylor, is studying the contemporary lesbian feminist community.

DOROTHY E. SMITH is author of *The Everyday World as Problematic: A Feminist Sociology, The Conceptual Practices of Power: A Feminist Sociology of Knowledge,* and *Texts, Facts, and Femininity: Exploring the Relations of Ruling.* She is currently a professor in the Department of Sociology in Education and head of the Centre for Women's Studies in Education at the Ontario Institute for Studies in Education.

ROBERTA SPALTER-ROTH is director of research at the Institute for Women's Policy Research and Sociologist-in-Residence at the American University. She has written extensively on women's policy issues, including "Science and Politics in the Dual Vision of Feminist Public Policy Research: The Case of Family and Medical Leave," "Mothers, Children, and Low Wage Work: The Need for a Family Wage," and "Dependence on Men, the Market, and the State: The Rhetoric and Reality of Welfare Reform," co-authored with Heidi Hartmann and others at IWPR.

JUDITH STACEY has written widely on feminist thought, family change, and family policy. Her publications include *Brave New Families: Stories of Domestic Upheaval in Late Twentieth Century America* and *Patriarchy and Socialist Revolution in China.* She teaches sociology and women's studies at the University of California at Davis.

RONNIE J. STEINBERG has written one book, *Wages and Hours: Labor and Reform in Twentieth Century America,* edited two books, *Equal Employment for Women,* and *Job Training for Women* (with co-editor Sharon Harlan), and is the author of "The Social Construction of Skill: Gender, Power, and Comparable Worth." Her current research focuses on the design of gender-neutral compensation systems and on the containment of sexual harassment and sexual assault policies in the university.

VERTA TAYLOR is the co-author, with Leila J. Rupp, of *Survival in the Doldrums: The American Women's Rights Movement, 1945 to the 1960s* and the coeditor, with Laurel Richardson, of *Feminist Frontiers: Rethinking Sex, Gender, and Society*. Her current research focuses on lesbian communities and culture and on postpartum depression and the women's self-help movement.

Index

12.63